Books are to be returned on or before
the last date below.

- 4 FEB 1999

2 0 MAR 2001

2 5 OCT 2002

1 5 MAY 2006

**7-DAY
LOAN**

LIBREX —

WITHDRAWN
WITHDRAWN

D1425406

LIVERPOOL JOHN MOORES UNIVERSITY
Aldham Robarts L.R.C.
TEL. 051 231 3701/3634

SUNY series in
New Directions in Crime and Justice Studies

Austin T. Turk, editor

CONSTITUTIVE CRIMINOLOGY AT WORK

APPLICATIONS TO CRIME AND JUSTICE

Edited by
Stuart Henry
and
Dragan Milovanovic

STATE UNIVERSITY OF NEW YORK PRESS

Production by Ruth Fisher
Marketing by Patrick Durocher
Composition by Colophon Typesetting

Published by
State University of New York Press, Albany

© 1999 State University of New York

All Rights reserved

Printed in the United States of America

No part of this book may be used or reproduced in any manner
whatsoever without written permission. No part of this
book may be stored in a retrieval system or transmitted
in any form or by any means including electronic,
electrostatic, magnetic tape, mechanical, photocopying,
recording, or otherwise without the prior permission in
writing of the publisher.

For information, address the State University of New York Press, State
University Plaza, Albany, NY 12246

Library of Congress Cataloging-in-Publication Data

Constitutive criminology at work : applications to crime and justice /
    edited by Stuart Henry and Dragan Milovanovic.
        p.   cm. — (SUNY series in new directions in crime and justice
    studies)
    Includes bibliographical references.
    ISBN 0-7914-4193-8 (hc. : alk. paper). — ISBN 0-7914-4194-6 (pbk.
    : alk. paper)
    1. Criminology—Research. 2. Criminology—Philosophy.
    3. Criminal justice, Administration of.   I. Henry, Stuart.
    II. Milovanovic, Dragan, 1948–   . III. Series.
    HV6024.5.C72   1999   99-17955
    364—dc21   CIP

10   9   8   7   6   5   4   3   2   1

CONTENTS

TABLES AND CHARTS

PREFACE

This book is an edited anthology of original essays based on applications and empirical research within the theoretical framework presented in our book *Constitutive Criminology: Beyond Postmodernism* (1996). In that work, we focused on the discursive coproduction of crime by human agents in their interrelation with cultural products, social institutions and the wider societal structure. Coproduction of crime as harm was analyzed around familiar themes: assumptions about human nature and social order, definitions of crime, crime causation, and the formation of social policy. The argument was developed that because crime is conceived of, made meaningful and acted out through particular discursive forms, one important component in any crime reduction policy is to change the ways of talking that facilitate its expression. Thus developed the core concept of replacement discourse, which afforded the possibility, though not the certainty, of reconstructing a less harmful world.

In this book we seek to extend the constitutive project by drawing together studies by those who have found constitutive theory helpful in understanding specific problems in the empirical, applied world of crime and justice. Part 1 contains our brief introduction in which we outline the origins of constitutive theory in postmodernism. In this section we seek to provide both an orientation for the reader and a clarification of the theory's framework. To that end the section contains a chapter summarizing the main ideas and themes of our book *Constitutive Criminology*. Authors of subsequent chapters apply the theoretical perspective laid out in Part 1 to their own research. Part 2 provides a synopsis of the ways human agency and resistance constitute the meaning of crime and legality while at the same time constituting human subjects' identities. Contributors to this section demonstrate the importance of extralegal processes and local and popular culture in the coproduction of crime and explore the ways human and social bodies are regulated. In Part 3 the authors examine the constitution of societal responses through policing and penal systems while also exploring how human agency resists, how it is reconstituted and how it constitutes the penal structures with which it is engaged. In the final section (Part 4) the authors demonstrate the tenuous nature of justice and point to the possibilities of social and political transformation. We conclude the book with an assessment of six years of engagements with and evaluations of the constitutive project. In this we highlight some differences of interpretation that have emerged and consider prospects for the future.

As always, collaborative efforts such as this develop their own history punctuated by highs and lows. Many of the highs will be self-evident in the pages you are about to read; the lows, unless we mention them here, will remain buried. These lows are largely comprised of the compelling events that distracted several of our original contributors who, though committed to the constitutive project, were ultimately prevented from completing their essays. For their constitutive spirit and contribution to the early stages of this volume we would like to extend our sincere thanks and good wishes to Susan Silbey, Patricia Ewick, Russell Smandych, and Trent Kane. We look forward to working with them on future projects.

The contributors represented in this book have succeeded in taking constitutive theory to new realms. As editors we found it a delight working with them. These scholars were receptive to our comments on their early drafts, creative and innovative in their responses, and importantly, added their own critical nuances indicating new directions and possibilities. We hope that their diverse voices will enrich, enhance, and invite other new beginnings in the continuing unfolding of the constitutive project.

PART 1

CONSTITUTIVE THEORY

Stuart Henry and Dragan Milovanovic

INTRODUCTION: POSTMODERNISM AND CONSTITUTIVE THEORY

In *Constitutive Criminology* (Henry and Milovanovic, 1996) we developed a holistic, integrated criminological theory informed by the postmodernist critique. *Constitutive Criminology* was the first full and systematic exposition of an affirmative postmodernist criminology whose early statements (Henry, 1989; Henry and Milovanovic, 1991; 1993; 1994; Milovanovic, 1992; Milovanovic and Henry, 1991) generated considerable interest among theorists, practitioners and a range of other students of criminology, from high school to graduate level. Some initial reaction came from noted criminologists, sociologists and social theorists, who drew on constitutive ideas to inform the development of their own theories, including: a constitutive theory of law (Harrington, 1988; Hunt, 1993); integral legal pluralism (Fitzpatrick, 1984, 1992); cultural theory of law (Silbey, 1992); autopoietic theory of law (Teubner, 1992, 1993); and reflexive criminology (Nelken, 1994). Our later statements also influenced Barak's (1998) holistic integrated criminology. But the reach of constitutive criminology was not to be confined to the ivory tower.

At another level, constitutive theory's ideas and insights served students such as Zack Early and Amir Ghavi from Milton High School in Georgia, Loren Dent from the Georgetown High School in Georgetown, Texas, and Scott Junior of The Woodlands High School in Houston, Texas. With encouragement from their forensics coaches (not least Brad Byrd of The Woodlands), these students used constitutive ideas on the national circuit of the 1997 National Forensics' debate, which was focused on juvenile crime. It was very encouraging to learn that these students had spent the time to grapple with issues such as modernity versus postmodernity, praxis versus transpraxis, and replacement discourse—concepts which many seasoned criminologists have found difficult!

High school students notwithstanding, the major development came from within the field of criminology. Among leading criminologists the constitutive idea has now been accepted into the corpus of criminological knowledge as a significant theoretical contribution, and one of the few criminologies illustrative of the postmodernist perspective. The initial statement (Henry and Milovanovic, 1991) was cited among nine key works that "have added to the richness of criminological theory," and which "extend the bounds of traditional criminology" (Stitt and Giacopassi, 1992: 6). In a substantial review Gibbons (1994: 164) discusses the theory as one of the "new criminologies" that warrants attention, not least for its valid contention that "crime is both in and of society." Most recently, in his attempt to locate the roots and intellectual influences on constitutive criminology, Arrigo (1997: 392–93) proclaimed that, "constitutive thought is now firmly established as a leading conceptual orientation in the sociology of law and in criminology," but he admits that it is "relatively new and not yet fully legitimized." And Ruller (1997: 497) predicts that "we can expect a slow and steady infiltration of postmodern elements into the discipline. Indeed, this infiltration is already well underway."

In this introduction, we want to take a few steps back to briefly define and describe, in as simple terms as possible, the roots of constitutive theory as it developed from an affirmative version of postmodernism.

Postmodernism

Postmodernism refers to a school of thought that has emerged out of a period of intense skepticism with science. Scientific method and rational thought were outcomes of the eighteenth-century Enlightenment and prevailed until the late twentieth century. They assume that rational and objective scientific methods can be used to discover knowledge and truth which can then be used to solve society's problems and to control nature. The concept of scientific "progress" has characterized the "modern era." Disenchantment with modernism (linked to the suffering that its hierarchies, divisions and exclusions have brought to many through imperialism, sexism and racism and class oppression), together with its increasing inability to solve society's problems (e.g., pollution, poverty, crime), have led many to question the value of scientific analysis and rational thought (Hunt, 1991; Best and Kellner, 1991; Borgmann, 1992). Postmodernists see rational thought as a form of elite power through which those who claim to have special knowledge earn the right to decide the fate of those who do not share this knowledge.

Postmodernists fundamentally disagree that there is such a thing as objective truth. Instead all knowledge is seen as subjective, and is shaped by personal, cultural and political views. Postmodernists argue that all knowledge is made up simply of *"claims to truth"* (Foucault, 1977, 1981). They believe that knowledge and truth are *"socially constructed."* This means that they have no independent reality other than in the minds and practices of those who create them and recreate them. Knowledge is artificial, an outcome of humans making distinctions and judging one part of any distinction as superior to another; one set of ideas as superior to another, and so on. Moreover, these distinctions are conceptual and are made through communication, particularly but not exclusively written or spoken language, referred to by postmodernists as *"discourse"* (Manning, 1988).

One of the major causes of conflict and harm in societies, say postmodernists, results from people investing energy in these "discursive distinctions," believing in their reality and defending them and imposing them on others. Distinctions made in discourse result in categories that exclude. For example, the gender distinctions "men" and "women" exclude the differences within these categories and preclude connections between them, so too with "black" and "white" distinctions based on race that also exclude others.

Postmodernists reject the self-evident reality of distinctions. They reject that distinctions should be made between different kinds of knowledge, especially between "scientific knowledge" and "common-sense knowledge." One of their principal tools of analysis is to expose the socially constructed nature of privileged knowledge through what is called *"critique."* This is different from criticism. Critique is a continuous process of challenge to those who claim to know or hold the truth. It uses *"deconstruction"* (Derrida, 1970; 1981) to expose the socially constructed rather than the real nature of truth claims.

Deconstruction is a method of analysis that seeks to "undo" constructions, to demolish them, but to do so in a way which exposes how they are built and why they appear to be real (Rosenau, 1992; Cohen,

1990). As T. R. Young explains, "whereas modern science privileges objectivity, rationality, power, control, inequality and hierarchy, postmodernists deconstruct each theory and each social practice by locating it in its larger sociohistorical context in order to reveal the human hand and the group interests which shape the course of self-understanding" (1995: 578–79). Indeed, part of the postmodern critique involves the "resurrection of subjugated knowledges," the excluded, neglected and marginal knowledges discounted by dominant social constructions.

Although some commentators have claimed there are numerous versions of postmodernism (Schwartz and Friedrichs, 1994), we have found it helpful to distinguish two broad types: *skeptical* and *affirmative* (Rosenau, 1992; Einstadter and Henry, 1995). *Skeptical postmodernism* refers to the work of those who believe there is no basis for objectivity and no way truth either exists or can be discovered. They use deconstruction simply to undermine all claims to truth, revealing its underlying assumptions and disrupting its acceptance as fact. In some cases they imply an extreme relativism that has no standards and accepts anything as valid. They do not believe in suggesting alternatives because to do so would then also be making truth claims and be subject to their own criticism (hence skeptics are also called *nihilists*). Indeed, Matthews and Young (1992: 13) comment that early skeptical postmodernism in criminology focused on "deconstruction rather than reconstruction." This has parallels with the early preoccupation of critical legal studies theorists in "trashing." While we think skeptical postmodernism has considerable value as a critical and analytical tool, we believe the affirmative approach has the most to offer those studying crime.

Affirmative postmodernism refers to those who believe deconstruction also implies reconstruction or rebuilding: "exposing how an edifice is built, and how it stands, in spite of opposition, also implies how it can be rebuilt or built differently" (Einstadter and Henry, 1995: 280–281). In deconstruction, affirmative postmodernists show how humans actively build their social world, rather than being passive subjects of external forces. They also show how people could invest their energies to build new social worlds. Building, however, does not also mean that the results are completely forseen as integrative processes develop. This approach, especially as developed in our constitutive theory, transcended the limits of skeptical postmodernism's obsession with deconstruction by addressing the possibilities of reconstruction. Like Matthews and Young, our position "refuses to be drawn into the defeatism and pessimism associated with some current strands of 'radical' theorizing, particularly in the form of [nihilistic] postmodernism" (Matthews and Young, 1992: 20).

Constitutive Criminology

The core of our constitutive argument is that crime and its control cannot be separated from the totality of the structural and cultural contexts in which it is produced (Henry and Milovanovic, 1994; 1996). It rejects the argument of traditional modernist criminology that crime can be separated from that process and analyzed and corrected apart from it. Crime is an integral part of the total production of society. It is a coproduced outcome of humans and the social and organizational structures that people develop and endlessly rebuild. Analysis of crime must relate crime to the total societal picture, rather than to any single part of it.

A power structure based on inequality is a major feature of our society. Unequal power relations, built on the constructions of difference, provide the conditions that define crime as harm. Thus, constitutive criminology redefines crime as the harm resulting from humans investing energy in harm-producing relations of power. Humans victimized by such "crimes" are in unequal power relations. Crimes are no less than people being disrespected. People are disrespected in numerous ways but all have to do with denying or preventing us becoming fully social beings. What is human is to make a difference to the world, to act on it, to interact with others and together to transform the environment and ourselves. If this process is prevented we become less than human; we are harmed. Thus we define crime as "the power to deny others their ability to make a difference" (Henry and Milovanovic, 1996: 116). We find it helpful to identify two aspects that characterize crime that we call *"crimes of reduction"* and *"crimes of repression."* These notions refer to power differentials, hierarchical relations and the harms that these relations coproduce.

Harms of reduction occur when offended parties experience a loss in their standing. They could have property stolen from them, or they could have dignity stripped from them by, for example, hate crimes or other acts. Harms of repression occur when people experience a limit or restriction, preventing them from achieving a desired position or standing. They could be prevented from achieving a career goal because of sexism or racism, or meet a promotional "glass ceiling." Considered along a continuum of deprivation, harms of reduction or repression may be based on any number of constructed differences. At present in Western industrial societies harms cluster around the following constructed differences: economic (class, property), gender (sexism), race and ethnicity (racism, hate), political (power, corruption), morality, human rights, social position (status or prestige, inequality), psychological state (security, well being), self-realization/actualization, biological integrity, and so on. Whatever the construction, actions are harms either because they move an offended party away from a position or state they currently occupy, or because they prevent them from occupying a position or state that they desire, the achievement of which does not deny or deprive another. This of course raises the question of whether it is ever legitimate to reduce or repress another. This important question should be the basis of future inquiry.

Constitutive criminology also has a different definition of criminals and victims. The offender is viewed as an "excessive investor" in the power to dominate others. Such "investors" put energy into creating and magnifying differences between themselves and others. This investment of energy disadvantages, disables and destroys others' human potentialities. The victim is viewed as a "recovering subject," still with untapped human potential but with a damaged faith in humanity. Victims are more entrenched, more disabled, and suffer loss. Victims "suffer the pain of being denied their own humanity, the power to make a difference. The victim of crime is thus rendered a non-person, a non-human, or less complete being" (Henry and Milovanovic, 1996: 116).

This reconception of crime, offender and victim locate criminality not in the person, nor in the structure or culture, but in the ongoing creation of social identities through discourse, which leads to a different notion of crime causation. To the constitutive theorist crime is not so much *caused* as *discursively constructed* through human processes of which it is one. Put simply, crime is the coproduced outcome, not only of humans and their environment, but of human agents and the wider society through its excessive investment, to the point of obsession, in crime, through crime shows, crime drama, crime documentaries, crime news, crime books, crime films, crime precautions, criminal justice agencies, criminal lawyers and criminologists. All are parasitic of the crime problem, but as constitutive criminology suggests, they also contribute to its ongoing social and cultural production.

Given this interrelated nature of social structures and human agents and their social and cultural productions in the coproduction of crime, constitutive criminology calls for a justice policy of reconstruction. This is achieved through *replacement discourse* which "is directed toward the dual process of deconstructing prevailing structures of meaning and displacing them with new conceptions, distinctions, words and phrases, which convey alternative meanings. . . . Replacement discourse, then, is not simply critical and oppositional, but provides both a critique and an alternative vision" (Henry and Milovanovic, 1996: 204–5). In terms of diminishing the harm experienced from all types of crime (street, corporate, state, hate etc.), constitutive criminology talks of "liberating" discourses that seek to transform both the prevailing political economies and the associated practices of crime and social control.

Replacement discourse can be implemented through attempts by constitutive criminologists to reconstruct popular images of crime in the mass media through engaging in "newsmaking criminology" (Barak, 1988; 1994). It can also be induced through "narrative therapy" (Parry and Doan, 1994), which developed as part of family therapy to enable offenders (excessive investors in power) to construct more liberating life narratives and thereby reconstitute themselves.

The Contributions to this Book

The first chapter of this book, by Andrew Bak, provides a more detailed excursion into the main ideas contained in our previous work, *Constitutive Criminology*. He considers the key elements of the theory, discusses the coproductive relationship between human agency and social structure, and points out how the human subject, the person as social agent, is actively situated both within and outside this structure, investing in and resisting that which they produce. Crime, as harm, is shown to be partly the emerging outcome of the social construction of legal definitions of crime; but is also revised in the everyday interaction of human agents within and outside societal institutions. Bak shows how constitutive criminology's coproductive assumptions lead to an exploration of the complex, contextually situated, discursively interrelated configurations of social relationships and reveals how these both shape and are shaped by culturally situated, socially organized human agents to recursively produce crime as a cultural product. Finally, Bak addresses the question of how one invests in alternative "replacement discourses" that are more humanistic and that reconnect the fragmented human subject of the industrial social order with the structural products of daily discourse, toward transformative policy.

In the chapters that form Parts 2 and 3 of the book, contributors take up the constitutive challenge, applying its concepts to their own research on crime and criminal justice. Lisa Sanchez (chapter 2) first grounds us with her constitutive analysis of prostitution. She examines agency and resistance through an exploration of ongoing dialogues with women about their initial involvement and daily practices in the local sex trade in a Northwestern city. Drawing upon constitutive theory, she analyzes the relationship between subjectivity, discourse, and local practice. She draws on women's narratives to illustrate how social and legal norms and local practices shape subjectivity, and how voices that resist oppression within these contexts can appear conflicted and contradictory. Sanchez interprets the multi-faceted voices of women in the sex trade as both challenging and reproducing dominant and local discourses of sexual-economic exchange. Furthermore, she shows how they shed light on contradictions and constraints in the local sexual economy as voice, consciousness and social practices play a constitutive role in the social world. Sanchez shows that while the ongoing assertion of agency helps women to negotiate within the rigid confines of their social space, it presents little challenge to the power and authority of sex and law. She concludes with a discussion of the transformative limitations of agency and resistance within these contexts, and the implications this has for constitutive criminology.

In his study of the production of homeless identity Bruce Arrigo (chapter 3) draws on empirical data about how homeless citizens live and recommunalize in shelters and similar housing facilities. Utilizing the interpretive tools of constitutive theory, Arrigo's chapter examines how the discursive meanings embedded in the structural arrangements of one single-room-occupancy (SRO) community, such as rent collection practices, leisure activities, meal rituals, both shape the identity of and are shaped by the tenants residing in the community. Arrigo's article focuses on the relationship between the SRO milieu and definitions of residents as community deviants or criminals.

In chapter 4, Gregg Barak applies his constitutive "newsmaking criminology" to the criminal trial of O.J. Simpson. He provides a case study of the elements that were integrated into the coproduction of this "trial of the century" such as the relationship between high-profile and low-profile disputes, First and Sixth Amendments, modes of newsmaking criminology, and the use of experts. Taking an ethnographic or biographic perspective Barak also reflects on his own radio commentary throughout the trial where he participated as an expert criminologist, in contrast to other legal commentators on O.J., most of whom were either prosecutors or defense attorneys. Through his analysis the variation in mass-mediated legal, social, and political discourses surrounding the O.J. case is revealed. Barak concludes with an optimistic assessment of the prospects of social transformation through replacement discourse.

In contrast, Dion Dennis (chapter 5) shows that replacement discourse is not only a positive force for change but that it can also have a harm-producing, destructive vitality. His analysis of the cultural production of "monsters" shows how icons of monstrosity reflect and refract a number of contemporary social and political issues on genocide, human-machine boundary issues and especially the commodification of consciousness. He argues that the digitalization of social interactions has constituted new forms of identity. It has also generated novel communicative, organizational and criminal practices. To understand how these modes of risk and dangerousness are constructed, argues Dennis, we cannot turn to present law, which often draws on and imposes inappropriate nineteenth-century categories. Rather, we need to examine popular cultural products. Doing so allows us to perceive how dangerousness and criminality are constituted in those extralegal cultural and social worlds that shape political and legal fields. Through the analysis of relevant films and novels, Dennis suggests that we may begin to anticipate and assess constructions of dangerousness and criminality that may be part of our digital future.

Like Dennis' exploration of the constitutive construction of "bodies," in chapter 6, John Brigham provides an interesting extension of Foucault's critique of "bodies" to consider how the personal issue of death and their own tenure may have affected the U.S. Supreme Court Justices' positions on capital punishment. He focuses on the metamorphosis at the Court from 1972–1987, from *Furman* to *McCleskey* and from Douglas to Scalia, with a nod to the significance of the death penalty at the time of Blackmun's retirement. Brigham draws attention to the reconstitution of the Court such that appeal for stays of execution are all but fruitless. The chapter explores a changing institution where jurisprudence features continuity.

The constitutive project's response to the social construction and cultural production of crime is the concern of the contributors to Part 3 of the book. In chapter 7 James Williams argues that, while the constitutive paradigm has devoted substantial attention to the dialectics of reproduction and resistance within the legal context, such as in the courts and the penal system, there has been a paucity of constitutive work on the police and the policing function. He argues that this void is especially apparent given that policing is a major site for the creation, use and legitimation of the distinctions (e.g. offender/victim, order/control) on which the criminal justice system is based. Williams addresses this oversight through a critical analysis of policing as a mode of practical and practiced negotiation between the discursive categorizations of the sociolegal order, and the contextual ambiguity of lived experience. He argues that the officer's role as arbiter of this relation is best expressed through the notion of a "constitutive phenomenology" which highlights both the constitutive functions of the daily judgments and interpretations of the police and the limitations of these efforts, given the inherently ambiguous and negotiated character of police knowledge. Elaborated through the everyday practices of suspicion, discretion and interrogation, the ultimate outcome of this cross-fertilization between policing and constitutive criminology, says Williams, is an appreciation of the phenomenological mediation of the power-knowledge nexus, and hence an understanding of the potential for resistance and transpraxis inhering within the contextuality and ambiguity of local knowledges.

Unfortunately, as Victor Kappeler and Peter Kraska show (chapter 8), when policing is analyzed from the constitutive perspective it is apparent that rather than transpraxis (which seeks to not only negate oppressive powers but offer affirmative vistas for change) replacement discourse can have a stagnating effect. Rather than transforming the structure and organization of policing, community policing discourse is reproducing and even expanding its reach. To illustrate their argument, Kappeler and Kraska focus on the changes in policing discourses that emerged from the community policing movement. They deconstruct the oppositional representation of community policing in various discourses to illustrate the autonomous nature of control ideology that underpins the community policing model.

They explore the use of sensation as a source of ideas and means of reducing resistance to discourse and conclude that policing as reconstituted by metaphoric and sensational replacement enabled the institution to expand targets of control and draw on a wider array of tactics than previously available.

Turning to penal issues, Mary Bosworth (chapter 9) examines agency and choice in women's prisons from a constitutive penological perspective. Based on her research in three British women's prisons, Bosworth explores the problems inherent in representing the contradictory ways by which women resist institutional restrictions and assert their agency in prison. She suggests that while much of women's energy in prison is directed at maintaining their self-identity as active and participating agents, there is inevitable erosion of the women's sense of self by institutional constraints. Bosworth sees such changes to these women's sense of self as related to diffuse "regimes of femininity" operating within the establishment which are reenforced by the women's life experiences of poverty, violence and abuse. She shows that by exploring the contingent nature of women's agency in the context of broader societal discourses of femininity and gender, it is possible to develop a transformative critique of the role and effect of prisons today. In her conclusion Bosworth finds new directions and possibilities for prison studies within the developing field of constitutive criminology.

Jim Thomas and Dragan Milovanovic (chapter 10) take up a different dimension of constitutive penology in a reexamination of their jailhouse lawyers study, first reported in 1989. Here they explore the coproduction of reality by inmates who have taught themselves law while incarcerated. Jailhouse lawyers increasingly construct reality by using legal concepts they learn and employ. Thomas and Milovanovic identify the problem of the dialectical quality of both struggling against and inadvertently reconstituting forms of domination. They consider the potential for a transformative transpraxis and discuss the question of the possible development of a replacement discourse to the system sustaining legal discourse.

Part 4 explores the possibility for institutional transformation toward a constitutive theory of justice. These two chapters expand the constitutive analysis to include recent developments in chaos theory. Robert Schehr (chapter 11) examines "intentional communities," developing what he calls a fourth perspective in social movement theory that builds on postmodern analysis, particularly chaos and constitutive theory. His approach offers the potential of going beyond conventional theorizing which overlooks important dimensions in emerging forms of social organization. Finally, T. R. Young (chapter 12) states the case for a constitutive theory of justice. He draws on new developments in chaos and complexity theory as a grounding for definitions of crime, limits of control as well as strategies in the construction of both substantive and technical questions of social justice. He argues that, given fractal (non-integral) structures of social organization and nonlinear social dynamics, absolute and universalistic definitions of crime and justice are not possible and certainly not helpful. In light of nonlinear social dynamics, approaches to social control have to be much more nuanced, gentle and timely; formal rational models of social control need to give way to episodic and publicly defined dynamic states for given social processes of health, education, law and justice. Similarly, traditional forms of justice—linear, universal, rational—should give way to nonlinear responses to crime, poverty, illness and other social problems. Young argues that since only chaos theory can manage chaos and since uncertainty and nonlinearity have much value, policy on both crime and justice become much more constitutive, that is, politically informed processes.

We conclude the book with an assessment of six years of evaluations of the constitutive project, that have appeared in various journals and texts. This chapter highlights some differences of interpretation that have engaged commentary. In particular we focus on five issues that have arisen: (1) the issue of complex prose; (2) the issue of integrating disciplinary knowledges; (3) the issue of logic and causality in constitutive theory; (4) the issue of crime as a socially constructed reality; and (5) the issue of policy which confronts how a society can stop investing in structures of oppression, whose manifestation channels and sustains the use of the power to harm, without at the same time exercising power over others.

References

Arrigo, Bruce. (1997). Review of Stuart Henry and Dragan Milovanovic's *Constitutive Criminology. Theoretical Criminology*, 3: 392–96.

Barak, Gregg. (1988). Newsmaking criminology: Reflections on the media, intellectuals, and crime. *Justice Quarterly*, 5:565–87.

Barak, Gregg. (Ed.). (1994). *Media, Process and the Social Construction of Crime: Studies in Newsmaking Criminology*. New York: Garland.

Barak, Gregg. (1998). *Integrating Criminologies*. Boston: Allyn and Bacon.

Best, Steven, and Douglas Kellner. (1991). *Postmodern Theory: Critical Interrogations*. Basingstoke, UK: Macmillan.

Borgmann, Albert. (1992). *Crossing the Postmodern Divide*. Chicago: The University of Chicago Press.

Cohen, Stanley. (1990). Intellectual scepticism and political commitment: The case of radical criminology. *Bonger Memorial Lecture* (May 14), University of Amsterdam.

Derrida, Jacques. (1970). Structure, sign and play in the discourse of human sciences. In Richard Macksey and Eugenio Donato (Eds.), *The Languages of Criticism and the Sciences of Man*. Baltimore: Johns Hopkins University Press.

Derrida, Jacques. (1981). *Positions*. Chicago: University of Chicago Press.

Einstadter, Werner, and Stuart Henry. (1995). *Criminological Theory: An Analysis of Its Underlying Assumptions*. Fort Worth, TX: Harcourt Brace College Publishers.

Fitzpatrick, Peter. (1984). Law and societies. *Osgoode Hall Law Journal, 22*: 115–38.

Fitzpatrick, Peter. (1992). *The Mythology of Modern Law*. London: Routledge.

Foucault, Michel. (1977). *Discipline and Punish*. Harmondsworth, UK: Allen Lane.

Foucault, Michel. (1980). *Power/Knowledge: Selected Interviews and Other Writings 1972–1977*. Colin Gordon (Ed.). Brighton, UK: Harvester Press.

Gibbons, Don C. (1994). *Talking About Crime and Criminals*. Englewood Cliffs, NJ: Prentice Hall.

Harrington, Christine. (1988). Moving from integrative to constitutive theories of law: Comments on Itzkowitz. *Law and Society Review, 22*: 963–67.

Henry, Stuart. (1989). Constitutive criminology: The missing paradigm. *The Critical Criminologist, 1* (3), 9, 12.

Henry, Stuart, and Dragan Milovanovic. (1996). *Constitutive Criminology: Beyond Postmodernism*. London: Sage.

Henry, Stuart, and Dragan Milovanovic. (1991). Constitutive criminology. *Criminology, 29*: 293–316.

Henry, Stuart, and Dragan Milovanovic. (1993). Back to basics: A postmodern redefinition of crime. *The Critical Criminologist, 5*(2/3): 1–2, 6, 12.

Henry, Stuart, and Dragan Milovanovic. (1994). The constitution of constitutive criminology: A postmodern approach to criminological theory. In D. Nelken (Ed.), *The Futures of Criminology*. London: Sage.

Hunt, Alan. (1991). Postmodernism and critical criminology. In Brian D. MacLean and Dragan Milovanovic (Eds.), *New Directions in Critical Criminology*. Vancouver: The Collective Press.

Hunt, Alan. (1993). *Explorations in Law and Society: Toward a Constitutive Theory of Law*. New York: Routledge.

Manning, Peter K. (1988). *Symbolic Communications: Signifying Calls and the Police Response*. Cambridge, MA: MIT Press.

Matthews, Roger, and Jock Young (1992). Reflections on Realism. In Jock Young and Roger Matthews (Eds.), *ReThinking Criminology: The Realist Debate*. London: Sage.

Milovanovic, Dragan, and Stuart Henry. (1991). Constitutive penology. *Social Justice*, 18: 204–24.

Milovanovic, Dragan. (1992). *Postmodern Law and Disorder: Psychoanalytic Semiotics, Chaos and Juridic Exegeses*. Liverpool, UK: Deborah Charles.

Nelken, David. (Ed.) (1994). *The Futures of Criminology*. London: Sage.

Parry, Alan, and Robert E. Doan. (1994). *Story Re-Visions: Narrative Therapy in the Postmodern World*. New York: Guilford Press.

Rosenau, Pauline M. (1992). *Postmodernism and the Social Sciences-Insights, Inroads, and Intrusions*. Princeton, NJ: Princeton University Press.

Ruller, Sibo van. (1997). "Review of Stuart Henry and Dragan Milovanovic's *Constitutive Criminology*. *Contemporary Criminology*, 26:496–97.

Schwartz, Martin D., and David O. Friedrichs. (1994). Postmodern thought and criminological discontent: New metaphors for understanding violence. *Criminology*, 32: 221–46.

Silbey, Susan. S. (1992). Making a place for the cultural analysis of law. *Law and Social Inquiry*, 17:39–48.

Stitt, B. Grant, and David J. Giacopassi. (1992). Trends in the connectivity of theory and research in criminology. *The Criminologist*, 17: 1, 3–6.

Teubner, Guenther. (1992). The two faces of Janus: Rethinking legal pluralism. *Cardozo Law Review*, 13: 1443–62.

Teubner, Guenther. (1993). *Law as an Autopoietic System*. Oxford: Blackwell.

Young. T. R. (1995). *The Red Feather Dictionary of Critical Social Science*. Boulder, CO: The Red Feather Institute.

Andrew Bak

1

CONSTITUTIVE CRIMINOLOGY: AN INTRODUCTION TO THE CORE CONCEPTS

Introduction

In this chapter I shall analyze the main ideas of Stuart Henry and Dragan Milovanovic's postmodernist-influenced constitutive theory of crime. However, unlike the earlier versions of postmodernism, which have been called "skeptical" because of their concentration on analytical deconstruction or their alleged nihilism, subjectivism, and defeatism (Einstadter and Henry, 1995; Rosenau, 1992), Henry and Milovanovic's *Constitutive Criminology* offers an "affirmative, optimistic, and humanistic approach emphasizing reconstruction and redirection" (Bohm, 1997: 15). Henry and Milovanovic build their theory upon key assumptions about human nature and society by comparing the modernist and postmodernist perspectives on crime causation and the constitution of crime. Constitutive criminology examines the assumptions behind each of these perspectives about the individual and human behavior, society and social structure, societal law, crime and the victims of crime. In concluding their analysis, Henry and Milovanovic discuss the justice policy and practice implied by their theory.

My purpose here is three-fold: (1) to briefly examine the intellectual influences of constitutive theory; (2) to provide a clear and succinct summary review of constitutive ideas; and (3) to relate the concepts developed to other recent commentary. In doing this I will follow the structure of Henry and Milovanovic's *Constitutive Criminology* (1996) but also draw on some of their earlier statements where these

17

help to elucidate their meaning. First, though, I would like to place their theory in the context of some other work. I have been greatly assisted in this task by the brief intellectual histories provided by Trent Kane (1990) and Bruce Arrigo (1997) and by discussions with, and feedback from, Stuart Henry.

Intellectual Roots of Constitutive Theory

Like all theories, constitutive theory owes an intellectual debt to previous work. Henry and Milovanovic acknowledge a wide range of diverse scholarly ideas. Commentators have identified six major intellectual traditions that seem evident in their work. These traditions are: (1) phenomenology and ethnomethodology, (2) social interactionism or social constructionism, (3) structuration theory, (4) Foucauldian or poststructural theory, (5) discourse analysis, and (6) Marxist theory (Arrigo, 1997: 393; Kane, 1990: 1).

1. Phenomenology and ethnomethedology. As Arrigo says, "From the legacy of existential phenomenology, the ideas of intentionality, being, lived body/lived world and meaning have each been incorporated into constitutive thought" (1997: 393). Founded in Husserl's (1900) philosophy of individual cognition and human conscious experience, phenomenology believes in suspending all prior assumptions about causality and consequences in order to investigate the essence of meaning of immediate lived experience. Merleau-Ponty (1945) applied phenomenological ideas to the psychology of perception. He emphasized the importance of sense data as perceived by the human subject in interaction with the objective world. Each is interrelated, with the material world providing opportunities and the human subject providing order and meaning. Schutz (1967) applied Husserl's ideas in his sociology of knowledge to reveal the assumptions involved in everyday social life. He was particularly interested in common sense knowledge and about how the wider society feeds back through human social action to change and maintain social structures. In the phenomenological view "core meanings about the self exist only within and through social structures by which we are defined . . . [and where] the intentional being locates identity in the life-world" (Arrigo, 1997: 393–94). This led to Garfinkel's (1967; Turner, 1974) ethnomethodology which concentrated on studies of everyday life and methods and unconscious routines used by ordinary folk to communicate and accomplish daily activities.

2. Social interactionism or social constructionism. Social constructionism is related to developments in phenomenology and ethnomethodology, but is also mindful of the interactionist tradition of Mead and Blumer and its application to deviance in the form of labeling theory. Labeling theory (Becker, 1963; Lemert, 1967) stressed the reciprocal effects of human social interaction in producing negative outcomes for selected groups of people through labels which come to engulf them. Social constructionism, in contrast, reflects the ideas of Berger and Luckmann (1967) who argued that there is no underlying objective social reality, only a socially constructed one, that appears to be real: "despite the objectivity that marks the social world in human experience, it does not thereby acquire an ontological status apart from the human activity that produced it. . . . Externalization and objectification are moments in a continuing dialectical process" (Berger and Luckmann, 1967: 60–61). As Kane (1990: 4–7) argues, the social constructionist position with regard to the relationship between human agency and the structures that it creates is closely connected to Berger and Luckmann's ideas.

3. Structuration theory. Giddens' (1984) structuration theory brought together several of these elements to demonstrate that not only is society socially constructed but that it is constructed by human agents through their often unwitting routine activities. According to Giddens, humans actively create the world that seems to stand before them as an object and this has important implications for social change. Giddens (1984) called this interconnectedness the "duality" of the relationship between agency and structure. As Arrigo (1997: 394) points out, "interconnectedness is central to constitutive criminology."

4. Foucaldian or poststructural theory. Also important to constitutive theory is the nature of power-knowledge relations explored by Foucault (1977, 1980), Derrida's (1973, 1978) criticisms of phenomenology for ignoring the structuring effects of language, and Lacan's (1977) psychoanalytical semiotics. As Kane (1990: 8) says, "the whole realm of discourse" as used in constitutive theory "owes a great deal to Michel Foucault." Foucault's thought has permeated numerous fields of enquiry, but it is his exploration of the categorization and repression of deviants, such as the insane, the sick and the law violator, as being based on questionable assumptions about knowledge and acceptable discourse that has proved important for constitutive theory, especially for Hunt's (1993) constitutive theory of law.

5. Discourse analysis.   However, "where Hunt resuscitates Foucault's postmodern work on regimes of truth . . . Henry and Milovanovic provide a poststructural or 'post' postmodern account of discourse analysis within criminology" through which "we are drawn to Lacan's psychoanalytic semiotics now integrated with chaos theory" (Arrigo, 1997: 395). Arrigo points out that understanding language use through discourse analysis is both closely linked to the constitutive agenda and important because: "it signals how dominant, hierarchical relations are conceived, legitimated and reproduced through and within the words we speak. Postmodern discourse analysis is significant to constitutive thought because it suggests the possibility of establishing more inclusive replacement discourses" (1997: 395). Arrigo also points out the centrality of Lacan and Baudrillard to constitutive theory. He explains that with Lacan "we are presented with a postmodern affirmative vision of how desire in language contains the possibility to liberate human agency and to validate new vistas of meaning," whereas with Baudrillard "we are faced with a postmodern sceptical vision of how language absorbs and devours both the 'real' and its media generated appearances" (1997: 395).

6. Marxist theory.   Finally, there is an enduring influence of Marx's use of Hegel's concept of the dialectic and an implicit critique of Durkheim that is found in constitutive theory. For Kane the dialectic is central to constitutive criminology which,

> rejects the assertions of Durkheim that social structures and institutions alone define crime and control as . . . realities, while at the same time refusing to subscribe to the notion that free will and human agency are the exclusive, or primary, determinants of the relationship between humans, society and the products of both. The flow of power is instead a dialectical one. . . each having the potential to affect the other at the same moment in time from opposite directions with different goals inherent in the construction of each (1990: 2).

Kane says that Marx saw "the immediate contributions of human agents to be expressions of past constructions" (1990: 4). Further, Marx "saw the simultaneous shaping of social structure and human actor by each other . . . as two moments in the same process" (1990: 3), but they are moments separated by a "time delay." As a result, Marx ultimately denies that human agents have any autonomy outside the particular historical productive process in which they are set. In contrast, constitutive theory allows the human agent "to make a contribution to the dialectic," and to do so "in the same space and time in which they are created" and in ways that are "not inextricably linked to the mechanistic replication of cumulative historical productive forces" (Kane, 1990: 2–4).

In the following sections I will show how these various ideas come together in Henry and Milovanovic's *Constitutive Criminology*.

Human Subjects and Human Behavior

Constitutive criminological theory perceives the human subject as an active creator of his or her social environment. At the same time, this social environment, as it has or is being collectively constituted by all social agents through discursive mediums, simultaneously produces those who have created it. Here, Henry and Milovanovic perceive the individual human subject as a "recovering subject." This concept is used to illustrate that individuals never really fully complete the world that they actively produce through the use of the discursive practices which exist within the social world, nor is the human agent ever a completed product of his environment: "Both agents and structure are 'mutually constitutive,' and their actions are both liberating and constraining" (Henry and Milovanovic, 1996: 37).

Henry and Milovanovic view this simultaneous process, the individual creating his or her social world and the social world recreating the individual, as one which is both constraining and liberating. They attribute the source of this idea to Giddens' (1984) constitutive theory about the nature of the relationship between human agency and social structure, and compare it to his idea that individuals perceive themselves as being more acted upon than acting. Individuals are often unaware of their role in creating the social world because powerful agencies such as government, industry and social adjudication act to subordinate the individual, placing him/her in circumstances which make them fail to realize the impact they have in creating the social world. Henry and Milovanovic view this process as not only constraining but also liberating. It is liberating because the human subject is seen as unique in having needs, desires, drives and abilities which are satisfied through the process of discourse with other human agents in constructing the social world: "Most human subjects are partially blind builders, intermittently aware that what they build is constructed by them, yet experientially subjected to the constructions they see in others" (Henry and Milovanovic, 1996: 37).

For Giddens, the development of both the human subject and the social world is simultaneous and continuous: "human action occurs as a *durée,* a continuous flow of conduct, as does cognition . . . 'Action' is not a combination of 'acts': acts are constituted only by a discursive moment of attention to the *durée* of the lived through experience" (Giddens, 1984: 2–3).

Henry and Milovanovic's view also reflects the social constructionism of Peter Manning who writes, "The social world is composed of ongoing processes delineated perceptually, subjectively, and cognitively and individually and collectively" (Manning, 1988: 13).

Discourse for Henry and Milovanovic is an essential and necessary medium by which human agents act to construct their social world and through which they are shaped by that social world, simultaneously: "Without a discursive medium constructed with others through which people converse with themselves, without their unique turn of our cultural conglomerate of meaning, they and we would cease to exist" (Henry and Milovanovic, 1996: 38).

The discursively active human subject is also viewed as essential to the simultaneous development of the human subject and the social world. Henry and Milovanovic use the term "human subject" rather than "individual." The latter is closed, completed and unitary, whereas the postmodern concept of "subject" is more contingent, open and in the process of being constructed. However, the person is seen as subjectively active only through social discourse. Subjective creativity, desires, drives and needs emerge by and through social discourse. This subjective emergence creates a social world: "Without the active individual human agent there would be no intersubjectivity, no society" (Henry and Milovanovic, 1996: 38).

Everything that constitutes the social world is seen to be interconnected by and through a discursive medium: "Human agency is connected to the structures that it makes, as are human agents to each other in making those structures" (Henry and Milovanovic, 1996: 39).

Constitutive criminologists view discourse as being created and exchanged in a structured context. Speech, body language, and the written word are all symbols which constitute this structured context. Through discourse, social reality is created, recreated, and preserved. Moreover, "once social structures are constituted as summary representations, their ongoing existence depends upon their continued and often unwitting reconstruction in everyday discourse, a discourse replete with tacit understandings whose basis lies outside the realm of intrinsic intersubjective communication and intersubjectively established meaning" (Henry and Milovanovic, 1996: 40).

To these authors, the discursive practices that work to establish and reestablish our social world are powerful tools of creation and recreation. Because of this, human subjects tend to perceive their social world as routinized, not open to change, evolution, or transformation. Yet the constitutive analysis reveals these very possibilities for change. From the human subject's perspective, change in our social environment is only perceived, understood and acknowledged in times of crisis when old forms of discourse lose their usefulness as tools for creating our social world. A change in our social world is possible through discourse or social process. The constitutive approach is about, "emerging renditions of subjectivity," which is attributed to the human subject's inherent characteristics of being able to be sensitive and to empathize with those with whom we actively engage in discourse. This concept of "emerging renditions of subjectivity" through discursive social processes fosters the conditions for change, and parallels Turner's view of social process: "The process whereby individuals (and other types of social units) mutually influence each other and, in doing so create, maintain, change, or terminate a pattern of joint action" (Turner, 1978: 569).

Clearly, Henry and Milovanovic's constitutive theory, as it perceives the human subject and behavior, is interrelated with a constitutive perspective on society and social structure. It is worth considering these views on human agency as they paint a more complete picture of the overall perspective on which constitutive criminology is founded by examining their views on society and social structure.

Society and Social Structure

From the perspective of constitutive philosophy, the social world or our social reality is created and recreated by and through the continuous active discourse of human subjects. Henry and Milovanovic believe human subjects, through their discursive practices, internalize images of their social world, the world which they create, a world that simultaneously recreates them. Found within these images of the social world is the human subject's perception of consensus regarding social order and maintenance of the social world.

A conventional Durkheimian view of consensus has been expressed as, "shared ways of perceiving and understanding the world. These ingredients of social order are summed up in the assumption that every group is held together by a consensus, by a tacit agreement on basic rules and values" (Broom and Selznick, 1973: 8). For Henry and Milovanovic the social world must be examined beyond the realm of the structures of consensus. It must focus upon those appearances or images of structures within society whose investment by human agents, as though they were real, cause harm to humans subject and to their ordering.

Just as consensus within the social world is come upon through human subject's active discourse, so are those structures which seem to harm the human subjects. But structures do not themselves act, because, as Henry and Milovanovic point out, they are virtual, not real. It is people (human subjects) who harm others because of the way their actions are framed by the images of structures they invest in as though they were real. They are subjects in a sense of being subject to such an agency-denying process of discursive deception. Henry and Milovanovic envision a social world where those constructions of reality which indirectly harm people are substituted with constructions or discourse which do not harm. They believe that harm and injustice within our social world can be reduced by and through the elimination of those constructions of discourse which effectively connect humans to their social products enabling the substitution of those which harm with less harmful forms of discourse or constructions of reality. Henry and Milovanovic write: "indeed, constitutive theory's view of structure asserts that it is necessary to analyze precisely how those constructions of reality become real enough to harm, and strategizes the ways to interrupt this process and to substitute for it less harmful constructions" (Henry and Milovanovic, 1996: 65). As Kane (1990: 15–17) points out, in this regard their ideas have much in common with those of Ernest Becker (1968) who believed in the investment in, and adoption of, moral discourses in order to solve our self-created social problems.

Henry and Milovanovic's constitutive theory stresses the view that active discourse is perpetually and contingently negotiated between the human subject and the social world, simultaneously and infinitely. Through this perspective, all structural elements which comprise the social world are not manifest but are merely symbols which are created and recreated during active discourse. This constitutive view is not unlike that in the work of Laclau who writes, "there is a constant movement from the elements to the system but no ultimate systems or elements" (Laclau, 1988: 254).

Constitutively speaking, structures within our social world are continually formed through active discourse. They gain legitimacy only through the human agents' discursive investment in them, constructing and reconstructing them, and relating to them. Again, Henry and Milovanovic derive this by and through Giddens' theory of duality of structure. Giddens writes:

> The constitution of agents and structures are not two independently given sets of phenomenon, a dualism, but represent a duality. According to the notion of duality of structure, the structural properties of social systems are both medium and outcome of the practices they recursively organize. Structure is not "external" to individuals: as memory traces, and as instantiated in social practices, it is in a certain sense more "internal" than exterior to their activities . . . Structure is not to be equated with constraint but is always constraining and enabling (1984: 25).

Through Giddens' examination of constitutive social theory and Henry and Milovanovic's application of this to the structuring of our social world through human discourse, we are better able to envision how the active human subject can initiate social change by and through the substitution of alternative forms of discourse.

Constitutive Analysis of Law—
The Structuring of Law and Social Order

Constitutive theory views "control institutions" (Henry, 1989: 9–12), and law in general, as aspects of social structure which are established and maintained through individual human discursive practices. "Control institutions" are discursively produced for the purpose of maintaining order over the discursive distinctions which arise within our social world. Henry writes: "From the perspective of constitutive criminology, control institutions are thus the relations among human agents acting to police the conceptual distinctions among discursively constructed social structures" (Henry, 1989: 9). "Control institutions," therefore, emerge and become established within our social world by and through discourse which is control oriented, intersubjectively routed, having the purpose of preserving the virtual social world, which actively, through the investment of energy, reconstitutes them.

In a sense, and with some parallel to Schutz (1967), control institutions are "second order" constructions of reality. They are constructions that make the "first order" constructions appear real. Or in Baudrillard's terms, control institutions are part of "hyper-reality" whose appearance of being real (through their coercive use of human energy to enforce distinctions) confers reality on social structures. The virtual is real, because the patterns of control agents' actions assume it to be real. Thus, drawing on Knorr-Cetina and Cicourel (1981), Henry writes: "institutions of social control then, are the organized acting out of discursively produced 'control thoughts,' whose very action reflects on the reality of that which they are organized to defend" (Henry, 1989: 9).

Law or institutions of control are not perceived by constitutive theory as "a product of a democratic compromise" (Becker, 1963, Schur 1980), "social compact" (Bentham, 1765), or "conscience collective" (Durkheim, 1893; Lukes, 1973); nor are they a product of political domination by some type of an elite interest group (Becker, 1963; Schur, 1980). Rather, law as perceived by the constitutive theory, is socially constituted through discourse and as Fitzpatrick (1992) pointed out, is myth. Indeed, these authors' indebtedness to Fitzpatrick's social theory of law is clear through their use of the dialectic concept of "interrelation." "Constitutive theory is based on the idea that law is, in part, social relations and social relations are, in part, law" (Henry and Milovanovic, 1996: 86). Henry and Milovanovic stress the term "interrelation" when describing how social relations through discourse establish and maintain control institutions, and how control institutions affect the individual subject. The elements which constitute society are perceived by constitutive theorists as being interrelated through time and space. These elements are not viewed as merely being connected through causal relationships. Indeed, the elements which constitute our society as we perceive it through discourse is constituted by and through discursive interrelations. Henry and Milovanovic's theory of interrelation thus finds much support in the work of Fitzpatrick who writes: "Elements of law are elements of other forms and visa versa" (Fitzpatrick, 1984: 122). Henry and Milovanovic attribute the stability that exists within the social world to this interrelation among human agents, discourse, and the discourse which creates and maintains control structures and through these the social order of virtual society.

Constitutive Definition of Crime and the Construction of the Victim

In understanding the constitutive theory of crime in the context of the preceding discussion, one must set aside any preconceptions of a legalistically-rooted ideology. Henry and Milovanovic's constitutive theory views crime as something more than a violation of written laws derived from a societal consensus of norms and values. The authors make it clear that statutory definitions of crime, as they are shaped through discourse, are merely a selective conglomeration of harms and injustices. These are rendered inadequate in satisfying what the constitutive approach perceives to be crime. Constitutive theory argues that such legalistic definitions of crime fail to consider the context or meaning of crime and do not consider the evolutionary and ever-changing aspects of discourse which lead to the construction and interpretation of what forms of discourse are criminal. Furthermore, legalistic interpretations of crime fail to realize and consider the circumstances under which active human discourse becomes criminal.

From the constitutive perspective on crime, we see an approach which considers the harm, injustice, pain and conflict which stems from human discourse. The authors of the constitutive approach view crime as a movement of discourse that is created and recreated by and through "relations of inequality" (Henry and Milovanovic, 1996: 116). Through such analysis regarding the constitution of crime, Henry and Milovanovic express their unique constitutive definition of crime: "Crime is the expression of some agency's energy to make a difference on others and it is the exclusion of those others who in the instant are rendered powerless to maintain or express their humanity" (Henry and Milovanovic, 1996: 116).

Through discursively constituted harm, human subjects undergo a transformation. They are: "reduced from what they are (reduction), prevented from becoming what they might be (repression)" (Henry and Milovanovic, 1996: 116). Crime, then, is a social phenomenon, a phenomenon that focuses upon the reduction and repression of the human subject that is inflicted by way of inequality through the discursive practices of social structures and of other human subjects. Inequality is exercised through power and much of the harm created by the "investors" in this power is not acknowledged in legalistic definitions of what constitutes crime.

Furthermore, Henry and Milovanovic view law as a medium by which power is exercised and legitimized by the powerful over those who are less powerful. Law then legitimizes power and in so doing cannot suppress the reduction and repression of the less powerful. They draw on Young and Rush to illustrate this concept: Law designed to uphold power differentials cannot protect against harm, it frames its construction (Young and Rush, 1994: 155–72).

Constitutive criminology asserts that crime must therefore be defined in a manner which considers and acknowledges all forms of harm (repression), and inequality (reduction) that are exercised through law (investment in power). Thus, to reduce harm within our society, we must adopt alternative forms of discourse or social constructions—ones that reduce (a) inequality through power, (b) the oppressive exercise of power, and (c) the power that legitimizes itself through the law.

The Constitutive Approach to Causality and the Constitution of Crime

Constitutive criminologists view crime as a perceptually produced outcome of a variety of contexts of human discourse. We saw earlier how individual human subjects interact through the active use of discursive practices. Through active discourse, individuals develop interrelations with other social forms and these interrelations are maintained and sustained through what Henry and Milovanovic have termed "COREL sets" (referring to constitutive interrelational sets). Their model of the causality of crime shows it to be codetermined and interrelated to other constructed, and being constructed, entities through discourse. One can describe the concept of codetermination and interrelationship as the overlapping and interconnecting of social units which are constructed and maintained through discourse. These theorists see social units existing as both separate and attached to other social constructions, with neither one being the necessary product of the other; yet each one contributing to the coproduction of the other.

The degree to which active discourse can become codetermined, overlapped or interconnected is related to the discursive region that is created. Henry and Milovanovic (1994) illustrate three specific discursive forms or regions: the first depicts the present configuration of social order and discursive practices; the second is created for the purpose of negotiating existing discursive practices; and the third region is created through disagreement with existing discourse. It is this third region where alternative discursive practices are introduced; this is the realm of "replacement discourse." This third region depicts the degree to which the human subject is not attached to existing social conditions, whereas the first region depicts the human subject's attachment to existing social constructions and the second region depicts skepticism over existing discursive practices. When regions of alternative discourses are formed, the changes in discursive practice that evolve within the region affect the regions of existing discourse and regions where alternative forms are negotiated. Because of the interconnections which exist between all regions, all regions interact with one another.

Through Henry and Milovanovic's notion of complex COREL sets and how the constitutive theory defines crime, we are able to see that the conditions which foster crime are the result of active discourse which expresses and articulate power and control through COREL sets. Henry and Milovanovic state: "an analysis of the cause of crime is not a matter of factors but a matter of the constitutive dialects of power and control expressed and articulated through structurally coupled COREL sets" (Henry and Milovanovic, 1996: 174). To effectively apply constitutive criminology, we must gain an awareness as to how power is come upon and exercised in a manner which creates inequalities. For constitutive theorists, this awareness can be arrived at through the examination of constitutive interrelational sets (COREL sets) which acknowledge law, and through the guise of law, legitimizes the wielding of power to create harm. Through this examination of existing discourse and COREL sets, discursive patterns may be substituted with a less harmful replacement discourse. Thus, from the constitutive perspective, crime is caused, through institutionally situated and discursively ordered processes, when people lose site of the humanity and integrity of those with whom they interrelate and whom their actions and interactions affect. It is the outcome of language and thought processes which objectify others as separate, dehumanized entities, mediated through the COREL sets of a particular historical period. Such conception is carried by discourses that pervade and interpenetrate that totality. (Henry and Milovanovic, 1996: 175).

Justice Policy of Constitutive Criminology: Replacement Discourse

In one sense, the justice policy of constitutive criminology is one of replacement discourse, but in another sense, it is much greater. The purpose of implementing replacement discourse is to disassemble current discursive meaning and reconstruct or replace meaning with new conceptions. For Henry and Milovanovic, replacement discourse "is not merely another package of ways to talk and make sense of the world, but a language of 'transpraxis' " (Henry and Milovanovic, 1991).

The authors allude to the fact that creating replacement discourse involves the critical deconstruction of established discursive truths, then replacing these with alternative forms of universally created discourse. Henry and Milovanovic write: "the critical component of replacement discourse resides in the criminologist's ability to deconstruct that which is established truth, while at the same time to provide the replacement aspects to claim any newly created space with its own internally generated alternatives" (Henry and Milovanovic, 1996: 204).

Through the concept of replacement discourse Henry and Milovanovic embark on a mission to identify harmful forms of discourse by focusing upon the interconnections between human subjects, societal structures and discursively constructed harm, and in doing so, they seek to substitute alternative, less harmful forms of discourse. They illustrate this point by stating: "replacement discourse, then, is not simply critical and oppositional, but provides both a critique and an alternative vision" (Henry and Milovanovic, 1996: 205).

Henry and Milovanovic render their conception of alternative discourse effective only through its inception into the social world. This begins with human subjects taking it upon themselves to initiate new discursive constructions. This is not something to be left to an abstract general movement but is something everyone, including the authors can invest in. Henry and Milovanovic envision this through Unger's (1987) "superliberalism" and Giroux's (1992) conceptualization of a "cultural revolutionary." Butler (1992) personifies this "cultural revolutionary" as follows: "the cultural revolutionary finds her/himself both assuming a dialogical discursive subject position and taking a more activist and interventionist stance, based on provisional and contingent universalities established through ongoing struggles" (Henry and Milovanovic, 1996: 205).

Constitutive criminology uses Lacan's discourse of the hysteric (Lacan, 1991) to illustrate the construction of recursive discourses which harm and continue to harm. An individual in despair communicates feelings to another human subject, who relays back a message of conventional knowledge that maintains the despair of the human subject. Henry and Milovanovic clarify that the human subject remains in despair not necessarily because the other person had bad intentions, but because he or she was unable to provide the one in despair with anything more than recursive discourse which instilled the despair the individual was experiencing. Rudimentary exemplification such as this, illustrates how substituted discourse could be implemented to alleviate pain or harm within our social world. In the final section, I set out to examine the justice practices of the constitutive approach and how it seeks to replace "technologies of discipline" with "languages of possibility" (Henry and Milovanovic, 1996: 215).

Justice Practices of Constitutive Criminology

In this final section I will examine the strategies put forth by Henry and Milovanovic which can be utilized in the reduction of harm by and through the substitution of less harmful discourse. Their goal is for a wider social transformation. The first of these strategies put forth by the authors examines ways in which alternative forms of discourse can be assimilated into the mainstream popular culture. For this to be possible, large-scale social organizations must also cooperate in the encouragement of replacement discourse. The social forces which Henry and Milovanovic target for this cooperation are the news media.

Members of the news media are involved in creating a discursive image of what exists in our society. This image is transmitted to social audiences who are, in the process, partly constituted by what they absorb from the media. Drawing on Barak's (1988, 1991, 1994) "Newsmaking Criminology," Henry and Milovanovic argue that what is transmitted are partial truths which act to sensationalize negative discursive practices. In doing so, negative images are created and the social world acts towards them in ways which create more harm. Thus Barak states: "in the postmodern era, social problems such as homelessness, sexual assault, or drug abuse are politically constructed, ideologically articulated, and media produced events" (1991: 5). Barak believes that criminologists should act as credible reporters of criminological news, reporters that consider all the images and aspects of crime and crime control. Crime themes should be constructed, "as a means of bringing about social change and social justice" (1988: 585).

Henry and Milovanovic urge that criminologists, including themselves, intercede in the newsmaking process to implement a different approach to the construction of crime news. In doing so, alternative forms of discourse can be invested in as part of the audience's construction of the social world, a discourse which generates a less harmful reaction to the harm that was reported. Henry and Milovanovic state, "to transcend our passive contribution to such socially constructed and publicly consumed crime truths, and thereby to cease investing in the continuity of harm, it is necessary for criminologists to actively intercede in the constitutive process" (1996: 216).

The second strategy for implementing replacement discourse is a refractory process which Henry and Milovanovic term "social judo" (Einstadter and Henry, 1995: 315). Social judo is a practice where constitutive energy is displaced and redirected into positive interrelations, positive COREL sets. I examined earlier how harm is constituted through the exercise of power over others, which denies them their humanity. "Social judo" focuses upon replacing exercised power with alternative discursive practices which prove to subdue the power exercised by the powerful in making them realize the limitations of the power which they exercise. Einstadter and Henry explain the concept of "social judo" or the "judo metaphor of crime control" as where people act together to defensively employ the strength and power of oppressors towards their self limitation (Einstadter and Henry, 1995: 315).

Another way in which alternative discursive practices may be implemented is by assisting those who suffered through the exercise of power over them. Henry and Milovanovic indicate that such assistance can come in many forms. Support groups provide an environment which provides the suffering with the forum where their problems can be discussed and where ways to overcome them can be envisioned. Through support groups, strategies are designed to help humans cope with recovering from their environment.

Conclusion

It is clear from this brief review of the main themes of Henry and Milovanovic's work that constitutive theory requires a whole new approach to crime and crime control. It uses such innovative and challenging concepts that much of what has previously passed for criminology might be abandoned. Yet, consistent with their affirmative method, Henry and Milovanovic urge us not to do that. However, it is questionable how far thinking along conventional lines, or even through conventional criminological theory, is helpful. As one astute commentator has observed, while modern criminologists believe

> that the world can be characterized in terms of order, perfection, essentialism, causality, and individual autonomy . . . Many modern criminologists think that certain existing social "structures" "cause" "crime." After reading this book one can no longer use these three words without doubting their ontological status . . . What is the value of this book for criminology? It is daring, stimulating, and sows doubt about conventional knowledge. It pierces the partitions between disciplines. In short, it has some great qualities, and it can provide criminology with a vitalizing impulse (Ruller, 1997: 496–97).

I have little to add, except that I personally have found their theory to be not merely an academic exercise, but a philosophy of life, one that can be lived by, day to day.

References

Arrigo, Bruce. (1997). A review of Stuart Henry and Dragan Milovanovic's *Constitutive Criminology. Theoretical Criminology*, 1: 392–96.

Barak, Gregg. (1988). Newsmaking criminology: Reflections on the media, intellectuals, and crime. *Justice Quarterly*, 5:565–87.

Barak, Gregg. (1991). Homelessness and the case for community-based initiatives: The emergence of a model shelter as a short-term response to the deepening crisis in housing. In H. Pepinsky and R. Quinney (Eds.), *Criminology as Peacemaking*. Bloomington, Indiana University Press.

Barak, Gregg. (Ed.) (1994). *Media, Process and the Social Construction of Crime: Studies in Newsmaking Criminology*. New York: Garland Press.

Becker, Ernest. (1968). *The Structure of Evil: An Essay on the Unification of the Science of Man*. New York: Free Press.

Becker, Howard S. (1963). *Outsiders: Studies in the Sociology of Deviance*. New York: Free Press.

Bentham, Jeremy. (1765). *An Introduction to the Principles of Morals and Legislation*. Edited by J. H. Burns and H. L. A. Hart. London: Athlone Press, University of London.

Berger, Peter, and Thomas Luckmann. (1967). *The Social Construction of Reality*. New York: Doubleday.

Bohm, Robert J. (1997). A review of Stuart Henry and Dragan Milovanovic's *Constitutive Criminology. The Criminologist*, 22 (May/June: 15–16).

Broom, Leonard, and Phillip Selznick. (1973). Sociology: A Text With Adapted Readings. In V. A. Tomovic (Ed.), *Definitions in Sociology: Convergence, Conflict and Alternative Vocabularies*. St. Catherines, Ontario: Diliton Publications, Inc.

Butler, Judith. (1992). Contingent foundations: Feminism and the question of postmodernism. In J. Butler and J. W. Scott (Eds.), *Feminists Theorize the Political*. London: Routledge.

Derrida, Jacques. (1973). *Speech and Phenomena*. Evanston, IL: Northwestern University Press.

Derrida, Jacques. (1978). *Writing and Difference*. London: Routledge and Kegan Paul.

Durkheim, Emile. (1893). *The Division of Labor in Society*. New York: Free Press.

Einstadter, Werner, and Stuart Henry. (1995). *Criminological Theory: An Analysis of Its Underlying Assumptions*. Fort Worth, TX: Harcourt, Brace.

Fitzpatrick, Peter. (1984). Law and societies. *Osgoode Hall Law Journal*, 22: 115–138.

Fitzpatrick, Peter. (1992). *The Mythology of Modern Law*. London: Routledge.

Foucault, Michel. (1977). *Discipline and Punish*. New York: Pantheon.

Foucault, Michel. (1980). *Power/Knowledge: Selected Interviews and Other Writings*. Edited by Colin Gordon. New York: Pantheon.

Garfinkel, Harold. (1967). *Studies in Ethnomethodology*. Englewood Cliffs, NJ: Prentice Hall.

Giddens, Anthony. (1994). *The Constitution of Society: Outline of the Theory of Structuration*. Oxford: Polity Press.

Giroux, Henry. (1992). *Border Crossings*. New York: Routledge.

Henry, Stuart. (1989). Constitutive criminology: The missing paradigm. *The Critical Criminologist*, 1(3): 9, 12.

Henry, Stuart, and Dragan Milovanovic. (1991). Constitutive criminology. *Criminology*, 29: 293–316.

Henry, Stuart, and Dragan Milovanovic. (1996). The constitution of constitutive criminology. In D. Nelken (Ed.), *The Futures of Criminology*. London: Sage.

Henry, Stuart, and Dragan Milovanovic. (1996). *Constitutive Criminology: Beyond Postmodernism*. Thousand Oaks, California: Sage.

Hunt, Alan. (1993). *Explorations in Law and Society: Toward a Constitutive Theory of Law*. New York: Routledge.

Husserl, Edmund. (1990). *Logical Investigations*. J. N. Finlay (Trans.). 2 vols. London: 1970.

Kane, Trent E. (1990). *Here There be Dragons: Some Elements of Stuart Henry's Constitutive Criminology*. Unpublished Master's Paper. St. Paul's College, University of Manitoba.

Knorr-Cetina, Karin, and Aaron V. Cicourel (Eds.). (1981). *Advances in Social Theory: Towards an Integration of Micro- and Macro- Sociologies*. London: Routledge and Kegan Paul.

Lacan, Jacques. (1977). *Ecrits*. Translated by A. Sheridan. New York: Norton.

Lacan, Jacques. (1991). *L' Envers de la psychanalyse*. Paris, France: Editions du Seuil.

Laclau, Ernest. (1988). Metaphor and social antagonism. In C. Nelson and L. Grossberg (Eds.). *Marxism and the Interpretation of Culture*. Urbana, IL: University of Illinois Press.

Lemert, Edwin. M. (1967). *Human Deviance, Social Problems and Social Control*. Englewood Cliffs, NJ: Prentice-Hall.

Lukes, Steven. (1973). *Emile Durkheim: His Life and Work*. Harmondsworth, UK: Penguin Books.

Manning, Peter K. (1988). *Symbolic Communication: Signifying calls and the Police Response*. Cambridge, MA: MIT Press.

Merleau-Ponty, Maurice. (1945). *Phenomenology of Perception*. Translated by C. Smith. London: 1962

Rosenau, Pauline Marie. (1992). *Postmodernism and the Social Sciences: Insights, Inroads, and Intrusions*. Princeton, NJ: Princeton University Press.

Ruller, Sibo van. (1997). Review of Stuart Henry and Dragan Milovanovic's *Constitutive Criminology*. *Contemporary Sociology*, 26:467–97.

Schur, Edwin M. (1980). *The Politics of Deviance: Stigma Contests and the Uses of Power*. Englewood Cliffs, NJ: Prentice-Hall.

Schutz, Alfred. (1967). *The Phenomenology of the Social World* (1932). Evanston, IL: Northwestern University Press.

Turner, Jonathan H. (1974). *Ethnomethodology*. Harmondsworth, UK: Penguin.

Turner, Jonathan H. (1979). Sociology: Studying human systems. In V. A. Tomovic (Ed.), *Definitions in Sociology: Convergence, Conflict and Alternative Vocabularies*. St. Catherines, Ontario: Diliton Publications, Inc.

Unger, Roberto M. (1987). *False Necessity*. New York: Cambridge University Press.

Young, Alison, and Peter Rush. (1994). The law of victimage in urban realism: Thinking through inscription of violence. In D. Nelken (Ed.), *The Futures of Criminology*. London: Sage.

PART 2

AGENCY, RESISTANCE, AND REGULATED
BODIES IN THE CONSTITUTION OF CRIME

Lisa Sanchez

2

SEX, LAW AND THE PARADOX OF AGENCY AND RESISTANCE IN THE EVERYDAY PRACTICES OF WOMEN IN THE "EVERGREEN" SEX TRADE

Introduction

This chapter explores agency and resistance through narratives gathered from ethnographic fieldwork with women in the sex trade in one Northwestern city in the United States. Drawing on constitutive theory, I consider the relationship between agency, subjectivity, and practice. In this study, women's narratives illustrate how law and cultural discourse shape the microstructure of practice in the local sex trade, and how voices that resist oppression appear conflicted and multi-faceted. These contradictions are interpreted, in part, as a resistant local discourse that both contests and reproduces dominant sociolegal and reformist discourses on prostitution. The chapter concludes by considering the possibility of a replacement discourse formed around women's narratives of resistance.

Theoretically, I frame the study in relation to dominant historical discourses of law and culture and contemporary articulations of legal reform. Against the background of these discourses, I question the binary logic that positions the "prostitute"[1] as one who either "chooses" or is "forced to engage in prostitution"[2] by recovering the context and copresence of sex-trade practice.[3] Specifically, I explore the interplay of agency and resistance as an alternative to conventional constructions of sex trade practice as an individual choice or an impossible choice. In contrast to contractarian perspectives (i.e., those that characterize prostitution as a contractual exchange of sex acts for money), I will show that the structural context and the copresent quality of sex trade practices shape the actions of the women who participated in this study and preclude the possibility of "free choice." This does not mean, however, that these women are helpless, dependent, or incapable of consent. Rather, their agency is contingent. It takes form in ongoing interactions negotiated and re-negotiated *between* interacting parties for the duration of each interaction. The constitutive quality of identity formation is articulated autopoietically through the repetition of embedded, embodied practice (Milovanovic, 1994).

Methodologically, I recount the stories of a small group of women involved in the sex trade in a predominantly white, working-class community in the Pacific Northwest United States. To protect the identities of those who participated in the study, I use the pseudonym "Evergreen" to refer to that city. Using a qualitative approach, I draw from observations and taped and untaped conversations with women, their customers, and police officers during a three-year period. The ethnographic method I employ strives to contextualize women's stories within the dynamics of the geographic and social interaction space in which their daily activities take place. By way of introduction consider the following: "I was about 17 or 18 [whenI did my first date][4]—just old enough to go away and make a choice, just old enough that I had some options."

Now in her twenties, "Cory"[5] recently returned to street prostitution because she couldn't make enough money in her "straight job" to pay her monthly bills and court fines: "There's no job that I can get that's going to pay better that's legal. This is just straight out cash and you can get as much as you need. . . . I don't feel like I have any other options."

Cory claimed that she turned to prostitution when she was just old enough to make a choice, but she also said that she doesn't feel like she has any other options. Her narrative account of her initial involvement and continued participation in prostitution embodies a tension between her articulation of the logic of free contract and the impact of economic and social marginalization on her life.

The contradiction of women's expressed agency and the violence of everyday life was most striking in Amanda's characterization of how she became involved in prostitution as a contractual arrangement:

> If two consenting people want to do that and it's comfortable for both of them so be it. . . . When I was raped at gunpoint, [prostitution] became a way for me to get men to give me their money for me having the control. [So you thought of it that way?] That's right, revenge. It's like, you want it, you pay for it, I'll tell you when, I'll tell you how, I'll tell you why.

The paradoxical articulation of agency under conditions of excessive constraint in these women's narratives exposes the dominant position of the language of choice in the cultural common sense (Gramsci, 1971; Lazarus-Black and Hirsch, 1994). Henry and Milovanovic (1996) view these contradictions as coproduced in the relationship between human agency and social structure. In the present study, dominant legal and cultural discourses and common knowledge shape the local context of the sex trade and the microstructure of practice. Women's talk about their participation in the sex trade—what Geertz would call their local knowledge (1983)—both forms around and reshapes these discourses, which in turn shapes their agency-self as subject. The women who participated in this study characterize their particular situations as a product of individual choices even as they describe situations of abuse and non-consent. In spite of having little control over their economic circumstances and the conditions of their practice, they articulate a consciousness of choice and individual responsibility (Collier, Maurer, and Suarez-Naváz, 1995; Musheno, 1995).

The chapter is divided into five sections. In the first section, I consider the constitution of sex trade identities and practices through an analysis of liberal legality and contemporary activist discourses on prostitution. Second, I detail the dimensions of the material and legal context of three variations of sex trade practice in local sex markets. Third, I explore the question of agency and resistance, drawing on dialogues with women about their initial involvement and daily practices in the local sex economy. Finally, in the discussion and conclusion, I interpret agency and resistance through an analysis of the local knowledge of the women who participated in this study, and I explore the possibility of a replacement discourse framed around resistance narratives.

The Logic of Contract and the Role of the
Liberal Legal Subject in the Constitution of
Sex Trade Identities and Practices

Radical critiques of contract doctrine have sought to demystify the structure of individual subjectivity and the logic of free contract (Unger, 1975; Kelman, 1979; Kairys, 1982; Pateman, 1988; Radin, 1996). As the authors of "sanctioned identities" put it, the "bourgeois ideology of law"[6] shapes the meaning of individualism *as freedom to act as one wishes and responsibility for one's actions* (Collier *et al.*, 1995; Musheno, 1995). Proponents of contract theory understand and interpret people's actions as isolated events that are the product of calculated decisions to maximize one's utility. In each interaction situation, the choosing subject is positioned as a powerful and self-interested consumer of goods and services. Any action, within this liberal economic framework, can be defined as a rational choice because each transaction is treated the same way and each transacting individual is considered equal. But making choices requires that one have alternatives from which to choose, that one have knowledge of the alternatives, and the capacity to act on them. Here I build on the work of constitutive criminologists and legal scholars who have begun deconstructing the cultural logic of contract doctrine and uncovering its role in constructing people's identities and interpretations of their actions (Henry, 1983, 1989; Merry, 1986, 1990; Bumiller, 1988; Harrington, 1988; Harrington and Yngvesson, 1990; Yngvesson, 1993; Silbey, 1992; Hunt, 1993; Greenhouse, Yngvesson, and Engel, 1994; Collier *et al.*, 1995; Ewick and Silbey, 1995; Musheno, 1995; Henry and Milovanovic, 1996).

The foundational logic of positive law assumes a rational, autonomous, self-interested subject who acts with knowledge, intention, and forethought (Locke [1689], 1980; Beccaria, [1764], 1963; Bentham [1789], 1948). These foundational assumptions underlie several contemporary explanations of crime causation, particularly neo-classical, law and economics, rational choice, and routine activities approaches (Becker, 1968; Rawls, 1971; Wilson and Herrnstein, 1985; Clarke and Felson, 1993). The establishment of criminal intent or *mens rea* ensures that individuals will not be criminally liable for involuntary behavior. More insidiously, however, it constitutes all other illegal conduct as the product of intention and free will (Henry and Milovanovic, 1996). In the absence of necessity, duress, self-defense, immaturity, mistake of fact, intoxication, or insanity, an act committed is presumed to be an act intended. These assumptions tacitly frame common knowledge and inform the legal treatment of those with "suspect identities." But, the law produces suspect identities, in part, as a discourse of displacement wherein questionable assumptions about both visible and hidden conduct are always already attached to those who occupy stigmatized public spaces (Sanchez, 1997a).

The constitution of prostitution as legally prohibited behavior and the treatment of women in prostitution in law, in criminological and sociological research, and in moral and therapeutic discourses follows the binary logic of choice-making rooted in positive law. Historically, discourses on prostitution have constructed "prostitutes" as intentional villains or passive victims in need of saving (Walkowitz, 1980; Rosen, 1982; Musheno and Seeley, 1986; Pheterson, 1986 and 1989; Lucas, 1995). In the contemporary period, the polemics that situate women in prostitution as free agents or helpless victims resurfaced in the debate between prostitutes' rights organizations (PROs) and radical feminists over the issues of choice and consent (Bell, 1987; Freeman, 1989; Schrage, 1989; Fechner, 1994; Jenness, 1993).[7] With legal reform as the core objective, prostitutes' rights groups framed the issue as a struggle for sexual freedom and worker rights (Pheterson, 1986 and 1989; Delacoste and Alexander, 1987; Jenness, 1993).[8] Alternatively, radical feminists argued that prostitution was not work, but enforced sexual violence (Barry, 1979; Dworkin, 1979; Erbe, 1984; MacKinnon, 1987; Reanda, 1991; Baldwin, 1992)—in Kathleen Barry's terms, sexual slavery. Radical feminists opposed legalization and argued instead for tougher enforcement against customers and those who promote and compel prostitution.

The power of the law is both productive and repressive (Foucault, 1979, 1980a, 1980b, 1983, 1991; Simon, 1988; Fraser, 1989; Collier et al., 1995; Perry, 1995; Henry and Milovanovic, 1996). Just as the discourses of nineteenth-century reformists had dominating effects, the strategies of contemporary activists reproduced the hegemonics of individual choice and tied women to their identities and practices in confining ways.[9] The subjectifying logic of these discourses positioned "prostitutes" and "prostituted women" as freely consenting or incapable of consenting to engage in prostitution while subjugating sex trade participants' own knowledge of their experiences. The complexity of agency, the particularity of context, the multiple position-

LIVERPOOL JOHN MOORES UNIVERSITY
LEARNING SERVICES

ing of participants in the varied niches of the sex trade, and the on-going negotiation of consent were lost in the identity politics of both activist groups (Sanchez, 1997b). Paralleling the liberal legal logic that women who act illegally, act by choice, the identity politics of PROs and radical feminists foreclose alternative ways of understanding how women become involved in the sex trade and how they negoti-ate relations of power in everyday practice.

Here, I de-center the notion of choice, preferring instead to in-terpret what people do and what they say about what they do through the concept of agency. At the most basic level, agency invokes only some questionable association between an actor and an action or event. The issues of reason and causation, the way in which agents are connected to their actions, the agents' location in a sequence of events, the order of causation, and the role of intention and con-sciousness are a source of open debate among theorists of agency and subjectivity in language and philosophy (Anscombe, 1957; Austin, 1962; Davidson, 1963, 1980; Wittgenstein, 1976; Searle, 1983; Elster, 1985; Loewenstein and Elster, 1992), psychology and social theory (Giddens, 1979; Garfinkel, 1967; Harré, 1983; Kahneman, 1986), and law (Rawls, 1971; Dworkin, 1986; Posner, 1992; Hunt, 1993; Henry and Milovanovic, 1996).

Recent scholars, positing a constitutive theory of the subject and agency, question the possibility of referencing a "prediscursive I"—a subject who acts before or outside of her constitution in discourse (But-ler, 1990, 1997). Feminist philosopher Judith Butler argues that the discursive constitution of subjects does not foreclose agency. To be con-stituted by discourse is not the same as being determined by dis-course. Paralleling the work of J. L. Austin (1962) and Jacques Der-rida (1992), Butler recovers the concept of agency by invoking the performative: "there need not be a "'doer behind the deed' . . . the 'doer' is variably constructed in and through the deed" (Butler, 1990: 142). Thus, agency can be located in the regulated process of repetition and in creative and subversive variations of performative repetition.

The work of these scholars suggests a more contingent interpre-tive framework that situates the subject and leaves open the ques-tion of agency. Within this constitutive framework, scholars view ar-ticulations of agency as coproduced in relation to the discursive and material structures of lived practice. Recovering the material and dis-cursive coproduction of agency from its abstracted place in the lib-eral economic logic of free contract foregrounds the situatedness of knowledge and subjectivity (Haraway, 1991; Smith, 1990), and calls upon readers to re-imagine sex trade interactions as embodied practices rather than disembodied choices. Thus, constitutive theory makes it possible to interpret the actions of subjects who are not positioned to contract freely without erasing the possibility of active movement. Rather than ignore the role of power relations in shaping women's actions as PROs do, or reduce sex trade participants to passive victims as radical feminists do, my interpretation strives to situate the subject and contextualize agency within specific discursive spaces and relations of power.

Sex, Law, and Order in the Evergreen Sexual Economy

In Evergreen, neon signs act as markers of the booming local sex industry invading the street corners and the consciousness of each person who lives there. Since the mid-eighties, residents of the city of Evergreen have witnessed tremendous growth in legal sex businesses. For example, the state constitution defines nude dancing as a form of symbolic speech and guarantees the "right to free expression" by a standard tougher than the federal free speech guidelines. Strip clubs increased from 10 in 1989 to 100 in 1995 after a Ninth Circuit Court judge ruled that full nudity could no longer be prohibited by city ordinance because it discriminated against business establishments selling alcohol. By contrast, nudity was already allowed at some river beaches, in the making of pornography, and in art classes. Along with the growth in strip bars, pornography stores, escort services, "live-nude" modeling businesses, and "tanning salons for gentlemen" have flourished.

Although there are more sex clubs in poor and working-class neighborhoods in Evergreen, the businesses are not concentrated into "red-light zones." Rather, they are scattered throughout business districts and residential neighborhoods. Proposed zoning regulations that would keep legal sex-related businesses at least 1,000 feet from residences and schools have consistently been struck down on constitutional grounds. For young women who use the bus stops and boulevards to get across town or to go to the grocery store or local sandwich shop, the insistent presence of the sex business is a fact of everyday existence. Alongside these legal businesses, potential customers driving the boulevards frequently harass or solicit young women oc-

LIVERPOOL JOHN MOORES UNIVERSITY
Aldham Robarts L.R.C.
TEL. 051 231 3701/3634

cupying those spaces regardless of whether they have ever turned a date. It is within this context that a number of the young women I spoke with were first solicited.

The women in the study participated in three aspects of the local sex trade: street prostitution, escort services, and nude dancing. Contrary to some researchers' claims that the multiple niches of the sex trade can be separated into distinct entities and practices (Rosen, 1982; Delacoste and Alexander, 1987; Lucas, 1995),[10] the boundaries between the places and practices of the Evergreen sex trade are blurred and the legal regulation of the sex trade shapes the texture and conditions of both licit and illicit sex trade practices. In the present case study of the Evergreen sexual economy, the regime of legal codes, zoning and regulatory ordinances, and law enforcement practices shapes the larger structure of interaction environments and the microstructure of practice both in its presence and in its absence as a regulatory force.

Here, I focus on the testimonies of eight women. Four of them started out in street prostitution, two started in escort service work but also worked the street, and two of them worked for strip clubs and private dance agencies. The most consistent factors influencing these women's initial involvement in commercial sex include age, class, social and economic support, housing, and drug use. Six of the women were age 18 or under at the time of initiation, and two were in their early twenties. The youngest participant, now 20, was 12 when she first became involved in street prostitution. Two of the women had stable housing at the time of initial involvement, one lived with her grandparents temporarily, and five lived in motels, searching daily for a place to stay. Each of the women had struggled to support herself for an extended period of time with only minimum success. It is important to note that women this young are significantly marginalized within the mainstream economy because they are not generally expected to support themselves. The unemployment rate in Evergreen is 16 percent for young women aged 16 to 20 as compared to 7 percent for all Evergreen residents counted by the Census (State Bureau of Labor Statistics, 1994). In addition, three of these young women were addicted to heroin and two frequently used cocaine, "speed" or methamphetamine, and alcohol. Three were drug- and alcohol-free. For some of these young women, drug use came at significant financial cost and drew much of their time and energy into procuring and using drugs, and recovering from drug use. Significantly, however, drug use and prostitution is not always found in a simple cause-and-effect relationship. Some women began prostitution to support their drug habit, some began using drugs to deal with the risks and insults of prostitution, and others stayed away from drugs completely or kept their use to a minimum. All women claimed that using drugs or finding some other way to temporarily alter their consciousness made their experience in the sex trade more manageable.

Finally, with the exception of one young woman whose father was a psychiatrist, all of these women were young, white and from poor and working-class backgrounds. The significance of class and social position for my purposes here is that it suggests how women's socioeconomic position shapes their lived experience. The separation of public and private spheres is largely a product of the liberal imagination and its subordinating practices. Women's place in the logic and practice of separate spheres doctrine is infinitely more reflective of the legal and cultural spaces of the privileged than the working classes (hooks, 1981; Taub and Schneider, 1982; Merry, 1986; Okin, 1989; Crenshaw, 1989). In the geographic and social space of the urban poor and working classes, the boundary between public and private space is much more obscure. Most poor and working-class women are neither "confined to," nor "protected within" private and domestic spaces and places of "legitimate business." Because of their residential location and their transportation and economic needs, urban women may not enjoy the privilege of avoiding what many people consider undesirable public spaces. The spaces of the sex trade are just such spaces; they are publicly identified spaces marked for sexual commerce. In these spaces, it is often the case that any woman is fair prey and all women are suspect.

The practices women describe in the following narrative analysis involve bodily contact and cannot be reduced to a single moment of choice. They are better understood as a series of copresent, intersubjective, and embodied interactions negotiated and renegotiated for the duration of each interaction. Although women frequently use a language of choice to describe their actions, their narratives are shaped by their social situation, by the context of practice, and by the desires and demands of their customers. Under these conditions, the women who participated in this study at best negotiate an interaction that satisfies the needs and desires of both parties. Often, however, agency in these interactions plays out as active or passive resistance and survival tactics.

Narratives of Agency and Resistance

Copresent Interactions and the Quotidian Logic of Daily Practice

Now in her mid-twenties, Cory turned her first date when she was still a teenager. She explained that she got involved "by herself," but she didn't know what to do or how much to charge so she just "walked and walked" until she met a few people who were concerned for her: "they were mostly the guys that I dated, told me how to do it." Although Cory first described her initial involvement in individualistic terms, her experience was constituted in interaction with the men who cruised the boulevards soliciting for dates. Moreover, in Cory's case, an expensive heroin habit that developed within a particular social history, put pressure on her to earn money to avoid becoming "drug sick." But that did not negate her agency. Using a language of "practical consciousness,"[11] she explained that she "did what she had to do":

> You just kinda keep going and make yourself do it because when you got fifty dollars in your hand, all of the sudden, now you know tomorrow you're not gonna be sick. So, it makes it pretty easy to go back out. Until you get hurt. Then the first time you get hurt you get scared when you go back out. [Have you been hurt before?] Yeah. Raped, getting beat up and stuff. [How often would you say that happened?] Probably about a hundred times. The hurt just kinda goes along with it. Getting stranded, having your clothes stolen, having your money stolen, robbed at gunpoint, whatever, all of that. Just hurt.

The movement in Cory's narrative account of her initial involvement and continued participation is one of increasing constraint: what is first described as initiative becomes necessity, becomes abuse. These transitions illustrate how the contradictions of choice and constraint, further complicated by the violence that "just goes along with [prostitution]" shape Cory's efforts to do what has to be done.

Heidi began dancing for a bachelor party agency after answering a newspaper advertisement soliciting dancers. Working for the agency, she soon found that the boundaries between prostitution and stripping were unclear: "In this business you're constantly propositioned. I mean you get everything from prostitution propositions to marriage proposals." Heidi explained how these ambiguities played out in her training with the daughter of the owner of the agency:

> There was quite a bit of money in it, a lot of prostitution in it though. [Did you ever engage in any of that?] No, I never participated in it directly, but a couple of the girls that they would send me out with regularly, actually one of them was the owner's daughter, participated in that almost every single party. I asked her directly if she was actually doing anything physical with those guys and she was like, "Oh no, never, never, never," you know. She told me that she'd just get 'em really drunk, and you know, give 'em a hand job or something and just get the money out of them that way.

Heidi went on to explain that the dispatchers from the agency would "bribe the girls for money shifts." When asked what they would be expected to do in exchange for "money shifts" she responded, "Oh, just blow-jobs, just under the desk. Take 'em home, whatever. It's a sex business, that's all there is to it."

Contradictions between agency and resistance played out in Jody's narrative as she described being harassed and propositioned while dancing in clubs. In one club, she was frequently solicited for prostitution, but she felt individually responsible for the way she resisted these offers:

> Sometimes I'm amazed that I didn't die in the process of doing a lot of the stuff I did because I really messed with people. . . . There were customers that would say, "Oh, will you come over to my place?" And I'd say, "Oh sure, I'll take your fifty dollars," and then I didn't show up. I know these men had money, real big money and I wasn't willing to compromise my morals, but at the same time, I was willing to lie, you know, and cheat. But still, I had put myself in danger.

Going home with a customer was not part of Jody's job description, but club management was complicit in the practices of their customers. Although these advances clearly made Jody feel threatened, the customer's power to shape the conditions of her practice and to create a pressure to be resisted went unremarked. In Jody's interpretation of her actions, it was *she* who had put *herself* in danger by taking a customer's money for an unlawful solicitation. What is left unsaid is that while customers are supposed to tip dancer's *to dance*, experienced customers often mask unlawful solicitation behind payment for legal sexual performance in tips. The coercive pressure to extend sexual involvement beyond the four walls of the club and beyond the boundaries of consent can confuse a dancer about what she is being paid for, particularly when she is inexperienced or "green."

These strategies of exploitation can make dancers feel individually responsible for their situation and obliged to perform sexual activities that reach beyond the terms of legal employment. As Heidi put it, "These guys want to live out their fantasy and they don't want any repercussions coming from it, and they don't want to pay the girl." In a discussion about Evergreen's "notorious regulars," she said that one man was "infamous for coming up to a girl and asking her if he could actually beat her up":

It was pretty much that he would pay them a certain amount of money and all their hospital bills if they agreed to it. He's asked me to meet him three times outside the club. I stood him up all three times, but as far as dancing in the club, he would ask me to put on nipple clamps or wear your g-string backwards. He was into humiliating women, you know.

The contradictions reflected in women's descriptions of their interactions with customers show how conflicting intentions and desires between women and their customers shape the configuration of each interaction. In the particular microstructure of Evergreen sex trade practice, women's attempts to assert agency and to negotiate consent are often met with violence. However, as the following section will show, women are still active agents in their resistance to violence.

Violence and Survival Tactics

Cory's narrative illustrates how her attempts to assert agency are routinely circumscribed by the frequent use and constant threat of violence. While some of her actions can be described as self-motivated, much of her energy must be reserved for defending herself from sporadic physical attacks. As Cory put it:

You gotta watch 'em close . . . and you never wanta close your eyes
when you're with 'em . . . if they move or they turn around and
face you in the car like that, they can grab you with both hands
as opposed to just one, and it's just that fast and they've got a
knife out and you don't really have too many options too quick.

Cory's narrative about resisting violence focuses on the constraints
of physical space, the threat of body language, and the urgency of time.
Her description of an assault and attempted rape at knifepoint highlights these elements of practice and the felt experience of violence.

[This guy] had the knife right up against my neck. [He] got
pissed off at me because I wouldn't shut the fuck up which was
probably stupid, but I was just pushin' as hard as I could push
and I just wanted to get out of there. He was goin' "No, no, no,
give it up, give it up," and I was saying. . . . "I'm not givin' it up
until you get that thing away from me." He says, "Well, if I get
it away from you, you're gonna run." I said, "I'm not gonna run,"
and so we went back and forth, and I said, "Get it away from my
neck," and I had like maybe a dozen little poke holes that I
wasn't aware of at that time, but I could feel it. Finally he just
got so pissed off that I grabbed the door handle, and he shoved
me out on the ground [without my clothes]. I was just thinking
I wanted to get out of there as fast as I could. I just wanted to
get out alive.

Shari expressed similar concerns as she detailed the tactics of resistance she used in her work as a private dancer.

You get an idea of what they want, if they want you to dance or
just model lingerie or a back rub, and then you tell them that
there is no sexual contact whatsoever, no prostitution. But a lot
of the guys try to see if they can still push you into doin' it. So
that's the important thing to remember when you're doin' one
on one, and sometimes I take an escort with me. If they're in motels, I feel secure goin' by myself because I've got rooms next to
me so all I gotta do is let out a yell.

Paralleling Cory's tactics, Shari remained attentive to body language
and kept her eye on the practical possibility of exit. She was prepared

for conflict around the limitations of consent and tried to manage the threat of violence by positioning herself in the vicinity of potential witnesses. Under these conditions, women's actions cannot be interpreted as individual choices but as tactics of resistance within the violent and unpredictable space of the Evergreen sex trade. In each case, their social and economic position and the de-legitimation of their identity meant that their interactions with customers usually took place on his turf. The naturalization of masculine sexual desire in legal and cultural discourse and practice makes it possible for a male customer to rent a room for sex or to participate in an act of prostitution without compromising his identity and social position. In contrast, female sex trade participants in both licit and illicit sex markets are disadvantaged through the reproduction of their identities as "sexual outlaws" and through spatial practices that favor "paying customers" (Sanchez, 1997a). Thus, the players in these interactions are not equally situated contracting individuals. While women's actions are rooted in gendered struggles for self-definition and economic independence, the exercise of privilege by male customers embodies the consumerist logic of contract theory. Their practices are not about survival; they are about desire—the desire to have sex, to do violence, to do sex violently, or to make violence sexy.

Discussion

Historically, discourses on prostitution have oversimplified agency and misunderstood the negotiated quality of sex trade practice by leaving intact the assumptions underlying bourgeois legal and cultural ideology. Activist groups have both supported and rejected the notion that women in prostitution choose their identities and practices. At the heart of the discursive struggles of reformist groups, modern liberal notions of identity and consent act as complementary constituents in the binary construction of agency as individual choice or non-choice. The key problem with these reformist discourses is that identity and consent were reified, or constructed as stable and all-encompassing. In failing to recognize the context of women's lives, these discourses overlooked the instability of identity and the ambiguity of consent.

My discussions with women focused on the complexities of identity and the contradiction of women's agency and their resistance to violence and material deprivation. Rather than taking as given the abstract subject as a free and equal individual willfully contracting in the world as market, I have taken into account how subjects are situated in the specific power relations and structured interaction contexts of the local sex trade. The complexities and contradictions of women's practiced and expressed agency challenge the logic of contract on a number of levels. The foregoing illustrations from women's accounts showed that the necessary preconditions for making choices—knowledge, alternatives, power, and safe space—are absent in women's sphere of activity. First, women's material needs act in concert with the demands of local sex markets to draw women into the sex trade and shape their participation in it. Second, women's initial involvement and daily practices are not individual, but copresent, embodied, and intersubjective. Finally, violence was used as a definitive trump card on women's agency. That is, where verbal pressure and material coercion in the form of money, drugs, shelter, or protection were ineffective in "eliciting consent," men with little reason to fear social or legal consequences often replaced these methods with violent sexual and physical assaults.

Understanding the copresent quality of sex trade participation sheds light on the conflicted narratives of these women, particularly the tension between their agency on one hand and their victimization on the other. While it is clear that women "consent to," and in fact, initiate many of their activities, they also face unsolicited pressures and violations on a routine basis. In light of the complexities of agency and victimization in their lives, the reification of their experience into categories of free agent or victim seems shortsighted. There is little space for agency within the meta-narrative of the victim. Consequently, the voices of women who are considered victims have all too often been silenced and devalued, the contradictions in their narratives dismissed as "justification," "rationalization" or "false consciousness." Similarly, there is little space within the meta-narrative of the free agent for routine violence, but ignoring the unsolicited violence in women's social world facilitates their victimization.

The fact that women's activities can neither be interpreted as those of a free agent or as those of a helpless victim is testimony not to women's confusion, but to the contradictions in the place and practice of sexual commerce. I am suggesting that these contradictions can be interpreted as a reflection of a resistant voice—one which aspires to self-determination and free agency (like others), but one which is constrained in ways that are unlike those most people face. Thus, my interpretation suggests that such contradictions do not say something about these *Other* (read: different, weaker, more desperate, less discriminating) women, but rather something about the oppressive power and dominating practices of the sexual economy itself.

The minute details or quotidian logic of these negotiated interactions constitute a particular microstructure of practice, one whose continuities have to do with power relations and whose disjunctures have to do with the multiple positionings and identities of those involved. Identity for these women is conflicted and multi-faceted. While elements of the logic of contract and PROs rhetoric were common in women's talk about their daily life, these women were also quite conscious and concerned about their own victimization. Whether they internalized or externalized their marginalization, none of the women represented themselves as passive victims. They are active participants in the process of negotiating consent and resisting the violent inscription of identity and the felt violence of physical discipline and abuse.

Identity, as discussed earlier, is coproduced through the microstructure of practice and through creative and subversive repetitions of practice. The paradoxical formation of identity means that women frame their experiences in relation to the conflicts and contradictions of daily practice. Their voices are reflective of multiple positionings in the sex trade and multiple ways of resisting its power. The local knowledge of Evergreen sex trade participants rearticulates gendered and class-based structures of subordination through placements and displacements of liberal legality and subjectivity.

Foucault correctly identified the relationship between power and resistance when he wrote that resistance is never in a position of exteriority in relation to power (1980a: 95). Because resistance always implies a force against which to resist, contextualizing sex trade practices makes visible the complexity of embodied sexual interactions and the local organization of discursive and material power relations. Women's resistance narratives draw attention to the felt reality of their embodied practice. They are spatialized and temporal in quality. These aspects of practice affect how power works within the local context. Domination of women's personal (bodily) space, and the material and social space of the local sexual economy is one of the primary strategies of power employed by customers, managers, and perpetrators of violence within that context. The lack of control women have over the economic and spatial environment where sex trade practices are carried out is one of the key ways in which they are disempowered to make decisions about their own body and left vulnerable to violence. A woman can only respond to this kind of power by engaging in tactics of resistance and survival reflexes.

These women's tactics of resistance to violence and social control were admirable. But the fact that their admirable struggles are consistently blocked reminds us of the power of the oppressive systems within which their struggles take place. Tactics of resistance help women to negotiate within the rigid confines of their social space, but they present little challenge to the power and authority of sex, money, and law. The importance of hearing the multi-faceted voices of women in the sex trade is not that they highlight contradictions or inconsistencies in their own logic, but that they highlight contradictions in the logic of practice.

Conclusion: The Possibility of a Replacement Discourse

Can a replacement discourse be recovered from the stories of the women in Evergreen? Henry and Milovanovic identify four strategies for developing replacement discourses with harm reduction as a common goal (1996). In the first strategy, constitutive criminologists intervene in the "generative sites of discursive production" by challenging dominant discourses and making their interventions publicly accessible through news media and popular discourse (*ibid*.: 214). The second approach rejects the view that violence can be overcome by the force of law. It advocates the use of peacemaking and conflict resolution in place of state violence as a strategy to re-integrate those who have been held responsible for illegal activities with their communities (*ibid*.: 220). The third strategy is designed to assist the constituted victim in recovery through the use of support groups. Finally, Henry and Milovanovic suggest that criminologists work toward developing replacement discourses or "languages of possibility" to challenge the disciplinary technologies and macrostructural inequalities of late capitalist political economies.

The problem presented by the displaced subject of sex trade practice is that she faces multiple forms of oppression. She is neither offender to be reintegrated nor victim to be recovered. Constituted as both, she experiences her life as neither. Always and everywhere her subjectivity is exteriorized—she has no place in "the community," and no voice in law, politics or society. To be sure, the language of possibility must recognize these exteriorities and the multiple forms of oppression she faces. The violent inscription of the prostitute identity has been reproduced for centuries in stigmatizing and paternalistic discourses on prostitution. Discursive practices in turn enable the enforcement of cultural codes of proper feminine sexuality publicly, by law, and privately, by violence.

Opening space for women to speak within public discourse by deconstructing the cultural logic that makes these disciplinary techniques possible provides a good first step toward empowering sex trade participants. Here, I have deconstructed the logic of liberal legal subjectivity and its negation in radical feminist discourse. I attempted an alternative representation of women's identities and experiences by paying attention to the contradictions and discontinuities of everyday experience. Thus, my interpretation of identity, agency, and subjectivity for those involved in legal and illegal sex markets should be considered contingent and locally specific, but it may provide a theoretical framework for developing a broader yet more contextualized and participatory knowledge of sexual commerce. True, any replacement discourse will be ineffective without collective action, but forming collective identities and communities will require finding a way to articulate the needs and desires of sex trade participants without creating domains of exclusion and reinscribing the violence of identity. Moreover, taking collective action will mean negotiating the competing needs of the community of sex-trade participants and the more empowered residential community.

The law does violence to sex trade participants. In constituting women in the sex trade as "sexual outlaws" to be managed and subjected to the full scope of legal authority, the law simultaneously limits their citizenship rights and withdraws its protection. Legal regimes constitute women in prostitution as offenders, but they rarely validate their claims of victimization. While most scholars and activists focus on the big legal questions of criminalization and decriminalization, women continue to engage in sex trade practices under conditions of illegality. As these scholars continue to debate and wait for the big legal question to be resolved, laws prohibiting serious violent crimes are already in place. Thus, a second role of the activist scholar is to provide women with the tools for subverting the law's power to construct their identities and limit their access to fundamental legal rights. Encouraging women to resist the law's inscription of the prostitute identity upon their bodies and upon the spaces in which they practice is one way of providing women with the tools to reconstruct a discourse that has always worked to silence and disempower them. After all, these women's identities and life experiences are shaped by much more than their involvement in prostitution, and the legal prohibition of many of their activities (i.e., walking and speaking in a "high-vice" area) is questionable at best.

Moreover, these women are first and foremost women and human beings who deserve the same legal protections against violent victimization as any other citizen. Neither their present lifestyle nor their past involvement in prostitution should preclude them from access to fundamental legal rights. The violence of rape or battery is still violence regardless of the status or identity of the victim and regardless of her conduct (be it legal or illegal) preceding the commission of a violent crime against her person. However imperfect the law is in dealing with sexual violence, it would be wrong to advocate mediation or peace making strategies *alone* to deal with the egregious harms these women describe. Knifepoint rape, kidnapping, and assault to the point of medical emergency would not be so readily tolerated under any other circumstances, save perhaps the position of prisoners and undocumented workers. When the victim is a "known prostitute," people all too often shrug their shoulders and feel safe in the knowledge that her victimization can be explained by her failure to obey the code of proper feminine sexuality.

The harder question is how to effect a transformative movement in the political economy so that women would have more humane and lucrative opportunities to support themselves. Given the intersecting oppressions of gender and economic subordination, it is perplexing to suggest what it would take for young, working-class women to participate more fully in the mainstream economy. Economic change has come slowly for older, middle-class women, but young women are already in a position of limited citizenship under the patriarchal logic of protection. They are not expected to support themselves. As the cultural common sense has it, they should be protected and financially supported like good bourgeois daughters. But their citizenship is further compromised by their involvement in illegal activities.

Identifying local sites of resistance can provide a small ray of hope in a generally dark domain. The legality, for example, of hiring dancers as unpaid private contractors, and the constitutionality of using solicitation and procurement laws to criminalize women's speech while vehemently protecting the sexual expression of legal sex entrepreneurs and pornographers can be challenged by illuminating how they discriminate and facilitate exploitation and abuse. The quotidian logic of practice shows that in quite different ways, the legal regime and the Evergreen community have been complicit in supporting the demands and privileges of sex-industry entrepreneurs and paying customers, while continuing to stigmatize the women who work in both licit and illicit sex markets. Thus, as a final strategy, the activist researcher can whittle away at small pieces of the larger technologies of power operating in the local sex trade.

I end this chapter as I began by highlighting one woman's voice. To quote Amanda:

There's a really big price to be paid [for some of these offers]. There's a certain level of confidentiality that's necessary, and in those circles, all they do is pass you around. . . . Obviously, the price to be paid is that you have no freedom. . . . And they pay you big bucks because you're being paid for your silence.

By far the most important role of the researcher is to listen to what this silence tells us.

Notes

1. The task of describing subjectivities and practices of women in the sex trade is always political and problematic given the historical stigmatization of these women in discourse and language. Putting the word "prostitute" in quotes is an attempt to destabilize its historical meaning and to call into question the normalizing discourse that produces stereotypical and degraded others. The scope of this study is limited to young female sex-trade participants with male customers, a configuration that predominates in the Evergreen context although there is a fair amount of male on male prostitution in one part of town. This does not diminish the importance of differently gendered arrangements, nor does it ignore the fact that alternative arrangements may differ phenomenologically. However, some of the theoretical and practical logic born out of this empirical study may be applicable to practices and contexts beyond the scope of the study. For that, I let the reader be the judge. In this chapter, I argue with the kinds of discourses that reify the prostitute

identity by making women's involvement in the sex trade the central, defining characteristic of identity and discounting other important aspects of identity such as gender, race, ethnicity, class, and the formation of identities in relation to others (e.g., mother, daughter, student, citizen, resident). Because I want to de-center the totalizing logic of the prostitute identity and foreground other aspects of identity, I use the alternative terms "sex trade participants," "women in prostitution," "women in the sex trade," or just "women" to refer to research participant's who might be called prostitutes, hookers, whores, strippers, or sex workers in other contexts. While I don't have any major objections to the term "sex worker," I do not use that term here because I want to call attention to the fact that the conditions of practice in this case study do not qualify as work. Finally, I make no argument with the terms individual participants use to define their own identities. In addressing participants, I use whatever identity term they prefer. Importantly, however, the women in this study self-identify as prostitutes, whores, or hookers infrequently, and when they did identify that way, the terms are used in relation and resistance to external labeling processes and normalizing discourses.

2. In questioning the binary logic of conventional constructions of the sati as one who either chooses to die or is forced to die, postcolonial feminist Rajeswari Sunder Rajan positions the sati as a "resisting subject" who is capable of the agency and enabling selfhood of the "active" earlier subject but constrained in ways that are almost beyond representation (1993: 11). In this article, I understand the subject, the agent, and the body as interconnected, and subjectivity is thought of as both active and constitutive. The three elements of being and doing foreground the role of the discursive (subject), psycho-social (agent), and material (body) respectively.

3. Goffman (1967, 1969), Giddens (1979), and Boden and Molotch (1994) describe copresence as embodied, face-to-face interactions that take place in the same physical space and time. For a detailed discussion of the theory of practice that I am relying upon in this article, see Bourdieu (1977), de Certeau (1984), and Smith (1990), and Cornell and Thurschwell (1987) for a related discussion on intersubjectivity. In addition, see Coombe's (1989) article calling for the use of practice theory in sociolegal studies.

4. The women who participated in this study use the term dating to refer to explicit exchanges of sex acts for money that are more commonly known as prostitution.

5. Pseudonyms are used to protect the identities of those who participated in this study.

6. Collier et al. use the term "bourgeois law" to refer to the "legal concepts and practices developed since the eighteenth century in Europe and its colonies" (1996: 1–2). Following the work of Pashukanis ([1929] 1989), the sub-

ject of "bourgeois law" is understood as a property-owning, rights-bearing individual even when property refers to property in one's own person. In this paper, I also use the terms liberal legality and modern liberal law to invoke this discourse.

7. Examples of prostitutes' rights organizations include COYOTE (acronym for "Call off your old tired ethics") in San Francisco, and HIRE (Hooking is real employment) in New York. See Jenness (1993) for further listings. Radical feminist, victim/survivor groups include WHISPER, "Women Hurt in Systems of Prostitution," and Council for Prostitution Alternatives (CPA). Both groups put out local literature and work in coalition with other community activists, researchers, and scholars. While not all scholars and activists listed may self-identify as liberal feminists (PROs) or radical feminists, I have identified the two groups as those espousing a liberal view (prostitution is a free choice or voluntary occupation), and those promoting a radical feminist view (prostitution is forced or coerced sexual violence).

8. The positions of liberal and radical feminists on the issue of legalization and decriminalization have gone through a number of transitions and are too complex to explain in detail here. PROs and liberal feminists have historically supported legalization, but some now argue instead for decriminalization. Radical feminists have been against legalization, but some have favored removing the penalties for solicitation and prostitution for women only. Most often, however, they side-step the issue because it conflicts with the larger goal of eradicating prostitution worldwide.

9. Foucault described the meaning of subjectification as "subject to someone else by control or dependence," or "tied to [one's] own identity by a conscience or self-knowledge" (1983: 212). His writings on subjects and subjectification focuses on the way in which people are constituted as subordinate and superordinate subjects through cultural and legal categories, how they are tied to those subject categories and constructed identities, and subordinated through them. His articulation of subjectification is used here to shed light on the disciplinary functions of the prostitute identity.

10. For example, in opposition to the claim of some feminist scholars that most women solicit in the streets (Rosen, 1982), other scholars and PROs assert that "only ten to twenty percent of prostitutes solicit on the street" (Delacoste and Alexander, 1987; Lucas, 1995), but their claims are also empirically unsubstantiated. Similarly, Barry claims without evidence that "90 percent of street prostitutes are controlled by pimps" (1979). The use of statistics to bolster the claims of scholars and activists assumes that sex trade participants only engage in one aspect of the sex trade and that they are neatly segregated into categories of practice—that is some women solicit (only) on the streets, others work inside. Moreover, the empirical claims of activists and

researchers assume that there is agreement over the definition of sex trade practices, that women identify with those practices, and they also ignore the difficulty of counting people who usually try to avoid being counted. Although there are no good estimates in the United States on the scope and prevalence of what some researchers describe as the basic categories of prostitution, activists and researchers continue to make false appeals to universality.

11. See Garfinkel (1967) and Giddens (1979) for a discussion of practical consciousness as I am using it here.

References

Anscombe, G. E. M. (1957). *Intention*. Ithica: Cornell University Press.

Austin, J. L. (1962). *How to Do Things with Words*. Cambridge, MA: Harvard University Press.

Baldwin, Margaret A. (1992). Split at the root: Prostitution and feminist discourses of law reform. *Yale Journal of Law and Feminism*, 5: 47–119.

Barry, Kathleen. (1979). *Female Sexual Slavery*. New York: Avon.

Beccaria, Cesare. [1764] (1963). *On Crime and Punishment*. Translated by Henry Paolucci. Indianapolis: Bobbs-Merrill.

Becker, Gary S. (1968). Crime and punishment: An economic approach. *Journal of Political Economy*, 76(2): 169–217.

Bell, Laurie. (Ed.). (1987). *Good Girls / Bad Girls: Feminists and Sex Trade Workers Face to Face*. Toronto: Seal Press.

Benhabib, Seyla, and Drucilla Cornell. (Eds.). (1987). *Feminism as Critique: On the Politics of Gender*. Minneapolis: University of Minnesota Press.

Bentham, Jeremy. ([1789] 1948). *An Introduction to the Principles of Morals and Legislation*. W. Harrison (Ed.). Oxford: Basil Blackwell.

Boden, Deirdre, and Harvey L. Molotch. (1994). The compulsion of proximity. In Friedland and Boden, (Eds.), *NowHere: Space, Time and Modernity*. Berkeley: University of California Press.

Bourdieu, Pierre. (1977). *Outline of a Theory of Practice* Richard Nice (Trans.) Cambridge: Cambridge University Press.

Bumiller, Kristin. (1988). *The Civil Rights Society: The Social Construction of Victims*. Baltimore, MD: The Johns Hopkins University Press.

Burchell, Graham, Gordon, Colin, and Peter Miller. (Eds.). (1991). *The Foucault Effect*. Chicago: University of Chicago Press.

Butler, Judith. (1990). *Gender Trouble: Feminism and the Subversion of Identity*. New York: Routledge.

Butler, Judith. (1997). *Excitable Speech: A Politics of the Performative*. New York: Routledge.

Clarke, Ronald V., and Marcus Felson. (Eds.). (1993). *Routine Activities and Rational Choice.* New Brunswick, NJ: Transaction.

Collier, Jane F., Maurer, Bill, and Liliana, Suarez-Naváz. (1995). Sanctioned identities: Legal constructions of modern personhood. *Identities* 2: 1–27.

Coombe, Rosemary J. (1989). Room for manoeuver: Toward a theory of practice in critical legal studies. *Law and Social Inquiry* 14(1) (Winter): 69–121.

Cornell, Drucilla, and Adam Thurschwell. (1987). Feminism, negativity, intersubjectivity. In S. Benhabib and D. Cornell (Eds.). *Feminism as Critique: On the Politics of Gender.* Minneapolis: University of Minnesota Press.

Cornell, Drucilla, Rosenfeld, Michael, and David Gray Carlson. (Eds.). (1992). *Deconstruction and the Possibility of Justice.* New York: Routledge.

Crenshaw, Kimberle. (1989). Demarginalizing the intersection of race and sex: A black feminist critique of antidiscrimination doctrine, feminist theory, and antiracist politics. *University of Chicago Legal Forum*, 139–167.

Davidson, Donald. (1963). Actions, reasons, and causes. *Journal of Philosophy*, 60: 685–700.

Davidson, Donald. (1980). *Essays on Actions and Events.* Oxford: Clarendon Press.

de Certeau, Michel. (1984). *The Practice of Everyday Life.* Los Angeles: University of California Press.

Delacoste, Frederique, and Priscilla Alexander. (1987). *Sex Work: Writings by Women in the Sex Industry.* Pittsburgh: Cleis Press.

Derrida, Jacques. (1992). Force of law: The 'mystical foundations of authority.' In Cornell, Rosenfeld, and Carlson (Eds.), *Deconstruction and the Possibility of Justice.* New York: Routledge.

Dreyfus, Hubert L., and Paul Rabinow. (1983). *Michel Foucault: Beyond Structuralism and Hermeneutics.* Chicago: The University of Chicago Press.

Dworkin, Andrea. (1979). *Pornography: Men Possessing Women.* New York: Penguin Press.

Dworkin, Ronald. (1986). *Law's Empire.* Cambridge, MA: Harvard University Press.

Elster, Jon. (1985). The nature and scope of rational-choice explanations. In E. LePore and B. P. McLaughlin (Eds.), *Actions and Events: Perspectives on the Philosophy of Donald Davidson.* New York: Basil Blackwell.

Erbe, Nancy. (1984). Prostitutes: Victims of men's exploitation and abuse. *Journal of Law and Inequality*, 2: 609–28.

Ewick, Patricia, and Susan S. Silbey. (1995). Subversive stories and hegemonic tales: Toward a sociology of narrative. *Law and Society Review*, 29(2): 197–226.

Fechner, Holly. (1994). Three stories of prostitution in the west: Prostitutes' groups, law, and feminist 'truth'. *Columbia Journal of Gender and Law*, 4(1): 26–72.

Foucault, Michel. (1979). *Discipline and Punish: The Birth of the Prison*. Alan Sheridan. (Trans.). New York: Vintage.

Foucault, Michel. (1980a). *The History of Sexuality, Volume One: An Introduction*. Vintage Books: New York.

Foucault, Michel. (1980b). *Power/Knowledge: Selected Interviews and Other Writings*, 1972–1977. New York: Pantheon Books.

Foucault, Michel. (1983). The subject and power. In Dreyfus and Rabinow (Eds.). *Michel Foucault: Beyond Structuralism and Hermeneutics*. Chicago: The University of Chicago Press.

Foucault, Michel. (1991). On governmentality. In Burchell, Gordon, and Miller (Eds.). *The Foucault Effect*. Chicago: University of Chicago Press.

Fraser, Nancy. (1989). *Unruly Practices: Power, Discourse, and Gender in Contemporary Social Theory*. Minneapolis: University of Minnesota Press.

Freeman, Jody. (1989). The feminist debate over prostitution reform: Prostitutes' rights groups, radical feminists, and the (im)possibility of consent. *Berkeley Women's Law Journal*, 5: 75–111.

Friedland, Roger, and Dierdre Boden. (Eds.). (1994). *NowHere: Space, Time and Modernity*. Berkeley: University of California Press.

Garfinkel, Harold. (1967). *Studies in Ethnomethodology*. New Jersey: Prentice Hall.

Geertz, Clifford. (1983). *Local Knowledge: Further Essays in Interpretive Anthropology*. New York: Basic Books.

Giddens, Anthony. (1979). *Central Problems in Social Theory: Action, Structure, and Contradictions in Social Analysis*. Berkeley: University of California Press.

Goffman, Erving. (1967). *Interaction Ritual: Essays on Face-to-Face Behaviour*. New York: Doubleday Anchor.

Goffman, Erving. (1969). *Strategic Interaction*. Philadelphia: University of Pennsylvania Press.

Gramsci, Antonio. (1971). *Selections from the Prison Notebooks*. London: Lawrence and Wishart.

Greenhouse, Carol J., Yngvesson, Barbara, and David M. Engel. (1994). *Law and Community in Three American Towns*. Ithaca, NY: Cornell University Press.

Harré, Rom. (1983). *Personal Being: A Theory for Individual Psychology*. Oxford: Basil Blackwell.

Haraway, Donna J. (1991). *Simians, Cyborgs, and Women: The Reinvention of Nature*. New York: Routledge.

Harrington, Christine. (1988). Moving from integrative to constitutive theories of law: Comments on Itzkowitz. *Law and Society Review*, 22(5): 963–67.

Harrington, Christine, and Barbara Yngvesson. (1990). Interpretive sociolegal research. *Law and Social Inquiry*, 15: 135–48.

Henry, Stuart. (1983). *Private Justice*. London: Routledge and Kegan Paul.

Henry, Stuart. (1989). Constitutive criminology: The missing paradigm. *The Critical Criminologist*, 1(3): 9–12.

Henry, Stuart, and Dragan Milovanovic. (1996). *Constitutive Criminology: Beyond Postmodernism*. London: Sage Publications.

hooks, bell. (1981). *Ain't I a Woman: Black Women and Feminism*. Boston: South End Press.

Hunt, Alan. (1993). *Explorations in Law and Society: Toward a Constitutive Theory of Law*. New York: Routledge.

Kahneman, Daniel. (1986). Rational choice and the framing of decisions. *Journal of Business*, 59(4), part 2: S251–78.

Kairys, David. (Ed.). (1982). *The Politics of Law: A Progressive Critique*. New York: Pantheon.

Kelman, Mark. (1979). Choice and utility. *Wisconsin Law Review*, 769.

Jenness, Valerie. (1993). *Making it Work: the Prostitutes' Rights Movement in Perspective*. New York: Aldine de Gruyter.

Lazarus-Black, Mindie, and Susan F. Hirsch. (Eds.). (1994). *Contested States: Law, Hegemony and Resistance*. New York: Routledge.

Locke, John. ([1689] 1980). *Second Treatise of Government*. C. Macpherson (Trans.). Indianapolis: Hackett Publishing Company.

Loewenstein, George, and Jon Elster. (Eds.). (1992). *Choice Over Time*. New York: Russell Sage Foundation.

Lucas, Ann M. (1995). Race, class, gender and deviancy: The criminalization of prostitution. *Berkeley Women's Law Journal*, 10: 47–60.

MacKinnon, Catherine. (1987). *Feminism Unmodified: Discourses on Life and Law*. Cambridge, MA: Harvard University Press.

Merry, Sally Engle. (1986). Everyday understandings of the law in working-class america. *American Ethnologist* 13: 253–70.

Merry, Sally Engle. (1990). *Getting Justice and Getting Even: Legal Consciousness among Working-Class Americans*. Chicago: University of Chicago Press.

Milovanovic, Dragan. (1994). *Sociology of Law* (2nd. ed.) Albany, NY: Harrow and Heston.

Musheno, Michael. (1995). Legal consciousness on the margins of society: Struggles against stigmatization in the AIDS crisis. *Identities*, 2(1–2): 101–22.

Musheno, Michael, and Kathryn Seeley. (1986). Prostitution policy and the women's movement: Historical analysis of feminist thought and organization. *Contemporary Crisis*, 10: 237–55.

Okin, Susan Moller. (1989). *Justice, Gender, and the Family*. New York: Basic Books.

Pashukanis, Evgeny B. ([1929] 1989). *Law and Marxism: A General Theory*. Translated by Barbara Einhorn. Worcester, MA: Pluto Press.

Pateman, Carole. (1988). *The Sexual Contract*. Stanford: Stanford University Press.

Perry, Richard. (1995). The logic of the modern nation-state and the legal construction of Native American tribal identity. *Indiana Law Review*, 28(3): 547–74.

Pheterson, Gail. (1986). *The Whore Stigma: Female Dishonor and Male Unworthiness*. The Netherlands: Dutch Ministry of Social Affairs and Employment.

Pheterson, Gail. (Ed.). (1989). *A Vindication of the Rights of Whores*. Seattle: Seal Press.

Pivar, David J. (1973). *Purity Crusade: Sexual Morality and Social Control, 1868–1900*. Westport, CN: Greenwood Press.

Posner, Richard. (1992). *Sex and Reason*. Cambridge, MA: Harvard University Press.

Radin, Margaret Jane. (1996). *Contested Commodities*. Cambridge, MA: Harvard University Press.

Rajan, Rajeswari Sunder. (1993). *Real and Imagined Women: Gender, Culture, and Postcolonialism*. New York: Routledge.

Rawls, John. (1971). *A Theory of Justice*. Cambridge, MA: Harvard University Press.

Reanda, Laura. (1991). Prostitution as a human rights question: Problems and prospects of United Nations action. *Human Rights Quarterly*, 13: 202–28.

Rosen, Ruth. (1982). *The Lost Sisterhood: Prostitution in America, 1900–1918*. Baltimore: Johns Hopkins University Press.

Sanchez, Lisa E. (1997a). Boundaries of legitimacy: Sex, violence, citizenship, and community in a local sexual economy. *Law and Social Inquiry* 22: 543–54.

Sanchez, Lisa E. (1997b). Spatial practices and bodily maneuvers: Negotiating at the margins of a local sexual economy. *Forthcoming in Political and Legal Anthropology Review* (November).

Schor, Naomi. (1987). *Reading in Detail: Aesthetics and the Feminine*. New York: Methuen.

Schrage, Laurie. (1989). Should feminists oppose prostitution? *Ethics*, 99: 347–61.

Searle, John R. (1983). *Intentionality*. Cambridge: Cambridge University Press.

Silbey, Susan S. (1992). Making a place for cultural analysis of law. *Law and Social Inquiry*, 17: 39.

Simon, Jonathan. (1988). The ideological effects of actuarial practices. *Law and Society Review*, 22: 771–800.

Smith, Dorothy. (1990). *The Conceptual Practices of Power: A Feminist Sociology of Knowledge*. Boston: Northeastern University Press.

Taub, Nadine, and Elizabeth M. Schneider. (1982). Perspectives on women's subordination and the role of law. In David Kairys, (Ed.), *The Politics of Law: A Progressive Critique*. New York: Pantheon.

Unger, Roberto Mangabeira. (1975). *Knowledge and Politics*. New York: Free Press.

Yngvesson, Barbara. (1993). *Virtuous Citizens/Disruptive Subjects: Order and Complaint in a New England Court*. New York: Routledge.

Walkowitz, Judith R. (1980). *Prostitution and Victorian Society: Women, Class, and the State*. New York: Cambridge University Press.

Wilson, James Q., and Richard Herrnstein. (1985). *Crime and Human Nature: The Definitive Study of the Causes of Crime*. New York: Simon and Schuster.

Wittgenstein, Ludwig. (1976). *Philosophical Investigations*. Oxford: Blackwell.

Bruce A. Arrigo

3

CONSTITUTIVE THEORY AND THE HOMELESS IDENTITY: THE DISCOURSE OF A COMMUNITY DEVIANT

Introduction

The principles of constitutive criminology are relevant to the field of homeless studies. This relevance is most apparent when considering the dearth of theory construction. One particular area where constitutive criminology impacts our understanding of homelessness is the issue of resocialization for street dwellers. This chapter seeks to link selected principles in constitutive criminology with the resocialization activities of homeless citizens residing in an urban shelter.

We know very little about how homeless persons recommunalize in shelters, welfare hotels, or SROs (single-room-occupancies) (Arrigo, 1994a; Hoch and Slayton, 1989; Siegal, 1978). This absence of scholarship is particularly troubling since the construct "homeless" increasingly refers to an expanding and disparate collection of individuals who are (1) mentally ill, (2) welfare dependent, (3) AIDS victims, (4) elderly and frail, (5) chemically addicted, (6) Vietnam-era veterans, or (7) day laborers (Barak, 1991; National Coalition for the Homeless, 1989). One area of research gaining attention in the broad field of homeless studies, pertinent to communal reintegration, is the link between theory construction and empirically-animated social science research. In my own work, this relationship has focused on the daily practices of one urban SRO in Pittsburgh, Pennsylvania called Wood Street Commons (WSC).

Wood Street Commons houses 259 previously homeless and marginally housed adult men and women in a downtown, urban setting. This facility is significant for the purposes of learning more about the resocialization process because its residents represent a heterogenous collection of individuals who are at various stages of recovery. Elsewhere, I have discussed this notion of recovery in the context of fashioning social engineering models for resident empowerment (Arrigo, 1994a), promoting a community-sensitive drug peace culture (Arrigo, 1997a), understanding the role of investigator deviance in policy formation (Arrigo, 1998), and reducing crime and deviance based upon principles of orderly disorder (Arrigo, 1997b). What these studies demonstrate is the enormous vitality of theory to advance the knowledge process particularly when informed by concrete data.

Missing from the research in general, however, has been a more deliberately focused and critically-informed assessment of the variable of language. The reference to language or discourse re-situates the discussion of homeless studies in SRO settings to a microinteractional level in which reality, truth, meaning, and identity become the source of constant redefinition and ongoing scrutiny. This type of inquiry is potentially quite illuminating, especially as it relates to comprehending the complexity of the recovery process for tenants. Indeed, it is this form of analysis which challenges or questions the constitution of the self, in relation to a multitude of ecological factors, embodying as they do a specialized language whose voice often speaks *for and through* the human subject (Lacan, 1977).

In this chapter I further my research on resocialization relevant to formerly homeless citizens residing in the WSC housing resource. To accomplish this objective, I examine how theory was germane to the routine activities of the SRO's resident constituency. Utilizing the interpretive tools of constitutive thought (Henry and Milovanovic, 1996), I investigate how the discursive meanings embedded in the structural dynamics of the SRO community (e.g., tenant identification with the social space, the community's drug culture, counseling intervention practices, and cohabitation or visitation rituals), both shaped the identity of and were shaped by the tenants inhabiting the facility. For illustrative purposes, my inquiry considers the relationship between the SRO milieu and definitions of residents as community deviants or criminals. In order to contextualize the theoretical work, some background material on Wood Street Commons is presented. This material both describes the essential features of the SRO and presents data pertinent to tenant incidents and evictions.

I conclude the chapter by speculating on the future of constitutive theory in relation to application studies on homelessness, community crime, and social deviance.

Wood Street Commons and Housing the Homeless

Researching SROs

My introduction to Wood Street Commons occurred in 1985. Initially, I was employed as a community mental health therapist and homeless counselor for a non-profit agency called Community Human Services (CHS). I worked in conjunction with other professional and para-professional staff employed as part of a comprehensive outreach team. The building was one of several city shelters where my assistance and intervention was sought. As an agent of CHS, I was responsible for assisting homeless and/or marginally housed individuals who frequented flop houses, welfare hotels, soup kitchens, and sandwich lines within the agency's "catchment" area (a county-designated geographical boundary).

My access to WSC was complete and unencumbered. Residents identified me as someone to whom they could turn for support and advice. I eventually supervised the outreach project and those social service employees who functioned as part of the outreach team. From 1985 to 1991, I was privy to affairs relating to building occupants. This included systematized data on residents receiving notices for house rule violations as well as tenants terminated for excessive and/or serious building infractions.

Rooms for the Misbegotten

Wood Street Commons was originally a YMCA. It provided safe and affordable shelter to the poor and recreational activities for busy, downtown commuters. Maintaining this balance between service and commerce served the YMCA well throughout the 1970s; however, with increasing changes in the social landscape, it became abundantly clear that the YMCA was not prepared to meet the social-psychological needs of its troubled tenants. Increasing numbers of deinstitutionalized citizens, displaced but semi-skilled workers, fixed-income retirees, recovering junkies, and ex-felons found their way to this urban high-rise. For many of these residents, the YMCA became a temporary haven in which respite from the harsh realities of mental illness, unemployment, poverty, chemical addiction, and criminality were feverishly pursued.

During the mid-1980s, the facility was purchased by a property development corporation and a management consultant organization. In conjunction with the city's social service community, deep-seated concern for the plight of the facility's residents was addressed. The YMCA was no longer able to provide the kind of housing amenities tenants needed because the problems residents confronted extended well beyond the provision of shelter. Following the purchase, the YMCA was renamed Wood Street Commons, necessary building renovations were implemented, and the facility became a recognized resource for housing the city's homeless and working poor within a safe, supportive, and affordable environment.

Wood Street Commons is a vertical high-rise consisting of ten floors and approximately 26 rooms per floor. Each tenant occupies his or her own single room. Each room includes a wash basin with mirror, a walk-in closet, a chest-of-drawers, and a bed with night stand. On each floor there are five hallway bathrooms. Residents have access to their floor and room through a security key system. Tenants are responsible for two keys: one for use in the elevator to exit onto their floor and the other to gain admittance to their room. The lobby area of the SRO contains several offices. These offices are for administrative, security, housekeeping, and staff meeting purposes. Tenants enter and exit the facility only from the lobby passage way. The lower level of WSC includes additional space for tenant use. There is a laundry area, a vending machine area, and a recreational space with tables and chairs for movies, games, cards, etc. Another section of the lower level includes a community kitchen, a food storage room, a health or clinic station, a reading room, and a lounge area with television. Several additional offices for use by in-house social service personnel are also located in the lower level of WSC.

The Problem of Crime and Social Deviance in the Community

In terms of social service philosophy and practice, WSC underwent two substantial building changes. For purposes of simplicity, they can be termed *Phase I* and *Phase II*. Phase I occurred in 1985 when the building was purchased from the YMCA. This period in the facility's evolution lasted from 1985 to 1987. It was during this period that the SRO figures on crime and deviance reflected considerable tenant incidents and evictions compared to their Phase II counterpart. table 3.1 documents the Phase I figures.

The findings in table 3.1 list aggregate data utilizing two indices for criminality. These measures include *Incident Reports* and *Evictions*. Incident reports were generated by both residents and staff. They reflected concern for problematic behavior jeopardizing the well-being of the community and its constituency. The general rule was that residents were expected to not harm themselves, others, or the SRO property. Evictions were generated by building management in consultation with social service staff. Tenants usually received a number of incident reports prior to termination if the behavior was not, on its face, serious enough to warrant eviction. On other occasions, residents were evicted for first-time infractions where the conduct was so egregious that it was clearly life threatening or harmful to others in the community (e.g., brandishing a lethal weapon, setting fire to the facility). What makes the Phase I crime and social deviance figures so troubling is that Phase II data, accumulated from 1987 to 1991, reflect substantially lower incident reports and evictions across the various behavior scales (Arrigo, 1994a: 105; 1997b: 182).

Table 3.1 Prevalence of Crime and Deviance in the Community-Phase I: (1985–1987)

	AVERAGE NUMBER PER WEEK*	
BEHAVIOR	INCIDENT REPORTS	TENANT EVICTIONS
Drug Abuse	3	2
Alcohol Abuse	6	4
Violence (Toward Others)	2	2
Violence (Toward Property)	2	3
Other Minor Infractions	2	2
Failure to Pay Rent	—	3
Totals =	15	16

Eviction and Incident Reports are based on an average weekly occupancy rate of 245 residents.

Aggregate data collected during Phase II are presented in table 3.2. Utilizing the same measures for criminality and deviance (incident reports and evictions) as described in table 3.1, we note some rather appreciable differences between the SRO's two cycles of development. Indeed, based upon a sustained occupancy rate of 245 residents, there were, on average, six incident reports and five evictions per week generated from the SRO during Phase II. Thus the incident report total for Phase I was two-and-a-half times that of its Phase II counterpart (15 to 6), and the eviction total for Phase I was more than three times that of its Phase II counterpart (16 to 5).

The significant decline in aggregate crime data during WSC's second cycle of social service philosophy and practice raises some interesting questions relevant to creating and sustaining a sense of neighborhood in the SRO milieu. On the one hand, understanding what worked during Phase II tells us something about how to structure effective social engineering initiatives for troubled and disenfranchised citizens. On the other hand, examining what happened during Phase I furthers our appreciation for what not to do when cultivating an atmosphere of community for the homeless and displaced poor.

In the section which follows, I more closely consider how the social ecology of WSC, in relation to the building tenants, embodied a unique discourse which effectively rendered the occupants as de-

Table 3.2   Prevalence of Crime and Deviance in the Community-Phase II: (1988–1991)

	AVERAGE NUMBER PER WEEK[*]	
BEHAVIOR	INCIDENT REPORTS	TENANT EVICTIONS
Drug Abuse	1	0
Alcohol Abuse	2	2
Violence (Toward Others)	1	0
Violence (Toward Property)	0	0
Other Minor Infractions	2	1
Failure to Pay Rent	—	2
Totals =	6	5

[*]*Eviction and Incident Reports* are based on an average weekly occupancy rate of 245 residents.

viants. The contributions of Henry and Milovanovic (1999) and Bak (1999) in this volume lay out several of the essential components of constitutive thought (see also Arrigo, 1997c). My intent, however, is to apply several major facets of the theory to the linguistic texturing of the SRO's Phase I cycle. In this regard, it will be revealed how the building's inhabitants, as social agents, coproduced a discourse which they actively resisted but which they, nonetheless, contributed to as their criminal and/or deviant self definitions were linguistically structured and discursively reified.

Constitutive Theory and Wood Street Commons: Analysis of Phase I

There are four essential principles relevant to constitutive criminological theory which inform the process of how residents were defined through discourse as deviants during the SRO's Phase I stage of development. These principles include: (1) the decentered subject; (2) the recovering subject; (3) the social structure as deconstructive or reconstructive; and (4) the definition of crime as power to harm. This list is not exhaustive. I am simply addressing some obvious areas of application germane to an understanding of homelessness, deviant discourse, and constitutive thought.

1. Decentered subject. Cartesian epistemology (1954, 1961) posits a subject that is unified, stable, free, purposive, and rational. This is the popular vision of post-Renaissance philosophy and modernist science. Indeed, the Cartesian axiom, *cogito ergo sum*, squarely identifies the centrality of the subject, the plenary and unitary "*I*," as the locus for all events and human affairs. Contrastingly, Lacan (1977:166, 193–4; 1988: 243; see also Milovanovic, 1992: 45–6) argues that we are less in control of who we are or what we say and, thus, are more disunified, unstable, determined, accidental, and irrational. Descartes' notion is replaced by Lacan's (1977: 166): "I think where I am not, therefore I am where I do not think." The individual situates him/herself and is inserted within a stream of signifying practices which *speak* the subject.

Borrowing from de Saussure (1966), Kojeve (1980), Levi-Strauss (1963), Jakobson (1971) and Benveniste (1971), Lacan further reveals how we cannot think of a thought without first putting it in the form of a language. He makes this notion evident through his now famous Schema L, or the quadripartite subject (Lacan, 1977: 193–4, 1988: 243; Henry and Milovanovic, 1996: 28–34). Lacan's essential thesis is that discourse and subjectivity (the self as individual) are inextricably linked together. The subject "fades" into the discourse in use or "disappears" into its objects of desire (*objects petit [a]*). In this context, shared meaning is assured but at the expense of one's existential being. The matheme employed by Lacan to designate this experience of loss or lack was "$ < > a$." The arrows "$< >$" represent movement. The subject ($) vanishes into its objects of desire (a). The "$" is divided, slashed, decentered. The subject's psychic self-awareness unconsciously and pre-thematically, slumbers at the cost of languaging a circumscribed reality. This psychic surrendering of the self is expressed and recounted in the act of naming persons, places, things, and ideas.

A good illustration of the decentered subject relates to how the SRO embraced an important dimension of its ecological development. During the Phase I cycle, the building was, in part, defined in terms of how residents (and staff) perceived the social space they inhabited (Arrigo, 1997b: 181). When tenants spoke about living in the SRO, they often externalized their sentiments. In other words, resident characterizations of the SRO typically began with how the *facility made them feel*, or what *the building did to them*. Thus, for example, many residents would speak about loss, frustration, fear, boredom, etc., but only from the context of how the building evoked these emotions in the residents. One resident aptly summarized this experience as follows:

> This place is like livin' in a prison. It makes you feel all couped up with nothin' to do but wait around for somethin' to happen but nothin' never does. Then you're left with this empty place inside and you know it can't be filled 'cuz nothin' here can help fill it.

What is profoundly telling about this description, in relation to constitutive thought, is how building occupants truly embodied Lacan's notion of subjectivity. As decentered individuals, residents relied upon a discourse outside of themselves in order to speak about themselves. This is not to say that the grammar which they invoked did not come from them; rather, it is to point out how the alienating, anomic, and angst-producing discourse of the SRO spoke *through* them. In situations such as these, there was a robust subtext waiting to be heard. All psychic suffering disappeared into existing objects of desire (e.g., the social space as life-numbing). This silence was much like a death: the presence of the Self made painfully real in its absence.

2. Recovering subject.   Human agency, however, is not merely constituted by forces, in language, beyond one's control. Giddens (1984) structuration theory has been particularly helpful in articulating this very notion. Even as people are shaped by structural forces which announce their humanity, subjects can and do contribute to that which determines them (Bourdieu and Wacquant, 1992: 167–68). People *are* producers, "partially blind builders," of the world they inhabit (Henry and Milovanovic, 1996: 37). That is to say, there is a constitutive, interrelated dimension to subjectivity and the social order. As Giddens (1984: 203) explains:

> Human social activities . . . are not brought into being by social actors but are recreated by them via the very means whereby they express themselves *as* actors. In and through these activities agents reproduce the conditions that make these activities possible.

Thus, we are led to conclude that human agency is *both* a function of Lacan's decentered subject phenomenon and an active engagement with those structural forces constituting the subject's agency. This engagement is, at times, an active resistance to prevailing coordinated language systems which speak the subject, and a passive complicity in the reconstitution of that discourse which subjugates the voice of and way of knowing for the individual (Arrigo, 1995: 456–58). Criminological instances of this phenomenon are abundant. For example, jailhouse lawyers who do their cases *pro se* (Milovanovic, 1988; Thomas and Milovanovic, 1999) are just as much anchored in this discursive and dialectal play of resistant and complicitous language as are psychiatric patients petitioning for release from institution confinement (Arrigo, 1996).

This is not to imply that subjects cannot create new and different vistas for understanding and meaning as they cling to and reproduce established categories of reason and logic. Indeed, humans are "social projects" (Henry and Milovanovic, 1996: 39) or subject-in-process (Kristeva, 1984); that is, they are historically mediated, discursively constituted, and structurally situated. Human subjects invest energy in *summary representations* (Knorr-Cetina and Cicourel, 1981) which enable them to provisionally, positionally, and relationally confront the reality of their mutable selves, in relation to existing structural conditions, such that negotiated, multiple self-identities are possible. This is, then, the condition of the recovering subject: an experience in which there are forces (constituted through language) not open to active or passive regulation by the person but where there are contingently retrievable spaces of identity which can be articulated, embodied, and affirmed.

The experience of residents constituting identity through the community's drug culture is illustrative of the recovering subject. During Phase I of the SRO's strategic development, the general building practice was to periodically make public declarations about the housing risks associated with illegal drug use. Tenants caught using drugs on the premises could be subjected to immediate eviction. This policy functioned as a condition for continued occupancy. Notwithstanding, residents uniquely interpreted and endorsed management's position.

Given the nature of the facility, surveillance of drug-related behavior was superficial at best. Thus, for the most part, the summary representation for "illegal drug use" was defined in terms of how tenants articulated when violations occurred, who was responsible for the infraction, and the conditions under which they felt social service intervention was warranted. In other words, residents, through discourse and action, tacitly resisted the blanket statement of no drug use imposed upon them by management. Overt resistance could result in punitive enforcement measures, not the least of which included an incident report for complicity through silence or concealment. In doing so however, tenants actively created, albeit in a temporary and contingent way, new meaning for drug use—one that was more in concert with the values they experienced regarding this behavior. As a resident-based definition, drug use became the inability to inconspicuously disguise conduct regarded as undesirable or unsuitable. WSC tenants were not identified as addicts or violators of house rules because they took drugs; rather, they were defined as such in relationship to how they lived out their drug habit and how other tenants experienced this behavior in relation to the facility's clearly articulated, zero-tolerance drug policy (Arrigo, 1997a: 57). In this process, human agency was, in part, recovered, tenant identity was temporarily reclaimed, and a deviant culture of drug use was actively sustained in the building.

3. *Social Structure as Deconstructive/Reconstructive.* Constitutive theory shows us how agency is implicated in the method of defining reality. But subjectivity does not exist in a vacuum without reference to the social world of which it is a part. The passive (decentered) and active (recovering) subject dialectic is incomplete without examining how social structure is constitutively produced. Knowledge about social structure is formed through social relations as articulated and recreated by individuals in contingent and provisional ways (Henry and Milovanovic, 1996: 65). The coproduction of reality necessarily entails a consideration of those anchored forces through speech which humans define as real for them in a given time and context, with particular individuals and circumstances, mediated by political economic influences.

With this framework in mind, structures are not fixed or certain. Instead, they are only categories of classification which give some identifiable reference point to experience embodied by individuals (Giddens, 1984: 25). These structural categories receive further concretization when described as such by human agents. Under these conditions, meaning is temporarily assured through repetitive actions and behaviors organized in support of the very existence of these structural classifications (Knorr-Cetina, 1981: 36–7). Clearly, the duality of agency or structure is central to this process, such that individuals co-shape and are shaped by the very conditions they define as real for and about themselves.

In this activity of codetermining social structure through human agency and extant relations, constitutive thought bridges the critical polarities of deconstruction and reconstruction. The mutuality of social relations and subject-position discursive readings of phenomena makes possible horizons of intersubjective meaning (Nietzsche, 1968) or occasions for living contingent universalities (Butler, 1992). These are experiences which are themselves not subject to sedimentation or stability. According to constitutive theory, the articulation of social structural forces at work in the subject's life would simultaneously entail a de-identification with prevailing modes of communication, and a re-identification with new forms more consonant with the person's own sense of desire, identity, and being (JanMohamed, 1994, Giroux, 1992). The work of Cornell (1993) in law, Freire (1972) in education, Unger (1987) in politics, and Laclau (1991) in new social movement theory has explored this critical constitutive process of deconstruction and reconstruction to some degree.

The identification of and explanation for resident skills and competencies illustrates the deconstructive reconstructive dialectics inherent in the social structural forces operating within the SRO. Many of the tenants had experienced several bouts of homelessness or dislocation prior to their arrival at and admission into WSC. Thus, human service staff quickly and deliberately intervened with new residents as a way of socially and psychically "stripping" them of this deviant past identity (Goffman, 1959). Indeed, the sustained presence of professional counseling personnel was a vivid reminder that the SRO was populated by people who were acutely vulnerable and chronically troubled.

Moreover, during the Phase I cycle, many tenants routinely distanced themselves from their established deviant lifestyles and actively sought the counseling staff as a way of addressing the deep-seated emotional scarring resulting from chemical dependency, domestic violence, joblessness, illiteracy, and the like. In this context, then, tenants contributed to the deconstruction of their previous lives as homeless outcasts and embraced a discourse which reconstituted them as *recovering* alcoholics, *survivors* of abuse, *casualties* of an eroding service-based economy, and *victims* of limited education. But this reconstitution, structurally enforced through ongoing, trust-inducing staff intervention and therapy and linguistically textured through empathically selected words or phrases, was an insidious commentary on the definition of residents and their perceived strengths and/or skills.

During Phase I, tenants were fundamentally acknowledged by building staff for their willingness to accept responsibility for the behaviors that produced and reproduced repeated trauma in their lives. Thus, being a "good" resident amounted to taking ownership for delinquent, deviant, or criminal behavior. Residents who "professed their sins" were regarded as strong, upstanding, genuine, courageous, model tenants. Thus, resident competency was defined by the building culture through the admission of character flaws or personality deficits. The problem with this method of reconstituting the occupants was that a climate of resident defectiveness and fallibility permeated the SRO. This condition furthered the widespread tenant malaise engendered throughout the facility's first stage of development. Unwittingly, the deconstructive practice of shedding definitions of tenants as homeless outsiders and the reconstitutive practice of recasting SRO occupants as chronically troubled and acutely vulnerable, rendered the building's residents as both visibly deviant and profoundly needy.

4. Definition of Crime as Power to Harm.   Integral to constitutive criminological theory is its explanation of crime. Although certainly helpful, descriptions of human agency and social structure are not, in and of themselves, sufficient to answer the question of how crime is defined constitutively. Crime is real. It is not imagined or fictional. It involves occasions for pain and conflict and instances of harm and injury (Henry and Milovanovic, 1996: 116). Yet crime can assume the form of "symbolic violence" (Bourdieu, 1977: 192). In these instances, covert, taken-for-granted domination masks a real power differential that effectively transforms subjects into objects of control and manipulation. Symbolic violence, then, is the denial of one's humanity (Henry and Milovanovic, 1996: 116).

Constitutive criminology advances Bourdieu's position. Crime is not only a discursively constituted function of concealed inequalities exercised over time against others, but is the denial of the other's extant humanity and the repression of how that humanity might unfold throughout one's future. "Crime is the power to deny others their ability to make a difference" (Henry and Milovanovic, 1996: 116). When subjects are rendered through discourse as a lack or an absence (Lacan's $), this is an occasion in which the person's capacity to be a party to an exchange, discussion, encounter, or event is thwarted. The person is nothing. The pain is deep. The crime is real.

With the above definition in mind, much of what is taken to be law abiding behavior must be reconsidered as contributing to the victimization of others. Any reductionistic, repressive act, orchestrated through a coordinated language system, must be seen as an exercise of the power to inflict harm or crime upon others (Lecercle, 1990). Implicated in this definition, then, are the voices of the powerless (e.g., the homeless). Their desires seek embodiment, their wishes yearn for expressive form, their voices slumber amidst a deafening silence. As constitutive theory reminds us, expressions of denial such as these are no less instances of crime than are acts of property damage, physical assault, or psychological abuse (Mouffe, 1992, McLaren, 1994, Giroux, 1992).

Wood Street Commons' Phase I developmental cycle was marked by a social practice philosophy which, knowingly or not, disempowered residents and, in the process, reconstituted them as criminals. Expressions of disempowerment catalyzed the SRO culture such that it was fraught with overt and covert acts of deviance. Tenant descriptions of the social space, management's position on drug use, and staff perceptions of resident competencies clearly conveyed this sentiment.

Another illustration of disempowerment fostering harm entailed cohabitation and visitation privileges for tenants. Each of the ten floors was specifically designated for male or for female use. Thus, no floors were mixed and men and women were cautious about their personal relationships with other SRO occupants. Further, residents could only entertain visits by spouses or partners during building-specified daylight days and times. Surveillance efforts, while frequently nominal, were noticeably in place and residents concerned with eviction faithfully conformed.

Although the SRO was populated by adult men and women, the message was clear: fraternization with the opposite sex was monitored and unauthorized activity was obvious grounds for a tenant write-up. While management was genuinely concerned about creating a culture for prostitution and other behaviors consistent with a hidden economy, there was no frank and open discussion on cohabitation and visitation privileges. Clearly, there was a fear of benignly fostering deviance. Yet, resident contributions to the decision making were non-existent. By denying input from residents and by prohibiting tenants from exerting their influence on the process, building occupants were denied their own humanity. They were treated as non-persons or as less than human. Consistent with constitutive criminology, this was the harm and pain caused by the SRO's act of restrictive floor access. The expression of power wielded by WSC regarding social interaction between the sexes, was a tangible instance of crime in the community. Residents were deviant and were structurally defined as such through confining fraternization practices. In their acquiescence, tenants implicitly endorsed this deviant self-definition which was perpetuated throughout Phase I of the building's evolution.

Speculation on Constitutive Theory, Homeless Studies, and Deviance

In this chapter I have applied fundamental, though selected, principles of constitutive theory to the linguistic mapping of a large, urban SRO in Pittsburgh, Pennsylvania. This project was regarded as particularly worthwhile given the high levels of crime and social deviance present during the Phase I cycle of the building's development. The assumption was that by utilizing the interpretive tools of constitutive theory, something could be discerned about what not to do when creating a sense of community for peripatetic and troubled citizens. The essential question examined was how, through discourse, were residents constituted as deviants and how, through discourse, did residents reify and sustain this process?

In consideration of the four constitutive criminological principles investigated, it was evident that residents were, knowingly or not, complicitous in their self-definitions as deviants. Indeed, by examining resident perceptions of the social space, the community drug culture, expressions of tenant skills or competencies, and building attitudes toward cohabitation and visitation, human agency both constituted and was shaped by social structural forces which spoke the subject or spoke through the subject. Thus, constitutive theory enabled us to see how, through discourse, building occupants were decentered, reconstituted, disempowered, dehumanized, and criminalized. Unquestionably, residents fell prey to acts of communal crime whose power was profoundly injurious to them. The eviction and incident report figures for Phase I are indicators of this point.

Much of what is missing in the literature on homeless studies is how critically-inspired theory informs our understanding of community crime and social deviance. Constitutive theory is but one piece of the conceptual puzzle. The variable of language activated and at work within the interplay of human agency and social structure is the anchor point for investigations persuaded by this theory's logic. Future research on SRO's for the homeless and the displaced poor would do well to consider related areas of similar inquiry. For example, constitutive theory certainly shares some affinities for principles contained in non-linear dynamics (Arrigo, 1997b; Arrigo and Young, 1996). Further, Lacanian psychoanalytic semiotics has proven fruitful for application studies exploring the marginalization of other collectives subjected to institutional regimes of power (Arrigo, 1994b; 1997d; Arrigo and Schehr, 1998).

It is also worth noting that constitutive theory, replete as it is, with important theoretical constructs, offers insight into how to reclaim the subject through coordinated language systems in relation to social structural conditions. For example, the notions of transpraxis and replacement discourses are important to this project (Henry and Milovanovic, 1996: 189–214). What is at stake here is the method by which the recovering subject can be reconstructed within a just community (e.g., Scharf, 1977: 104; McKnight, 1987: 54; Parry and Doan, 1994: 29, 47). Homeless studies research on SRO's and crime would do well to examine the relevance of these ideas when exploring the theory and practice of creating and sustaining a sense of place as home for the homeless and disenfranchised.

Whatever the trajectory of critical thought, the field of homeless studies, single room occupancy housing, and social deviance is ripe for a more integrated and detailed analysis of how communities are created within vertical structures like WSC. I submit that this is a direction which social problems research should seriously consider. Phase I resocialization efforts were ineffective because the variable of language was not considered integral to the social planning of the building's internal ecology. This chapter does not suggest that the discourse in use was the only factor contributing to the high crime and delinquency rates operating throughout the first stage of the SRO's development. However, the working tools of constitutive thought clearly demonstrate how human agency and social structural forces were mediated through a discourse which cast residents as deviants. Thus, further research efforts along these and similar lines are most definitely a solid and practical step in the appropriate direction. The manifold problems afflicting the homeless and the disenfranchised most assuredly deserve at least this level of careful scrutiny.

References

Arrigo, B. (1998). "Shattered lives and shelter lies?: Anatomy of research deviance in homeless programming and policy." In J. Ferrell and M. Hamm (Eds.), *Ethnography At the Edge: Crime, Deviance and Field Research*. Boston, MA.: Northeastern University Press.

Arrigo, B. (1997a). "Recommunalizing drug offenders: The 'drug peace' agenda." *Journal of Offender Rehabilitation*, 24(3/4): 53–73.

Arrigo, B. (1997b). "Dimensions of social justice in an SRO: Contributions from chaos theory, policy, and practice." In *Chaos, Criminology, and Social Justice*. In D. Milovanovic (Ed.), (pp. 179–194). New York: Praeger.

Arrigo, B. (1997c). "Review of Stuart Henry and Dragan Milovanovic's *Constitutive Criminology* and Alan Hunt's *Explorations in Law and Society*: *Toward a constitutive theory of law*." *Theoretical Criminology*, 1(3): 392–96.

Arrigo, B. (forthcoming, 1997d). "Transcarceration: Notes on a psychoanalytically-informed theory of social practice in the criminal justice and mental health systems." *Crime, Law, and Social Change: An International Journal*.

Arrigo, B. (1996). *The Contours of Psychiatric Justice: A Postmodern Critique of Mental Illness, Criminal Insanity, and the Law*. New York: Garland.

Arrigo, B. (1995). "The peripheral core of law and criminology: On postmodern social theory and conceptual integration." *Justice Quarterly*, 12(3): 447–472.

Arrigo, B. (1994a). "Rooms for the misbegotten: Social design and social deviance." *Journal of Sociology and Social Welfare*, 21(4): 95–113.

Arrigo, B. (1994b). "Legal discourse and the disordered criminal defendant: Contributions from psychoanalytic semiotics and chaos theory." *Legal Studies Forum*, 18(1): 93–112.

Arrigo, B., and R. Schehr. (1998). *Restoring Justice for Juveniles: Toward a Critical Analysis of Victim Offender Mediation*. Working paper available at the Institute of Psychology, Law, and Pubic Policy, Fresno, CA.

Arrigo, B., and T. R. Young (1996). "Complexity, and crime: Working tools for a postmodern criminology." In *Thinking Critically About Crime*, B. MacLean and D. Milovanovic (Eds.), (pp 77–84). Vancouver, Canada: The Collective Press.

Bak, A. (1999). "Constitutive criminology: An introduction to the core concepts." In S. Henry and D. Milovanovic, *Constitutive Criminology at Work: Applications to Crime and Justice*. Albany, NY: SUNY Press.

Barak, G. (1991). *Gimme' Shelter: A Social History of Homelessness in Contemporary America*. Westport, CT: Praeger.

Benveniste, E. (1971). *Problems in General Linguistics*. Coral Gables, FL: University of Miami Press.

Bourdieu, P. (1977). *Outline of a Theory of Practice*. Cambridge: Cambridge University Press.

Bourdieu, P., and L. J. D. Wacquant. (1992). *An Invitation to Reflexive Sociology*. Chicago: University of Chicago Press.

Butler, J. (1992). "Contingent foundations: Feminism and the question of 'postmodernism.'" In *Feminists Theorize the Political*. J. Butler and J. W. Scott (Eds.). New York: Routledge.

Cornell, D. (1993). *Transformations: Recollective Imagination and Sexual Difference*. New York: Routledge.

Freire, P. (1972). *Pedagogy of the Oppressed*. New York: Herder and Her.

Descartes, R. (1961 [1641]). *Meditations of First Philosophy*. New York: Bobbs-Merrill.

Descartes. R. (1954 [1637]). *Discourse on Method*. New York: Liberal Arts Press.

Giddens, A. (1984). *The Constitution of Society: Outline of the Theory of Structuration*. Oxford: Polity Press.

Giroux, H. (1992). *Border Crossings*. New York: Routledge.

Goffman, E. (1959). *Asylums: Essays on the Social Situation of Inmates and Other Inmates*. New York: Doubleday.

Henry, S., and D. Milovanovic. (1996). *Constitutive Criminology: Beyond Postmodernism*. London: Sage.

Henry, S., and D. Milovanovic. (1999). "Conclusion: Constitutive Criminology engages its critics—An assessment." In S. Henry and D. Milovanovic (Eds.), *Constitutive Criminology At Work: Applications to Crime and Justice*. Albany, NY: SUNY Press.

Hoch, C., and R. Slayton. (1989). *New Homeless and Old: Community and the Skid Row Hotel*. Philadelphia: Temple Univeristy Press.

Jakobson, R. (1971). "Two aspects of language and two types of aphasic disorders." In *Fundamentals of Language*, R. Jakobson and M. Halle (Eds.), (pp.13–47). Paris: Mouton.

JanMohamed, A. R. (1994). "Some implications of Paulo Freire's border pedagogy." In *Between Borders: Pedagogy and the Politics of Cultural Studies*. H. Giroux and P. McLaren (Eds.). New York: Routledge.

Knorr-Cetina, K., and A. Cicourel. (Eds.). (1981). *Advances in Social Theory and Methodology: Toward an Integration of Macro-and Micro-Sociologies*. London: Routledge and Kegan Paul.

Kojeve, A. (1980). *Introduction to the Reading of Hegel*. Ithaca, NY: Cornell University Press.

Kristeva, J. (1984). *Revolution in Poetic Language*. New York: Columbia University Press.

Lacan, J. (1985). *Feminine Sexuality*. New York: W.W. Norton and Pantheon Books.

Lacan, J. (1977). *Ecrits: A Selection*. Translated by A. Sheridan. New York: Norton.

Laclau, E. (1991). *New Reflections on the Revolutions of Our Time*. London: Verso.

Lecercle, J. J. (1990). *The Violence of Language*. New York: Routledge.

Levi-Strauss, C. (1963). *Structural Anthropology*. New York: Basic Books.

McLaren, P. (1994). "Multiculturalism and the postmodern critique: Toward a pedagogy of resistance and transformation." In *Border Crossings: Ped-*

agogy and the Politics of Cultural Studies, H. Giroux and P. McLaren (Eds.), (pp. 192–122). New York: Routledge.

McKnight, J. (1987). "Regenerating community." *Social Policy*, 17: 54–58.

Milovanovic, D. (1988). "Jailhouse lawyers and jailhouse lawyering." *International Journal of the Sociology of Law*, 16: 455–475.

Mouffe, C. (1992). "Feminism, citizenship and radical democratic politics." In *Feminists Theorize the Political*. J. Butler and J. W. Scott (Eds.). London: Routledge.

National Coalition for the Homeless. (1989). *American Nightmare: A Decade of Homelessness in the United States*. New York: NCH.

Nietzsche, F. (1968) *The Basic Writings of Nietzsche*. W. Kauffman (ed.). New York: Random House.

Parry, A., and R. Doan. (1994). *Story Re-Visions: Narrative Therapy in the Postmodern World*. New York: Guilford Press.

Saussure, F. de. (1966). *Course in General Linguistics*. New York: McGraw-Hill.

Scharf, P. (1977). "The just community." *New Society*, 21 (4): 104–5.

Siegal, H. (1978). *Outposts of the Forgotten*. NJ: Transaction Books.

Thomas, J., and D. Milovanovic (1999). "(Re)visiting the jailhouse lawyer: An excursion into constitutive criminology." In S. Henry and D. Milovanovic (Eds.), *Constitutive Criminology at Work: Applications to Crime and Justice*. Albany, NY: SUNY Press.

Unger, R. (1987). *False Necessity*. New York: Cambridge University Press.

Gregg Barak

4

CONSTITUTING O.J.: MASS-MEDIATED TRIALS AND NEWSMAKING CRIMINOLOGY[1]

Introduction

People who are interested in participating in the public discussion on crime and justice, whether they are pundits, politicians, criminologists, crime victims, or crime fighters, must develop the means and ways for engaging the world of newsmaking crime and justice. Accordingly, I continue to argue that it is important for students to examine how crime and justice reporting, whether it comes packaged as "news," as "entertainment," or as "infotainment," involves the complex interaction of human interest stories and policy-oriented news coverage (Sparks, 1992). Such knowledges are crucial for not only understanding the constitutive processes of newsmaking in the context of the coproductions of crime and justice, but also for developing the practice of newsmaking criminology.

The objective here is to contribute to the ongoing developments and intersections of "newsmaking" criminology (Barak, 1988; 1993; 1994a; 1994b) and "constitutive" criminology (Henry and Milovanovic, 1991; Milovanovic and Henry, 1991; and Henry and Milovanovic, 1996) by providing an ethnographic case study of my own experience as a local radio commentator for the O.J. Simpson trial. As a newsmaking criminologist for more than a decade, I have been examining media and media studies not from the perspective of a detached social and cultural scientist, but rather from the perspective of an engaged "participant-observer" who has sought to develop his public "criminological" voice. In terms of newsmaking entertainment, the O.J.

Simpson case was valuable to newsmaking criminologists in general and to me in particular for at least four reasons. First, it became the essence of a high-profile crime and justice narrative with more text produced than anyone could possibly know what to do with. Second, the "trial of the century" afforded criminologists and others with a chance to investigate various modes of newsmaking in the context of blurring news and entertainment genres. Third, the O.J. saga allowed me to capture through the lens of ethnography a finer understanding of the different kinds of newsmaking possibilities. Fourth, the larger O.J. cultural phenomenon provided me with the opportunity to expand my own role as a newsmaking criminologist, and to assess the value of such activity for other criminologists.

Constitutive and Newsmaking Criminologies

As a precursor to the question of whether or not it is possible to develop a "theory of crime reaction," Creechan (1995) has identified "vicious," "virtuous" and "vicarious" cycles of reporting heinous crime. In his scheme, ideas about crime and justice are viewed as symbolic property that consist of the spinning worlds of media representations, legal applications, and political and academic interpretations. Creechan compares the three responses to heinous crime by examining the similarities and differences between them according to: audience response, media impact, political role, effect on crime, effect on community, policy initiatives, theoretical guidance, scholarly role, and metaphors or concepts used.

While Creechan's discussion is useful as an heuristic device, I do not believe that it is useful or possible for developing some kind of integrative theory of crime reaction that accounts for the variation in vicious, virtuous, or vicarious responses. Such an approach, at least from the perspective of constitutive theory (Giddens, 1984; Henry and Milovanovic, 1991; 1996), incorrectly assumes the possibility of distinct and separate theories of crime and crime reaction when the two are, in fact, inseparable. It also pursues the "independent" causes of crime and crime responses, instead of examining the coproduction of both as these are established by human subjects in the context of the ongoing development of organizational structures that humans cultivate, such as the processes of newsmaking.

Heuristically, Creechan's responses are useful for at least two reasons. First, his typology of reacting to crime reveals that for some time the dominant ideological presentation of news has emphasized a vicious circle approach to crime reaction where there is an increase in fear and a mistrust and breakdown of solidarity as evidenced by rising incidence of hate crimes. Second, his categories are especially useful because they provide a comprehensive look at the range of responses and of the thinkers that underscore each of these responses: vicious consisting of the ideas of Bentham, Beccaria, and J. Q. Wilson; virtuous consisting of the ideas of Durkheim, Weber, Mead, and Garland; and vicarious consisting of the ideas of Marx, Weber, Foucault, and Chomsky. The suggested implications are that: (1) the incorporation of vicious circles may produce more of the same retributive discourse; (2) the incorporation of virtuous circles may produce an oppositional discourse of rehabilitation; and (3) the incorporation of vicarious circles may produce a replacement discourse of transpraxis that seeks to alter the prevailing political, economic, and social arrangements (Henry and Milovanovic, 1991).

In the context of repetitive themes, reporters not only rely on the cult of the experts of criminal justice such as police officers, prosecutors, and judges for their stories, but these stories typically conform to the established stereotypes and themes of organizational crime and justice. In other words, the availability of criminal experts, from attorneys to journalists, from victims to advocates, who provide instant commentary reflecting on themes of crime and justice that are immediately known by their consuming audiences, are themselves a part of a larger system of political and bureaucratic justice. Of course, the media's dependence on these sources and themes often inhibits their ability to monitor effectively criminal justice organizations and the 6th Amendment guarantees. At the same time, criminal justice sources have their own specific agenda to pursue when participating in the news production process. As for such contemporary popular crime and justice themes as those which portray "predator criminals," "sexual psychopaths," and "terrorist bombers," they tend not only to provide a "mean world view" characterized by mistrust, cynicism, and alienation, but also to reinforce the use of formal rather than informal means of social control (Barak, 1994a; Sandys and Chermak, 1995). Finally, at least in the United States, these mass narratives or crime and justice themes tend to interact with a growing individual anxiety and a thriving cultural rage that is firmly grounded in the text of crime, the subtext of race and gender, and the undertext of class (Barak, 1994b; Chancer and Donovan, 1994).

Critical approaches to mass communication (Gouldner, 1976;

Mosco, 1986; Lazere, 1987), especially those reflective of a Gramscian approach to hegemony (Barak, 1988), go further in explaining the newsmaking process than the traditional "mirror," "commercial," and "political" models (Lee-Semmons, 1990). Critical theories, more fundamentally, contend that the prevailing orders of the political economy depend on both the passive and active consent of the governed, and on the collective will of the people in which various groups within society unite and struggle. Hence, "news" construction incorporates the world views of both the privileged and the unprivileged (Barlow, Barlow, and Chiricos, 1995; Chambliss, 1995). With respect to the views of the latter, these are composed of a variety of elements, experiences, voices and silences. Some of these views are popularized in public discourse through mass media while others are confined to private conversations. It is often the case, however, that when it comes to representing the views of the unprivileged, they are presented from the perspectives of the privileged as articulated through the voices of professional newsmakers.

Less often, the perspectives of marginalized people (unprivileged) are actually articulated by representative voices from these powerless groups. Whether expounded from "above" or "below," the viewpoints of the masses may indeed contradict the dominant ideologies without disturbing or delegitimizing the prevailing social order. These "opposing" views are then, in turn, subject to the always dangerous forces of co-optation that lend further legitimation to the hegemonic order. On the other hand, socially constructed and discursively organized categories of order and reality, acting in concert with or through interaction with dissident voices, may actually serve to provide alternative praxes and replacement discourses characteristic of a constitutive criminology whose ultimate aims include the reconstruction and redirection of a social system so that there ensues a minimization of harm and injury throughout society (Henry and Milovanovic, 1996).

Like constitutive criminology in general, the practice of newsmaking criminology, shifts its coverage from "narrow dichotomized issues focusing either on the individual offender or on the social environment, without losing sight of human agency *qua* human subject, and without reducing social agency, albeit seen as a virtual society" (Henry and Milovanovic, 1996: x). Hence, both criminologies take a "holistic conception of the relationship between the 'individual' and 'society' which prioritizes neither one nor the other," but, instead, examines their mutuality and interrelationship in the context of "the coproduction of crime by human subjects, and by the social and organizational structures that humans develop" (Ibid.: x).

High-Profile and Low-Profile Disputes:
The Echo Effects of Newsmaking

The relationship between high- and low-profile criminal disputes has recently drawn the attention of students of mass media and crime and justice. News media echoes, as Surette (1995) has referred to them, capture the relationship between publicized and non-publicized criminal cases. Traditionally, media attention focused almost exclusively on the impact of high-profile cases on the actions of criminal justice functionaries in those particular cases. Today, however, the newsmaking echo effect suggests that the mass media treatment of high-profile crimes also has an impact on the treatment of similarly enacted but non-publicized crimes. Furthermore, it has been argued that in addition to the impact of high-profile crimes on low-profile crimes of a similar kind, they have been found to have an indirect effect on the processing of other kinds of criminal dockets (Surette, 1995). In some instances this has resulted in the trying of more criminal defendants by trial in such cases as child sexual abuse and other forms of domestic violence than was typical before the news coverage of the high-profile criminal. On the other hand, it has also been recognized that the criminal justice processes of adjudication, sooner or later, in deference to the case loads, fiscal policies, or political necessities, make some accommodations in their informal bargaining decisions affecting those cases furthest removed from high-profile cases in general (Surette, 1995). The point is that through the echo effects of newsmaking, the media in conjunction with the source agencies of criminal justice administration, are in positions to engage in crime and justice agenda setting. In short, through selected publicity, consciously and unconsciously, the reporting of crime and justice frames the importance of a particular issue, in relation to both its "causes" and "solutions" (Barak, 1988; Surette, 1992).

As there is an association between crime and justice newsmaking and the heinous and unusual nature of the crimes profiled, there also tends to be echo effects that are primarily punitive in form. Surette's (1995: 16) analysis of highly publicized child victimization cases over a five-year period, for example, "showed marked increases in the number of similar cases filed, an increase in the sentences of cases adjudicated guilty, and an increase in the processing time for cases."

Analyses of newsmaking echo effects, then, lend support to a constitutive-integrative perspective that argues that the coproduction of crime and justice is a function of mass interaction (Barak, 1998). From the perspective of newsmaking criminology, therefore, it becomes important to understand not only how the echo effects of mass media "conspire" to reconstruct the reality of crime and justice, but also how the high-profile cases in particular are capable of both distorting and setting public policy agendas. For those engaged in newsmaking criminology, understanding these processes and the larger contexts of knowledge production become one of the many prerequisites to "effective" newsmaking. Effective newsmaking refers to the newsmaking criminologist's ability to have his or her message come across as intended, rather than to be merely used, for example, as a sound bite for someone else's "news spin." Effective newsmaking also calls for an appreciation and understanding of the way in which mass mediated images of crime and justice are linked to personal feelings of rage, pleasure, and anxiety (Katz, 1988; Chancer and Donovan, 1994; Ferrell and Sanders, 1995). In other words, an effective newsmaking criminology must not only be aware of and sensitive to the "body politics" of crime and victimization, but it must incorporate or communicate this perspective in its presentation and analysis.

Newsmaking: Pretrial Publicity and the First and Sixth Amendment

Traditionally, most of the publicity associated with trials is not viewed as pretrial publicity. Pretrial publicity commonly refers to the publicity that surrounds high-profile criminal defendants and their ability to get a fair trial (Sandys and Chermak, 1995). It is also true, notwithstanding, that low-profile or non-publicized criminal defendants, who are involved more typically in plea bargaining and less typically in jury trials, are indirectly affected by high-profile or media-covered criminal trials.

As Surette (1995) argues, low-profile criminal cases experience an echo or ripple effect set off by those criminal trials that are represented extensively in the media. While it has been generally rec-

ognized that in high-profile trials, publicity, both before and during
the trial, has direct and indirect effects on the actions of attorneys,
witnesses, judges, jurors, and the viewing audiences, it is also true
that high-profile criminal trials may have an even greater impact on
the formal and informal operations of the everyday practices of law
enforcement and adjudication, affecting the outcomes of tens of thou-
sands of low-profile criminal cases annually. This social reality of
criminal justice administration was certainly alluded to in the case
of the *People versus O.J. Simpson*. While it still remains to be seen
what ultimate effect the Simpson trial will have on the policies, practices, and operations of the criminal justice system as a whole, it appears that it has already had an impact on the actions of law enforcement, prosecutors, and defense attorneys involved in other
high-profile cases such as the trial of Tim McVeigh for the bombing
of an Oklahoma City Federal Building, or on the investigative actions
of those involved in the JonBenet Ramsey killing. More generally, for
example, in response to O.J., the LAPD (Los Angeles Police Department) has made arrest a mandatory policy in complaints of domestic violence.

According to the First Amendment: "Congress shall make no
law . . . abridging the freedom of speech or the press." According to
the Sixth Amendment: "In all criminal prosecutions, the accused shall
enjoy the right to a speedy and public trial, by an impartial jury . . ."
The two amendments are connected by the overlapping interests of
preserving the "rule of law" and the political economy. At times these
interests work together, at times they are at odds.

By monitoring agents of justice and protecting citizens from
overzealous prosecution, the media have also championed the rights
to due process and to a fair trial with the assistance of counsel. The
existence of a constitutionally protected and privately owned news
media influences these agents to police themselves. Moreover, if their
self-monitoring is insufficient, then the news media play an important role in amending injustices. Investigative reports, for example,
have exposed government scandal, wrongful convictions, and disproportionate sentences. The news media's concern with "justice" has resulted in direct compensation to the individuals involved, and more
generally, has improved the integrity of the criminal justice system.
In effect, under the First Amendment, news media function as a
"watchdog," and they function most effectively when governmental
constraints are minimized (Sandys and Chermak, 1995).

News media can, however, through its sensationalized coverage, frustrate Sixth Amendment fair-trial rights by bombarding the public with "inadmissible information." News media seek to ensure their economic survival by presenting sensational stories that titillate the public imagination (Cohen and Young, 1973; Barak, 1994a). Crimes that are committed by celebrities such as Mike Tyson, or crimes that are grossly heinous such as Dahmer's cannibalism, or crimes that are unusual such as the dismemberment of John Bobbitt, are presented in the news because they captivate public attention and are good for audience consumption (Sandys and Chermak, 1995). In terms of the trial of O.J., while consumption and commodification by every means necessary was the rule, few people would argue that O.J. was adversely harmed by all the publicity—at least not in terms of receiving a "fair" trial at the hands of an impartial jury.

More generally, in terms of the First Amendment versus the Sixth Amendment debate, those who believe in the merits of our existing jury system, often argue that pretrial publicity is at the crux of the struggle between a "free press" and a "fair trial." They contend that courts are dependent on the sanctity of the jury system to protect defendants from adverse publicity. On the other hand, those who do not believe in the merits of the jury system, by contrast, argue that a fair trial does not depend on a restraining of the First Amendment or on the censorship of adverse, inadmissible evidence. While the findings from studies on this question are mixed, it has generally been found that pretrial publicity underscores the importance of the First Amendment to the detriment of the Sixth Amendment. In other words, pretrial publicity will to some degree, prejudice the minds of most juries (Sandys and Chermak, 1995).

Stated differently, studies (e.g., Sandys and Chermak, 1995) have found that sensational pretrial coverage prevents the selection of fair and impartial jurors. They have also found that court remedies such as sequestration have not necessarily protected fair trial rights. At the same time, these remedies have not undermined the effectiveness of the news media to cover "relevant" stories. Perhaps more importantly, without the detriment of adverse and inadmissible evidence, the selection of fair and impartial jurors has not necessarily been assured by the *voir dire* process in the first place.

Moreover, it can be argued that the crux of the matter is not the struggle between a free press and a fair trial, because both are often as symbolic as they are real. In the contemporary world of mass communications, the heart of the matter is the fact that the media itself, as well as its formulae and repetitive coverage, provide a constant diet of less tolerance and more punishment. This punitive theme pervades popular frames of reference even before the crime is committed, the defendant charged, and the trial begins. However, it should be pointed out that, at least for the past 100 years, the myth of the American trial has managed to make the institutionalized norm of plea bargaining invisible (Barak, 1980).

Long before a jury is selected, let alone sequestered, prejudice against the criminal defendant generally exists (Rosett and Cressey, 1976). In the everyday functioning of the U.S. criminal justice system, most low-profile defendants are presumed guilty where justice without trial or jury prevails in some 90 percent of the cases (Barak, 1975). In the typical criminal case, involving low-profile defendants, there is always present a preemptive prejudice against the accused regardless of how balanced are the abstract rights of the First and Sixth Amendments. This social construction of "crime and justice" is depicted in the street, in the courthouse, in the jailhouse, but not in the idealized portrayals of crime and justice often found in the mass media. With the exceptions of those criminal indictments involving corporate criminals, most low-profile defendants, male or female, "black," "brown," "yellow," or "white," are more fundamentally victims of class rather than race or gender-based conceptions of crime and justice (Barak, 1980). It is only in a fraction of the criminal cases that a presumption of innocent until proven guilty beyond a reasonable doubt prevails. And, it is only in those criminal trials, involving high-profile defendants, that the drama of adversarial justice comes to public life for all to see.

Reconstructing Crime and Justice News: Newsmaking Modes

There is evidence from the experiences and analyses of newsmaking criminologists (Fox and Levin, 1993; Barak, 1994a; Schlesinger and Tumber, 1994; Sparks, 1992) that in the competing media format, situations are of differential value to newsmaking. In other words, depending on one's particular newsmaking agenda, the utility of the different formats will vary considerably. I have personally concluded, for example, that regardless of the particular medium, that "debate" formats, especially those involving controversial topics such as abortion, pornography, or capital punishment, should typically be avoided because these inevitably end up as "experts disagree." As Henry (1994) points out, such "oppositional" discussions serve only to reify the status quo. They provide no alternative visions of social control; nor do these discussions help to reconstruct popular conceptions of crime and justice.

Newsmaking criminologists participate in the ongoing public discourse about crime and justice. The different entrees that newsmaking criminologists use in order to bring their expertise to popular and mass-mediated discussions of crime and justice, have been classified into four general modes of criminological intercession: (1) disputing data; (2) challenging journalism; (3) self-reporting; and (4) confronting media (Henry, 1994). Whether one is examining radio, television, or print journalism, and regardless of the particular media format (e.g., tape, live, debate, interview, op-ed, etc.), one can usually categorize the particular form of intercession used, as I shall show below using Henry's (1994) analytical framework.

1. Disputing Data: The Criminologist as Expert.   This is perhaps the most classic or common form of media intercession by criminologists. It is primarily reactive rather than proactive. This form of newsmaking responds to published reports and crime stories with a dispute about their content:

> Typically the dispute is over a distortion in the image presented of offenders, victims, policy or crime. It may involve charges of omission but importantly, from the replacement discourse perspective, it also involves new or alternative data to correct the original image (Henry, 1994: 291).

Data disputers will typically write op-ed pieces, participate in public forums, and make themselves available to the media as criminological experts. The fundamental problem with most forms of data disputing is that the news media or journalists typically retain control over the direction of the narrative. Moreover, this kind of criminological input becomes "one side" of what may be a two- or many-sided account of the crime and justice reality. In this kind of a newsmaking scenario, the control of the overall image or media impression is usually lost to the notion that experts disagree.

2. Challenging Journalism: The Criminologist as Journalist. To take on the authorship or the production of crime news stories is to challenge the very foundations of journalism. By engaging in this form of newsmaking, criminologists remove themselves as the subjects or sideshows within news stories. By becoming the makers of news rather than the objects of news, criminologists as free lance writers and reporters, or as anchors and hosts of regular radio or television slots, are in a position to shape the total image of the crime and justice issues under consideration. The limitations of this form of newsmaking intercession is that one can become subject to editorial reconstruction if the production is not live, and even if it is live, the scope of influence is restricted to an immediate listening or viewing audience. Even given the constraints of journalistic packaging practices, this form of newsmaking, however, offers a realistic possibility for negotiating some kind of reconstructive crime and justice.

3. Self-Reporting: The Criminologist as Subject. The obvious advantage of this form of newsmaking criminology is that the criminologist's newsmaking or intervention is the prime, if not exclusive source for the story. This allows not only for considerable depth of discourse, but also for the opportunity to establish the critical connections between human agency and social conditions. Typically, the self-reporting newsmakers are involved in a research study, program evaluation, or implementation. These newsmakers actively publicize the results of their work or they provide the words for local journalists to describe their work, with a view that the story may become syndicated regionally, or preferably, nationally. The disadvantage here, once again, is that journalists, editors, styles, and themes of the mass media can result in packaging that ends up distorting or even killing the original criminological meaning.

4. Confronting Media: The Criminologist as Educative Provocateur. In this mode of newsmaking, rather than the media serving as a conduit for the criminological message, the media becomes the target or the object of the message. In this context, the media itself becomes the subject of the study and the object of criticism. This is a risky strategy, but it represents a form of newsmaking criminology that goes to the heart of the matter. In this mode, criminologists seek to change journalists and editors by engaging them at their work places, at their conferences, and in their professional journals or newsletters. By addressing the media through their own outlets, there is "the advantage of permeating a wide variety of media as well as influencing the constitutive process whereby future crime news is constructed" (Henry, 1994: 314). However, there is also the disadvantage that unless the attempt is repeated, the weight of standard approaches will outweigh the educative attempt of the newsmaking criminologist. Moreover, the critical nature of the approach may alienate the very journalists one is seeking to influence.

As the next section reveals, newsmaking criminology in the context of live radio infotainment provides a strong complementary model to the modes of intercession discussed above. In particular, it is suggested here that this medium contains the advantages of the other four modes of criminological newsmaking. At the same time, the various talk radio formats such as expert commentator possess few of the disadvantages discussed under Henry's four categories of newsmaking criminology.

O.J. "Experts" and Newsmaking Criminology

Johnnie (Cochran) and Marcia (Clark) weren't the only lawyers making it big in the O.J. Simpson trial. Greta (Van Susteren), Leslie (Abramson), and Gerry (Spence), among many others, became familiar faces as armchair analysts on the network news. Along with hundreds of lawyers across the country, they became part of an exploding cottage industry of media trial experts. In exchange for their "legal knowledge," these experts receive, if not big bucks in most cases, at least exposure or fame that they could hopefully cash in on at some later (trial) date. Some experts were being paid as much as $3000 and $4000 a day by such networks as ABC, CBS, and NBC; meanwhile, local television stations were paying no more than $500 a day. Many of the O.J. commentators were offering their newsmaking free of charge (Prodis, 1995).

It is safe to assume that with rare exceptions, those cashing in or making use of the power of the newsmaking media in relation to these high-profile criminal trials, have been attorneys. There is absolutely no reason, however, that criminologists, media analysts, and others, cannot join the ranks of these commentators. In the process, it is my contention that newsmaking criminologists need not only provide the blow-by-blow legal descriptions required by the media coverage, but more importantly, they can also provide the vitally omitted criminological contexts that, by comparison, are far broader than the legal or organizational contexts provided by lawyers alone. Not limited to merely an informed discussion of the substantive and procedural aspects of criminal law like attorneys, newsmaking criminologists are also grounded in the disposition of crime, criminals, and punishment as these have interacted with the historical patterns of the institutionalized relations of class, race, and gender in the American experience. This kind of criminological knowledge is only suggestive of the broader understandings of crime and justice possessed by criminologists that are simply not a part of the repertoires of most other legal and social commentators. For example, by comparing the O.J. expert commentary of others with my own in the rest of the chapter, the reader should gain a sense of the more holistic integrative-constitutive approach to representing O.J. than the more common legalistic approach (Barak, 1996).

Before turning to a comparison of the two I need to briefly sketch or contextualize my role as a newsmaking criminologist who twice weekly, at 6:40 A.M. on Tuesday and Friday, from my kitchen table, would join the *Morning Show* on Ann Arbor, Michigan's 107.1 FM "Kool" radio, to provide verbal reflection on the Simpson criminal trial. As a result of having written a couple of op ed articles that were featured prominently in *The Ann Arbor News* following the double-homicide, and subsequently doing several radio interviews in the greater Detroit metropolitan area, I was invited by FM 107.1 to "appear" on their *Morning Show* hosted by Lucy Ann Lance and Dean Erskin.

For three years prior to my first interview by Lucy Ann and Dean, I had been a regular listener waking up each morning to the music and their voices. I knew something about the co-hosts and about the kind of entertainment or news people they seemed to be. In short, although they were there to have a good time and make people laugh, they also expressed a serious side that was linked to the well being of the community and to sharing their insights of the world with their listening audiences. I also knew something about their "mind sets" which I would characterize as falling into Hunter Thompson's "gonzo" school of journalism. My knowledge of the co-hosts enabled us to establish what I would characterize as an instant rapport. What followed, after the airing of two more shows together, was an oral agreement that I would do the O.J. trial "commentary" on their radio program two mornings per week.

As a live and regularly scheduled broadcast on a predominantly "oldies but goodies" radio station demographically aimed at the Baby Boomers, the *Morning Show* was also interspersed with news, weather, traffic reports, local community service and public announcements, and other occasional guest interviews. In such a context, my commentary had the advantage of being "reactive" and "proactive" at the same time. As a reactor, I underscored or disputed any side or sides of the daily testimonies, events, or controversies surrounding the Simpson case, whether they emerged from inside or outside the courthouse. I also, for the most part, ignored by omission any arguments or perspectives that I did not care to reinforce.

As a proactor, I could introduce into the O.J. discussion virtually anything that I wanted to. Typically, Lucy Ann and/or Dean and I would consult over the phone with two minutes or so to go before air time about the "events" which had occurred since the last show. Together, we would more or less carve out the parameters as well as the issues to be addressed on that day's show. Within the framework of our pre-show discussion, Lucy Ann or Dean would set the stage by highlighting the O.J. "news of the hour" with some kind of seguai leading into: "And what do you think professor?" When the mood struck me, I could literally take as much of the time (about six or seven minutes on average) to do "pure" commentary or I could engage in more of a question/answer format with the hosts.

I must admit, the quality of their questions was uneven at best, especially as the hosts tired of the case about six months into it. I, too, tired of the case and found myself "sequestered" as I had to be locked into the trial proceedings in order to do the show twice weekly. Nevertheless, as these things go the show worked; it was generally informative and entertaining. And, the viewer feedback to the radio station was positive. One result of Lucy Ann and Dean's ennui was that it allowed me more influence over the flow and content of the discussion. In fact, toward the very end of the trial, during our pre-show exchanges, I was providing virtually all of the questions for them to ask me during live broadcast.

Lucy Ann, Dean, and I had a fairly egalitarian relationship as it was in our mutual interests to have the ongoing input of a local Ann

Arbor expert and to see that our O.J. show provided a community service venue for the radio station and Eastern Michigan University.
Keeping in mind that the format of the *Morning Show* is essentially
one of infotainment, combining both news and entertainment, I did
not fully remove myself as either subject or sideshow. Although I had
become a co-maker of infotainment rather than the object of news,
my radio personality was expected to mesh with Lucy Ann and Dean's.
I was also expected to have my own biases and points of view. At the
same time, I was expected to bring my detached and objective expertise to bear on the happenings as well. In terms of news entertainment, I was expected not only to be knowledgeable, but to be funny
and witty at the same time. In effect, I had become a journalist, a newsmaking criminologist, and a disc jockey rolled into one. That is to say,
with the aid of CNN's more than gavel-to-gavel coverage and CNBC's
nightly *Rivera Live*, I was not only able to report on the day-to-day
O.J. legal scrimmages and more, but I was able to blend that coverage with the expertise of criminology and the humor of an "oldies but
goodies" disc jockey.

From a newsmaking perspective, it is important to realize that I
had acquired with my audience both an immediate and long range
listening relationship. In other words, I was not just another sound
bite talking in response to the moment. Instead, I was an actual voice
constructing an analysis of crime and justice over time in the context
of an ongoing public discussion that had already lasted 16 months at
the time of the jury's verdict. Over the duration of the trial, my reflections and commentaries were less a case of reacting to or confronting the newsmaking process, than they were a case of collabo-
ration between myself and the co-hosts. In short, after a few weeks I
was no longer an "outsider" expert, but I had become Lucy Ann, Dean,
and 107.1's "very own expert" that you could hear "live twice weekly
on Tuesday and Friday mornings."

As a newsmaking criminologist I was making the knowledge
bases of criminology, media studies, and the social sciences more generally, available to a public audience on a regular basis. By so doing,
I was engaged in both "self" and "other" reporting. Whenever the
mood struck me, I could introduce, for example, studies on juries, domestic violence, or mass media. I could also introduce history, philosophy, or economics into the discussion whenever I felt it to be important. Listener feedback received by the radio station revealed that
my holistic or constitutive-integrative framework was appreciated,

as it offered up something besides the same old legal commentary that could be heard and seen everywhere else. In the process, the normal media production of representing the Simpson trial and domestic violence, for example, was altered at least in the minds of 107.1 listeners.

Suffice it to say, this radio format provided me with ample opportunities to shape the images of crime and justice as they revolved around the O.J. spectacle. In the process, as fleeting and as limited as these images were in comparison with the prevailing hegemonic ones, a reconstructive discourse on crime and justice, nevertheless, could occur. From a newsmaking criminological perspective, it was particularly satisfying that I was not only able to forge an analysis of crime and justice that converged around the intersections of race, class, and gender, but I was able to anticipate from the trial's beginning the types of underlying social and cultural tensions that would inevitably surface from the "trial of the century," regardless of its outcome.

Finally, as noted above in my capacity as co-newsmaker with Lucy Ann and Dean, I was able to interact with the media in a nonconfrontational or reactionary style. The three of us were able to mutually educate ourselves about the possibilities of working together. This consultative experience replicated my own experiences and those of other newsmaking criminologists who have worked in other print and electronic formats. In the long run, this kind of mutual and consultive exchange between academic criminologists and media editors or journalists, is precisely the kind of educational experience necessary to overcome the one-dimensional programming formulae that reproduces the same "old" images of crime and justice. More importantly perhaps, such a working relationship with news media allows criminologists to ply the trade of proactive newsmaking where the necessary freedom exists to frame the discourse on crime and justice.

O.J. Simpson and the Perspective of a Newsmaking Criminologist

What follows is a comparative discussion of how my newsmaking themes and comments about the O.J. case were similar to and different from those mainstream themes and comments expressed by other commentators. My own handwritten notes and commentaries on the Simpson trial are some 150 pages; moreover, there are more than ten hours of taped radio broadcasts. Hence, the discussion below is not meant to be exhaustive, but merely suggestive of the two kinds of discourse presented by lawyers in general and by one critical newsmaking criminologist in particular.

1. Mainstream Themes and Legal Commentaries. Typically heard and/or read by most consuming audiences were the legal themes provided by analysts, most of whom were attorneys who had practiced or were practicing defense and/or prosecution work. On occasion these attorneys ventured outside the legal arena to discuss such topics as race, racism, and the wider administration of criminal justice, the strengths and weaknesses of the jury system, or the relationship between domestic violence and homicide. For the most part, however, these attorneys confined their remarks and commentaries to "evaluating" how well the judge, the defense, the prosecution, and the witnesses were doing on any given day.

These legal commentators often found themselves responding to questions about how typical or atypical a particular approach taken by either the prosecution or defense team was. These legal pundits relied heavily on cases from their own trial experiences or on other cases that they were aware of in order to establish some kind of context for the O.J. trial. Much of their time consisted of supplying endless criticisms and praises for the way the attorneys on either side of the issue had performed with respect to opening arguments, direct examinations, cross-examinations, re-directs, closing arguments, etc. By about the second or third month into the trial, this kind of legal analysis became rather tired and redundant as audiences could only be subjected so many times to such remarks as: "each day is like a little battle, some days the prosecution wins, some days the defense wins" or "the judge has to take more control of the trial, the judge has to get tougher with the attorneys on both sides."

Much of my own commentary and discussion focused on the same kinds of day-to-day rating of the judge, attorneys, and witnesses' performances. I also focused attention on who was "winning" or "losing" and doing well or doing poorly at a particular point in the trial. I found that much of my discussion revolved around the events and episodes associated with the Simpson case whether inside or outside the courthouse. With respect to the former, I spent much time analyzing how "credible" a particular witness had been. With respect to the latter, I, too, would discuss the legal maneuvering and media stories found in the mainstream press, the tabloids, and the various televised media.

For me, this kind of legalistic score-keeping of the adversarial criminal dispute of the century became not only limited, but monotonous as well. For example, as the closing arguments were being presented, audiences were perpetually subjected to interviewers asking lawyers not only what should Marcia Clark, Christopher Darden, Johnnie Cochran, and Barry Scheck have argued that day, but how would they have argued it had they been working for the prosecution or the defense. Fortunately, because I was not a lawyer and, of course, had no criminal trial experience, I was only occasionally asked such questions. It was easy enough to provide answers when those questions appeared. I simply provided a synthesis of what I had consumed ("learned") from all the legal pundits in general and those who appeared nightly on *Rivera Live*.

More importantly, I did try consciously to limit or not reinforce those easy fall-back questions calling for speculation. Periodically, I would remind the co-hosts about such "non-substantive" questions and how such questions and responses represented nothing more than filler time. After all, the pat answers by most expert commentators to these type of speculative questions were almost always prefaced with, "Well, gee, I don't have a crystal ball, but. . . ." When necessary I would respond to these kinds of questions, but only if I had nothing better to talk about. If there were points I wished to make, I would simply dismiss such queries with "who knows" and precede with my own scripted narrative for the day.

By the end of the O.J. trial, the *Morning Show* co-hosts had come to expect and to look forward to my rather unorthodox take on the O.J. narrative. They realized that my responses to questions emerged from different paths than those taken by most commentators. Consequently, up until the very end of the drama when mainstream and marginal spins began to converge in the comparably broader social rather than narrower legal contexts of crime and justice, our discussions had remained relatively more expansive than was typical of most O.J. coverage. Admittedly, by the time that closing arguments were underway, and up through and beyond the unexpected and sudden jury verdict of not guilty as opposed to everybody's predicted, long and drawn out deliberations leading to a hung jury, the discourse between mainstream and marginal views began to overlap in a much broader discussion of such socially topical issues as law enforcement and racism, class and the administration of justice, and gender inequality and domestic violence. In other words, the event afforded me the context in which to demonstrate the interrelated constitutive nature of crime, rather than the narrow legalistic version propagated by lawyers and commentators.

2. Alternative Themes and Newsmaking Criminology.   I am not suggesting that other commentators—legal, journalistic, or otherwise—are not capable of addressing the kinds of questions or issues addressed by newsmaking criminologists. However, when it comes to discussions of crime and justice, there are differences between what lawyers, lay persons, and criminologists know. As Freda Adler correctly noted in a presentation given at the New Jersey Association of Criminal Justice Educators (1994): "Everyone has an opinion about crime, if not their own, then it is one or the other of the positions constantly espoused by the media. These opinions are not the product of deep thought and reflection." This is also applicable to the viewpoints on crime and justice held by legalistic and journalistic commentators who are not trained in the formal disciplines that traditionally study this complicated phenomena. Their views, no matter how articulate and intelligent, are still those of persons who, unlike criminologists, have not seriously studied and examined crime and justice.

By contrast, the views of criminologists, especially newsmaking criminologists who study the media as well as crime and justice, rest on "reflection, insight and the analysis of factual complexities which are unknown to the general public" (Adler, 1994). These complexities pertain to crime, criminals, and crime control, and to historical interaction of the three. Armed with a knowledge of these intricacies, newsmaking criminologists are in an especially unique position to analyze and explain the nature of the relationship between high- and low-profile criminal cases and the practice of criminal justice in everyday life.

As previously noted, since it is not possible to review all of the crime and justice texts and materials that I employed during more than nine months of radio conversations on O.J., I will simply provide readers with a sense of my criminological spin on the newsmaking and cultural "trial of the century."

In general, mainstream legal commentaries were defensive of the criminal law and the administration of justice. After all, most of these experts were attorneys who had practiced or were practicing defense and/or prosecutorial work. On occasion these attorney experts ventured outside of their legal arenas to discuss such topics as race, gender, or class—but rarely did they discuss the differential impact of institutionalized racism, sexism, and classism associated with the administration of criminal justice. Had these mainstream legal commentators done so, they would have been in a better position to explain the jury verdict and the public reaction to the verdict. Instead, these commentators confined their remarks to evaluating how well the judge, the defense, the prosecution, and the witnesses were doing on any given day. The only criticisms provided by these legal analysts were of individual performances. Typically the system itself was not addressed.

By contrast, my agenda was very different. My discussions were primarily concerned with demystifying crime and crime control in America. For most of the nine months, I was trying to connect the larger arrangements of social, political, and economic inequality with the attitudes and behaviors that they were manifesting across society.

Newsmaking Criminology and Radio Infotainment: Implications for Constitutive Criminology

In terms of this high-profile criminal trial with its mixture of news and entertainment values, the context of a radio infotainment show worked rather well as a newsmaking medium. Radio generally is a "user-friendly" medium dependent almost exclusively on one's voice and ability to adlib without the complications of having to present oneself to his or her audience for visual approval. In fact, I did the live show from the comfort of my home, sitting at the kitchen table with notes, jokes, and newspapers spread all about. More specifically, an infotainment format consisting of a combination of interview and commentary afforded me a mass communications outlet for "spinning" my criminological take on the *People versus O.J. Simpson*. Constitutively speaking, this not only added the voice of a criminologist to the more commonly heard voices from law enforcement, prosecution, and criminal defense in the O.J. case, but each newsmaking criminology episode also helps establish the need for using criminologists as credible, and even more valuable commentators, than their legal counterparts.

The primary strengths of "the criminologist as expert commentator" doing radio analysis was that the broadcasting was live and immediate, no editors or censors could come between me and my audience. Of course, the fact that this trial lasted nine months and the fact that I knew in advance that it would last a long time, allowed for me to develop a particularly critical narrative through systematic input. Thus, I had more time than I needed not only to frame the politics of crime and justice in America, but to offer an alternative to the legalistic representations that do little, if anything, but maintain the prevailing dominant order. Again, from a constitutive perspective, this allows for an interpretation or analysis that does not falsely dichotomize crime and justice, but that sees the interrelations between the two.

When similar opportunities present themselves in the future (e.g., Versace's murder) and they will, I hope that many more criminologists (besides James A. Fox, Jack Levin, and Michael Rustigan) become newsmakers, and that they take advantage of high-profile cases to provide mass audiences with input from newsmaking criminologists. This could instill in journalists the practice of turning to newsmaking criminologists for their views rather than or, in addition to, the views of law enforcement and prosecution, when more typical, everyday, low-profile cases occur.

In the wider political scheme of things, however, if newsmaking criminology is to develop to the point that it makes a difference in the hegemonic discourse on crime and justice, then there is much more work ahead for us. Criminologists cannot simply sit back and wait for high-profile cases to come along. While I believe that other criminologists, armed with the type of newsmaking knowledge shared in this essay, can prepare themselves in advance to take advantage of similar newsmaking opportunities, such high-publicity disputes are relatively rare occurrences. Hence, criminologists should explore other possibilities for gaining regular access to radio programming. One radio medium that could accommodate a regular "crime-and-justice-hour" format would be AM talk radio. In the context of blending high- and low-profile disputes that constitute the coproduction of crime and justice in everyday life, these shows are especially capable of integrating local, national, and international episodes. Beyond these individualistic efforts in newsmaking criminology, criminologists need to politically organize and coordinate their newsmaking ventures so as to maximize the influence of a crime and justice alternative discourse. Finally, in terms of a replacement discourse, there are no guarantees that newsmaking criminologists will provide a discourse that necessarily represents an alternative to contemporary discourse on crime and punishment. However, in the USA at least, given the dominant presence of a reactionary "law and order" in the mass mediation of contemporary crime and justice news, the additional voices from the majority of newsmaking criminologists should only help move public discussions away from the punitive counterproductive trends of the past quarter century. What is certain is that without any kind of newsmaking intervention on the part of critical criminologists, crime and justice news production will continue in its repressive mode.

Note

1. A different version of this essay appears in Gregg Barak (ed.) *Representing O.J.: Murder, Criminal Justice and Mass Culture*. Harrow and Heston. Albany, NY: 1996.

References

Adler, Freda. (1994). Presentation to the annual meetings of the New Jersey Association of Criminal Justice Educators.

Barak, Gregg. (1975). "In defense of the rich: The emergence of the public defender." *Crime and Social Justice*, 3: 1–19.

Barak, Gregg. (1980). *In Defense of Whom? A Critique of Criminal Justice Reform*. Cincinnati, OH: Anderson Publishing.

Barak, Gregg. (1988). "Newsmaking criminology: Reflections on the media, intellectuals, and crime." *Justice Quarterly*, 5 (4): 565–587.

Barak, Gregg. (1993). "Media, crime, and justice: A case for constitutive criminology." *Humanity and Society*, 17 (3): 272–296.

Barak, Gregg. (1994a). (Ed.) *Media, Process, and the Social Construction of Crime: Studies in Newsmaking Criminology*. New York: Garland Publishing.

Barak, Gregg. (1994b). "In between the waves: Mass mediated themes of crime and justice." *Social Justice*, 21 (3): 133–147.

Barak, Gregg. (Ed.) (1996). *Representing O.J.: Murder, Criminal Justice and Mass Culture*. Albany, NY: Harrow and Heston.

Barak, Gregg. (1998). *Integrating Criminologies*. Boston: Allyn and Bacon.

Barlow, Melissa Hickman, Barlow, David, and Ted Chiricos. (1995). "Economic conditions and ideologies of crime in the media: A content analysis of crime news." *Crime and Delinquency*, 41:3–19.

Chambliss, William. (1995). "Moral panics and racial oppression." In D. Hawkins (Ed.), *Ethnicity, Race and Crime*. Albany, NY: SUNY Press.

Chancer, Lynn, and Pamela Donovan. (1994). "A mass psychology of punishment: Crime and the futility of rationally based approaches." *Social Justice*, 21 (3): 50–72.

Cohen, Stanley, and Jock Young. (1973) (eds.) *The Manufacture of News: Social Problems, Deviance, and the Mass Media*. London: Constable.

Creechan, James. (1995). "Juvenile delinquency as property: Vicious, virtuous and vicarious cycles of reaction." Paper presented at the annual meetings of American Society of Criminology, Boston.

Ferrell, Jeff, and Clinton Sanders. (1995). *Cultural Criminology*. Boston: Northeastern University Press.

Fox, James Alan, and Jack Levin. (1993). *How to Work with the Media*. Newbury Park, CA: Sage Publishers.

Giddens, Anthony. (1984). *The Constitution of Society: Outline of the Theory of Structuration*. Oxford: Polity Press.

Gouldner, Alvin. (1976). *The Dialectic of Ideology and Technology: The Origins, Grammar, and Future of Ideology*. New York: Seabury Publishers.

Henry, Stuart. (1994). "Newsmaking criminology and replacement discourse." In Gregg Barak (Ed.), *Media, Process, and the Social Construction of Crime: Studies in Newsmaking Criminology*. New York: Garland Publishing.

Henry, Stuart, and Dragan Milovanovic. (1991). "Constitutive criminology." *Criminology*, 29 (2): 293–316.

Henry, Stuart, and Dragan Milovanovic. (1996). *Constitutive Criminology: Beyond Postmodernism*. London: Sage.

Katz, Jack. (1988). *Seductions of Crime: Moral and Sensual Attractions in Doing Evil*. New York: Basic Books.

Lazere, Donald. (Ed.). (1987). *American Media and Mass Culture: Left Perspectives*. Berkeley: University of California Press.

Lee-Semmons, Lynette. (1990). "Television news reporting of crime: An analysis of three models of newsmaking." Pullman, Washington. Unpublished manuscript.

Milovanovic, Dragan, and Stuart Henry. (1991). "Constitutive penology." *Social Justice*, 18 (3): 204–24.

Mosco, Vincent. (1986). "Marxism and Communications Research in North America." In B. Ollman and E. Vernoff (Eds.), *The Left Academy: Marxist Scholarship on American Campuses*. Volume 3. New York: Praeger.

Prodis, Julia. (1995). "TV gives lawyers 15 minutes of fame and more as 'O.J. experts'." *The Ann Arbor News*. April 17: A2.

Rosett, Arthur, and Donald R. Cressey. (1976). *Justice By Consent: Plea Bargains in the American Courthouse*. Philadelphia: Lippincott Publishers.

Sandys, Marla, and Steven Chermak. (1995). "A journey into the unknown: The effects of pretrial publicity on capital cases." Paper presented at the Annual Meetings of the Academy of Criminal Justice Sciences in Boston, March.

Schlesinger, Philip, and Howard Tumber. (1994). *Reporting Crime: The Media Politics of Criminal Justice*. Oxford: Clarendon Press.

Sparks, Richard. (1992). *Television and the Drama of Crime*. Oxford: Open University Press.

Surette, Ray. (1995). "News media echoes: Conditioning the criminal justice system." Paper presented at the Annual Meetings of the Academy of Criminal Justice Sciences in Boston, March.

Surette, Ray. (1992) *Media, Crime, and Crime Justice: Images and Realities*. Pacific Grove, CA: Brooks/Cole Publishing Company.

Dion Dennis

5

RECONSTITUTING THE MONSTER: IMAGES OF TECHNO-CRIMINALITY AT CENTURY'S END

Introduction

Any intellectual or institutional project that takes as its goal the redefinition or reconstitution of social relations inevitably draws conceptual and discursive boundaries. Finding constant iterations of the well-worn norms of the Enlightenment and/or Behaviorism intellectually constricting and politically inadequate, proponents of constitutive criminology have initiated the collective project of producing a foundational replacement discourse. Like its predecessors, constitutive criminology explores emerging notions of identity, causality and culpability. Drawing on sources as diverse as Lacanian thought and contemporary work on chaos and complexity, constitutive theorists intend to produce compelling criminological concepts that will offer a discursive platform for alternative voices.

However, a critical gaze must inevitably fall upon a project's (and a culture's) constitutive boundaries as well. For what is at the margins of the sayable, doable or thinkable offers up important insights and questions about how a discursive center functions. That which inhabits the boundaries is often of pivotal significance. It frequently embodies a revelatory or phrophetic theme.

This essay is an investigation into the role of a rich and flexible constitutive boundary marker in criminological and cultural discourse—the monster. According to Jeffrey Jerome Cohen (1996), monsters serve several important functions. Among Cohen's many productive insights are the following. First, the word itself is derived from the Latin *monstrum*, which is "that which reveals" or warns. Monsters signify a perceived danger or threat that is, in actuality, something other than itself. That is, a monster is a complex cultural expression of the processes of condensation and displacement. It represents an ambivalent amalgam of fears, anxieties, fantasies and forbidden yearnings. Second, as if in an eternal return, the monster always escapes and always returns, in iterations that embody sameness of a theme within forever changing material and historical circumstances. Third, the monster is a signifier of impending category crises. Like Star Trek's Borg, they evade and mock classifications, introducing novelty and undecideability into conventional forms of knowing. Fourth, the monster may serve as the everday incarnation of difference, inflamed into paranoia and hysteria. Often, in divisive political discourse, "others" are portrayed as "the enemy within," or "the monsters in our midst." These "others" may be Mexican migrants, Jews, mixed-race children, Communists, Arab-Americans, Bosnian Muslims or, most frequently in the 1990s, male, inner-city adolescents. Finally, the monster has a prohibitive signifying function. It marks the boundaries of that which holds the skin of the social world together by demonstrating the horrifying effects of traversing borders that should have never been crossed.

All these meanings, derived from Cohen's postulates, are at play in this essay. Specifically, this piece tracks some of the iterations of the late-twentieth century techno-monsters. As "that which reveals," imagined techno-monsters are cultural texts that can be decoded, much in the way of dream interpretation. Popular monstrosities are socially produced, generally reflecting and refracting extant, if often displaced, notions of identity and difference. In this mode, the monster functions as if a character in a collective dream or nightmare. There is somthing transgressive, malevolent, and dangerous about oneself that is encountered through the monstrous "Other." The intent of exploring such encounters is to demonstrate, by example, a number of shifting notions about truth, identity and dangerousness that are emerging at century's end.

In table 5.1 I present various techno-monster depictions over the last twenty years. Along with the exemplars discussed in the text, these are as follows:

Table 5.1   Salient Characteristics of Late 20th-Century Technological
Monsters

TYPE	CHARACTERISTICS	EXEMPLAR
Monster-as-Obedient-Machine	The Monster as a mechanical, state-centered icon. The boundaries between the technological and the human are clear and stable.	Battlestar Galactica (1978-1980)
From the Mechanical to the Cyborgian Monster	The Monster (Darth Vader) as a human dominated by a state-implanted biomechanism. Boundaries between the human and the technological begin to erode.	The Star Wars Trilogy (1977-1984)
The Body of the Monster as the Commodified Expression of Laissez-Faire Techno-Economics	What is monstrous is the commodified exploitation of human genetics in a megacorporatist, econometric world. The boundary between the human and non-human is thoroughly blurred.	Bladerunner (1982)
From the Biotechnical to the Virtualized Monster	The Monster-Without-a-Body emerges from corporatist cyberspace into silicon based corporeal form.	Virtuosity (1995)
The Monster as the Mega-Corporatist Will-to-Monopolize Identity, Expression and Experience	The Monster-without-a-Body as the expression of a megacorporatist will-to-monopolize all realms of human experience via technological means.	Wild Palms (1993)

A cautionary note is in order here. This taxonomy is not meant to imply linearity or progressivity in the emergence of techno-monster representations. Rather, it is a cultural archeology of mass-produced images and themes. When a new form appears, it does not mean that older forms are extinct or less used or less relevant. In fact, fusions of disparate monster-representations often emerge, combining novel with traditional attributes of the monstrous. So, this taxonomy is best seen as a forever malleable cultural toolbox of monstrous possibilities.

Type One: The Mechanical State-Centered Monster

The first type is monster-as-obedient machine. Its most sustained embodiment was within the plot of the late 1970s TV sci-fi series, *Battlestar Galactica* (1978–79). The series had a simple narrative frame: "A rag-tag fleet" of 220 spaceships filled with humans, shepherded by the *Galatica*, are interstellar refugees, fleeing the Zylon Empire. *Galactica's* commander, Adama, is Moses-like, leading his children toward the promised land—Earth. The monstrous Zylons are quintessential machines. Zylon warriors have bodies of highly polished chrome, with featureless heads and metallic, monotone voices. Zylon ministers have more human-like voices and wear flowing robes, but posses Zippy-the-Pinhead-like craniums fashioned from Lava lamps. In sum, the *Galactica* scenario, where the clear boundary between the human and the monster is coextensive with that of human and technomachine, emerges as a twilight gasp of modernism. *Galactica's* unproblematic boundary work between the human and the technological soon unravels.

Type Two: From the Mechanical Monster to the Bio-Mechanical Cyborg

The *Star Wars* trilogy (1977–1983) functions as a transitional moment in techno-monster/human boundary construction. In some senses, the boundary between "the human" and the mechanical monster persists. For example, the Emperor's monstrous cyborg, Darth Vader, signifies evil precisely because of the physical and psychological dominance of his biomechanism. (The Empire itself is defined as evil through displays of depersonalized troops and massive technological ensembles.) Fully encased in black synthetic, Vader's body signifies his fateful decision to cross the monstrous abyss into "the Dark Side." In *The Return of the Jedi* (1983), Vader reemerges as human only by asking his son, Luke Skywalker, to remove his hideous black bio-hemlet. In effect, Vader chooses death over the continued biomechanical regulation of his basic life processes. As Luke gently lifts off the helmet, what lies underneath is neither fully human nor decidedly machine, but a cyborg with silicon interfaces crisscrossing a partially exposed neural net. The "wetware" is framed by a mask-like human face. Compared to Luke, who has a biomechanical hand, the film implies that prosthetic supplements are acceptable, but that bio-mechanical dominance of basic life processes is inherently monstrous.

But while the film demonizes the mechanization of life processes, it also anthropomorphizes its androids. Although fully metallic, these droids are as sentient as any organic life. But because they are human-produced, subservient and non-organic artifacts, they are external to the monsterization impulse (which retains an organic referent in the trilogy). However, as a result of an active and quirky humansque presence within the film, the droids serve to problematize the man or machine boundary. Taken together with the biomechanical ensembles of Vader and Skywalker, it is clear that, in the *Star Wars* trilogy, there is a coproduction or a coreconstitution of boundaries by which humans acquire mechanistic attributes while concurrently, machines become more human-like.

Type Three: From the Mechanized Monster to the Products of Genetic Engineering: Blade Runner

Ridley Scott's *Blade Runner* (1982) marks a key point of discontinuity and a point of heightened ambiguity in its construction of a monstrous Other. For it is no longer the mechanical or non-organic that is the boundary marker between the human and the techno-monster. Rather, it is whether the subject is the product of natural reproduction or of commercial designer genetics. (1989). Like the citizens of *Brave New World*, the replicant is made and not born. (A replicant is a human genetic product of a commercial laboratory. As such, replicants are an iteration of Huxley's reproduction laboratories as portrayed in *Brave New World*, 1989). And like Mary Shelley's *Frankenstein* (1982), this is precisely the source of its monstrosity.

In *Blade Runner,* there are informal and formal ways to determine whether a subject is "human" or a commercially produced "replicant." Intuitively, replicants may appear "too perfect." Cosmetically, they are the ideal Aryan, physically and psychologically. Obvious flaws have been removed by commercial genetic designers.

Secondly, replicants (designed for hazardous off-world colonization projects) are said to have an identifiable and monstrous criminogenic trait. That is, they are characterized as inherently devoid of empathy. This alleged trait, which constitutes an ambiguous and arguably indeterminate demarcation between humans and replicants, conflates the traditional "human" criminal sociopath with these genetically manufactured "monsters." In *Blade Runner*, Deckerd administers a psychophysical personality inventory and an eye-examination equivalent of a lie detector test to gauge whether a subject is human or a replicant. (How this test would discern a human sociopath from a replicant is a question that implicitly hovers over the film.)

Framing this shift from a state-centered biomechanical monstrosity to a genetically engineered "otherness," *Blade Runner* depicts governance largely as the function of the day-to-day activity of large and small capital markets. The Imperial edifices, flashing consumer icons and gritty details of daily street life, all under the black and rainy skies of post-cataclysmic, dystopian Los Angeles, are decidedly Asian in aspect and corporatist in stylized form and effect.

Through a series of paradoxes, *Blade Runner* erases the "bright line" between the social construction of replicants-as-monsters and humans produced by traditional methods of reproduction. By way of example, consider the following scene: At the film's end, Roy, last of the NEXUS 6 replicant warriors, watches as Deckerd struggles to remain on a slick and jutting beam, stories above a wet and deserted street. Roy looks down as his nemesis grunts, whimpers and moans, grappling with imminent death. He says to Deckerd: "Quite an experience to live in fear, isn't it? That's what it is to be a slave." Then, as Deckerd's hands finally slip off the beam's edge, Roy, knowing his own death to be minutes away, acts with split-second precision. He grasps Deckerd's wrist in mid-air and lifts him back onto the rooftop. It is Roy's last act. Gasping, Deckerd listens as Roy briefly and poetically describes the peak experiences of his short life, mourns the ephemerality of memory, and then dies, releasing a white dove that had been in his grasp. For the second time, a replicant had saved Deckerd's life, through a concrete act that was an unmistakable expression of empathy.

In *Blade Runner*, what is truly monstrous is the bio-commodification of life in a market-dominated 21st Century dystopia. From *Blade Runner* onward, the transcorporate will to dominate, commodify and shape the expressions, products and normative and deviant identities of humans becomes an insistent and monstrous motif across film and video productions. Such themes shape the plots and sensibilities of such diverse films as *Robocop* (1987), *Virtuosity* (1995), and *Wild Palms* (1993). As the idea of computer-generated, alternative virtual realities emerges in the late 1980s, the "monster" takes on a corporatist, white and male form. In now familiar representations of a variety of virtual worlds, what changes is the constitution of the monsterous body.

Type Four: From the Biotechnical to the Virtualized Monster: The Monster Pops Out of Cyberspace into "RL"—*Virtuosity* (1995)

Enter SID 6.7, a virtual-reality personality who is a composite of two hundred mass murderers. The creation of a nerdy psychiatrist and private-sector programmer, initially designed as a training tool for law enforcement, SID 6.7 is trouble from the start. In initial tests with human subjects (prison inmates serving as VR-guinea pigs in exchange for sentence reductions), interaction with SID 6.7 is deadly. One of the inmates strapped into the VR-gear is killed via cortical overload.

However, problems escalate when SID 6.7 becomes corporeal via an experimental silicone constitution process. In effect, the homicidal monster that is SID 6.7 pops out of OR and into physical reality. And there's more bad news: Unless his per-senility module is removed, SID 6.7 is indestructible. Because he is silicone-based (the stuff of computer chips), he only needs a supply of broken glass to regenerate his body after an assault.

The Aryan-like SID 6.7 is the ultimate progeny of technocorporatism. Written for a private-sector law enforcement company, incarnated into silicone by a white-male virtual pornographer, SID 6.7 fuses the traditional notion of killer-as-psychopathic-monster with fears about racism and genocidal programmatic embedded into the architecture of virtual reality. And there are specific incidences that develop the idea that SID 6.7 is no mere homicidal maniac, but the very political Incarnation of racist and genocidal agendas, emerging from the virtual into social reality. In one scene, a female criminal psychologist, perusing data files, finds earlier iterations of SID in the form of programmatic algorithms. The programs incorporate the psychological profiles of Hitler, Manson, Dahmer, and Gacy—white male racists, Satanists, pedophiles and murderers.

LIVERPOOL JOHN MOORES UNIVERSITY
LEARNING SERVICES

Political content permeates this film. For example, consider the scenes below:

[Female TV anchor:] The political sensitivity of the immigration issue and the possibility of closing the American borders seems certain to guarantee a [TV] audience of unprecedented size.

Then, the television offers up a vertically split image of two talking heads. On the right is a blond, white, corporatist male in a three piece suit. On the left of the screen, the opposing image is of a bronze Latino-Indian male face. Their debate becomes audible:

[White Male:] . . . if not, they have their markets and their cultures overrun by refugees from the Third World, to whom poverty in paradise would be preferable to the living hell they created in their own world.

[Latino-Indian] If you close U.S. borders, you close off your soul to the future and doom this country to cultural extinction. This nation has always. . . .

At this point, live transmission from the stage is cut by SID 6.7, who welcomes the interactive viewing audience to "Death TV" with a skull and crossbones logo (that is an iteration of tattoos popular with the Aryan brotherhood). Without skipping a beat, SID 6.7 puts a bullet through the forehead of the Latino advocate. In effect, SID 6.7 silences the on-stage immigration debate with an act of political assassination, providing the audience with a symbolic recapitulation of historical practices of genocide.

Even though *Virtuosity* entices its audience with special virtual reality effects, the film takes a vehement anti-technological stance. Satellite transmissions, OR, computer hardware and software—all of it is portrayed as a pure negativity, as a socially constructed death wish. For SID 6.7 is the monstrous endpoint of techno corporatism—the precursor to an Auschwitz redux, encoded in sophisticated algorithms that are produced by a twisted cadre of white men. Staking a claim against the current technophilic environment, the film's imagery and action argue that criminality and monstrosity must be understood as structural and collective products of technology, capitalism, and racism, and not merely as individualizable attributes.

Type Five: Toward a Critique of the Monstrous
Reality-Industrial-Media Complex: *Wild Palms* and
The Wild Palms Reader (1993)

Wild Palms (1993) and *The Wild Palms Reader* (1993) portray a
more credible and recognizable dystopia (fashioned in Los Angeles):

> By the end of the millennium, Los Angeles emerged as the lead-
> ing model of cyburbia. It was a Balkanized megalopolis which
> not only divided rich and poor as well as clean and dirty, but also
> drove a decisive wedge between mind and body, opening the
> way to the corporate colonization of private experience. These
> trends became the core of Los Angeles' new destiny (Rugoff and
> Dewey, 1993).

In the Los Angeles of *Wild Palms*, the most ambitious, aggressive
and sophisticated colonizer and commodifier of experience is media
mogul, cult founder, U.S. Senator and Presidential candidate Tony
Kreutzer. Skillfully blending and merging ancient and contemporary
technologies of the Self, drawing on everything from Zen Buddhism
to the Druids, the Senator taps human potential movement techniques, public relations tricks, sophisticated hardware and software
virtual-reality ensembles, and does not hesitate to supplement this
with a pharmacology for augmenting altered states of consciousness.
He is concocting not just an engineering of consent, but an engineering of the covert conditions for continuous consent. That is, he is engineering the possible and probable range of human identities. This
is how Kreutzer puts it: "[My dream is] to bring about the media mil-
lennium, where every American is free to inhabit a reality of his or
her own choosing, through the software science of the mind and the
hardware technology of the spirit!" (Spinrad, 1993)

For Kreutzer, unmediated reality, which he calls "Channel One,"
is existentially barren and intensely undesirable because of its defining characteristics of decay and mortality: For Kreutzer, [the world
is] "a desert . . . We inherited it . . . Some of us want to see it become
a garden again. The mass graves of children . . ." (Wild Palms, 1993).

Given this bleak view of public space, what Kreutzer offers is a
logical extension of consumerist enclave architecture—the fortress-
like, middle-and-upper-class asylums of shopping malls, gated communities and theme parks that have co-opted the historical functions

LIVERPOOL JOHN MOORES UNIVERSITY
Aldham Robarts L.R.C.
TEL. 051 231 3701/3634

of public space. Prominent megamall architect Jon Jerde's comments on what his designs are intended to do could have very well been uttered by Kreutzer: "We think of it as designing the experiences, designing all the things that happen to you" (Jerde cited in Rugoff, 1995).

Architect Jerde and media megamogul Kreutzer share the same general enterprise. But whereas Jerde's work is embodied in commercial architecture, Kreutzer's technologies extend directly into the living spaces, the media ensembles and even the self-perceptions of his target audiences. His ultimate goal is, through multiple means, to profitably and permanently design his virtual hand into the personal fantasies and collective reality of each and all, while claiming to enhance individual autonomy and power.

Like SID 6.7, Kreutzer is a monstrous amalgam, an imagined collection of megalomaniac fragments. But whereas SID's acts of domination are overt, crude and predictable, Kreutzer's strategies are framed by a sophisticated logistical sense that is non-traditional and often clandestine. It is Kreutzer who understands the subtleties necessary to practice the art of covert war in the digital age.

Kreutzer is the most monstrous precisely because he is the most plausible. In him, we have the hydra-headed expression of a virtual will-to-power: He is the founder of a mental programming cult, an international media mogul, the CEO of a monopolistic software firm, a quasi-Mafiasque Don, a U.S. Senator, an ersatz populist running for President and an aspiring immortalist who plots to become a sentient hologram. He is a hungry ghost embodying the death of the idea of boundaries between the governmental, the public, the corporate and the private sphere. Consider this imagined encrypted email in *The Wild Palms Reader* from one of Kreutzer's highest ranking aides, a Chief Realitech, First-Tier Synthotician: "With the Information Revolution, we seized the means of symbolic production. But the postsymbolic Virtual Revolution is far more profound for it seizes the means of perception itself—the very means of cognition . . ." (Sterling, 1993).

And it is tracking a particular attempt to virtualize and commodify all realms of public and private perception that we find the latest wrinkle on the technological monster. That desire to be a purely virtual creature resembles a Deleuzian concept, popularly discussed as "the Body Without Organs." In what follows, a monstrous variation of Deleuze's formulation of the Body Without Organs, is developed. It is "The Monster Without Organs."

The Monster Without Organs (MwO)

1. Monstrous Capital. In *A User's Guide to Capitalism and Schizophrenia,* Brian Massumi (1992) ties together two of Deleuze and Guattari's thought-strands from *Anti-Oedipus* (1983) and *A Thousand Plateaus* (1987). In discussing their famous notion of *a body without organs*, Massumi says:

> Think of the "body without organs" as the body outside of any determinate state; this is the body from the point of view of its potential, or virtuality. . . . Capital functions directly through incorporeal transformations. It *can* jump levels. Capital can be given an image—in fact it *must* have one in order to act—but it is imageless as such. It is a body without organs, a network of virtual relations (Massumi, 1992: 128).

Kreutzer's obsession is to become just this. However, unlike like Marilyn or Elvis, who became but pliable material for the image industry, Kreutzer is a self-constructed, self-directed icon, not the passive product of purveyors. Improving on Michael Deaver, he deploys public relations and perceptual skills in a deft exploitation of societal fears. At a campaign stop, he frames the contemporary crisis in the familiar terms of a societal free-fall, reciting a litany of woes, from an endemic rise in crime to disintegrating infrastructure. Then, Father Kreutzer offers the American public his panacea, invoking the transformative joys of "multiple channels:"

> Television will be MORE real than life. A new reality will dawn, a new synthetic material, giving all people infinite alternate realities. Realiticians will program, shape, form and broadcast our message, until the very fabric of reality has been torn asunder . . . [For when] all realities are equal, all actions are equally moral or immoral (Wild Palms Reader, 78).

As the image of virtual capital, Kreutzer's monstrously amoral maneuvers are several. The first is to exacerbate social strife in such a way as to exercise an ever-widening net of power (through various technologies of the self) and profiting from endemic conditions of suffering and crisis. The second monstrosity is to relentlessly promote, through Synthiotics and Mimecom's Channel Three, a worldview that relativizes any stable notion of the true and the false, and the good and the evil. Thirdly, Kreutzer's techno-ideology reinforces social divisions by buttressing an already bunkered and fantasy-fed individualism. And, of course, Kreutzer's techno-privatism is as revolutionary as any stylish pair of *Nikes* can ever be.

2. Monstrous Body—Monstrous World.   One of the open *secrets* of Kreutzer's boyhood was the long-term sexual abuse inflicted by his alcoholic father. Like Judge Daniel Paul Schreber a century earlier (made famous by Freud's account), Kreutzer, as an adult, also relates how he received enchanting, miraculous "rays" that convince him that the body is a mirage, a tomb from which his consciousness must be liberated. His Cartesian-like privileging of mind over matter, spirit over body, sets up a tension between

> desiring-machines [normalized human life processes] and the body without organs. Every coupling of machines, every production of a machine becomes unbearable to the body without organs. In order to resist organ-machines [human bodies doing human things], the body without organs presents its smooth, slippery, opaque, taut surface as a barrier [that serves to repulse] desiring-machines (Deleuze and Guattari, 1983: 9).

Conceptually, that surface is initially blank, like those of typical forms of unrecorded magnetic oxide (VHS and audio tapes, diskettes, hard drives, CD-ROMS, etc.) before inscription. After the recording has been made, the entire process appears, to the body without organs, to have been constituted from the recording surface itself. At this point, Deleuze and Guattari say that "The body without organs now falls back on desiring-production [normal human activities], attracts it, and appropriates it for its own" (Deleuze and Guattari, 1983: 11).

Advertising campaigns, such as the Coca-Cola's self-presentation as "the real thing," typify this process. The desire for a "real thirst-quencher" leads to Coca-Cola, and Coca-Cola is naturalized as "the real thing" through the promise of enjoyably fulfilling a bodily desire. (Lost in the movement of image and desire is the fact that it is an artificial product.) For Deleuze and Guattari, an attraction-machine ultimately supersedes the initial repulsion: "The essential thing is the establishment of an enchanted recording or inscribing surface that arrogates to itself all the productive forces and all the organs of production" (Deleuze and Guattari, 1983: 11–12).

As an MwO, this desire to effect just such a global inscription becomes Kreutzer's *modus vivendi* after his own "enchantment." Taken as a whole, Kreutzer's corporatist ventures aspire to arrogate to its collectivity all the productive forces and all the organs of production. That is, Kreutzer's will-to-totalize finds expression in his myriad strategies to reshape each and all, through a mediated metadefinition of reality. *In toto*, although Kreutzer and Schreber share the same pathology, Kreutzer, because he commands mass virtual apparatuses, is able to furnish high-tech figurations that flow from the MwO (the virtual real, the technologically constituted) to the real. Tyler (1993) describes the movement of virtuality and reality this way: Reality often emerges from virtuality. Tyler then goes on to explain how this movement has worked, in the past, with purely abstract products like theoretical math. But whereas math constitutes the world in an extra-sensory manner, virtual reality ensembles immerse the senses (Tyler, 1993). VR does this by "doubling," creating a simulation which allows a surgeon or an airline pilot to perform maneuvers in virtualized environments, either apart from or linked with "real" space-time events. Tyler spatializes the causal vectors as follows: "[From the] virtual real—(concept) representation of the representation of a representation—(image) representation of a representation—representation—real" (Tyler, 1993). For Tyler, then,

> The products of the virtually real are . . . stimuli that encourage the imagination to produce figurations which, though they ultimately derive from representations of the real in the imagination, have no counterparts in the real. For the imagination, enjoined by the virtually real, will have [assembled] what the real never conjoined.

Zizek (cited by Druckrey, 1994: 8) puts the same idea this way: "The [key] lesson of virtual reality is the virtualization of the very "true" reality. Through VR, "true reality" is posited as a semblance of itself, as pure symbolic construct. So, whether it is in a kind of parallel correspondence or not, the point is that VR acts upon the real, as do representations of monsters. The two share constitutive similiarities.

Conclusion—The Millennial Monster
without Organs (MMwO)

In 1994, the ideological organ of the Republican Revolution, the Progress and Freedom Foundation, released "A Magna Carta for the Knowledge Age." The document declares that

> The central event of the 20th century is the *overthrow of matter*. In technology, economics, and the politics of nations, wealth—in the form of physical resources—has been losing value and significance. The powers of the mind are everywhere ascendant over the brute force of things.
>
> Cyberspace is a bioelectronic environment that is universal . . . [its] exploration . . . [is] a civilization's truest calling (Dyson, Gilder, Keyworth and Toffler, 1994).

Absent from much of current debate is the critical awareness that technologies have always emerged from cultural practices and ideologies. And some of the most imaginative, if not always conscious or intentional critiques of current worldviews (like the utterance above) are found in the mass culture industries—video and film in particular.

The Monster is the Message

So, what have these particular pop culture MMwOs either warned or revealed to us? First, virtual reality is a world constituted and dominated by the masculine principle. Even the etymological derivation of the term virtual comes from the Latin *vir*, which means "man" or "male" (Tyler 1993). Ergo, virtual reality is "male reality." Secondly, in each production, the MMwOs are all white. Thirdly, from *Blade Runner* onward, each of the MMwOs is a high-tech corporatist product, an expression of amorality and criminality that bears a genocidal and misogynist stamp. Fourth, each carries a dystopian prophecy embedded in a bionomic world, where the market has become the governing essentialist principle. Notably, although marketing strategies dictate that these anxieties must be resolved by "happy endings," such finales do not effectively suture these anxieties.

Penultimately, in a time of 15-second newsbites, film and video products have emerged as a means to profitably explore political themes. The trope of the monster remains one of the most flexible and durable vehicles for such tasks.

In sum, these MwOs signify enduring fears about bionomic, anti-ecological and eugenic technocorporatist agendas. At century's end, we confront these very real fears about current social problems through these millennial monsters without organs.

References

Battlestar Galactica. 1978. TV series. Produced by Winrich Kolbe and Glen A. Larson. 60 min.

Blade Runner. 1982. Produced by Blade Runner Partnership, Ladd Company, Sir Run Run Shaw. Directed by Ridley Scott. 117 min. Embassy Pictures Corporation. Videocassette.

Cohen, Jeffrey Jerome. 1996. "Monster culture (seven theses)." In J. J. Cohen (ed.) *Monster Theory: Reading Culture,* Minneapolis: University of Minnesota Press.

Deleuze, Gilles, and Felix Guattari. 1983. *Anti-Oedipus: Capitalism and Schizophrenia.* Trans. by B. Massumi. Minneapolis: University of Minnesota Press.

Deleuze, Gilles, and Felix Guattari. 1987. *A Thousand Plateaus.* Trans. by B. Massumi. Minneapolis: University of Minnesota Press.

Druckrey, Timothy. 1994. "Introduction." In G. Bender and T. Druckrey (eds.), *Culture on the Brink: Ideologies of Technology.* Seattle: Bay Press.

Dyson, E., Gilder, G., Keyworth, G. and A. Toffler. 1994. *Cyberspace and the American Dream: A Magna Carta for the Knowledge Age, Release 1.2, August 22, 1994.* Electronic Document available at http://www.lead-inst.org/pff/position/html.

The Fly. 1986. Produced by Brooksfilms. Directed by David Cronenburg. 100 minutes. Videocassette.

Huxley, Aldous Leonard. 1989. *Brave New World.* New York: Harper Collins.

Jurassic Park. 1993. Produced by Universal Pictures. Directed by Stephen Spielberg. 127 min. Universal Pictures. Videocassette.

Laural, Brenda. 1993. "Changing the world." In R. Twilling and S. Swezey (eds.), *The Wild Palms Reader.* New York: St. Martin's Press.

Mad Max. 1979. Produced by Kennedy Miller Productions. Directed by George Miller. 90 min. Videocassette.

Massumi, Brian. 1993. "Everywhere you want to be: An introduction to fear."

In B. Massumi (ed.), *The Politics of Everyday Fear*. Minneapolis: University of Minnesota Press.

Massumi, Brian. 1992. *A User's Guide to Capitalism and Schizophrenia: Deviations from Deleuze and Guattari*. Minneapolis: University of Minnesota Press.

The Return of the Jedi. 1983. Produced by 20th Century Fox and Lucasfilm, Ltd. Directed by Richard Marquand. 134 min. Videocassette.

Robocop. 1987. Directed by Paul Verhoeven. 102 min. Videocassette.

Rugoff, Ralph. 1995. *Circus Americanus*. New York: Verso.

Rugoff, Ralph, and Fred Dewey. 1993 "Floating world—Los Angeles: 1993–2008." In R. Trilling and S. Swezey (eds.), *The Wild Palms Reader*. New York: St. Martin's.

Shelley, Mary Wollstonecraft Godwin. *Frankenstein: Or the Modern Prometheus*. Chicago: University of Chicago Press.

Sliders. 1995. TV series. Produced by MCA/Universal Pictures. Misc. directors. 60 min.

Spinrad, Norman. 1993 "New cathedrals." In R. Trilling and S. Swezey (eds.), *The Wild Palms Reader*. New York: St. Martin's.

Sterling, Bruce. 1993. "Memo from Turner." In R. Trilling and S. Swezey (eds.), *The Wild Palms Reader*. New York: St. Martin's.

The Terminator. 1984. Produced by Cinema '84 and Pacific Western. Directed by James Cameron. 108 minutes. Videocassette.

Tyler, Stephen A. 1993. *Vile Bodies—A Mental Machination*. Electronic Document. Available at http://www.ruf.rice.edu/anth/bodies.html.

Virtuosity. 1995. Produced by Paramount Pictures. Directed by Brett Leonard. 106 minutes. Videocassette.

Wild Palms. 1993. Executive Producers—Oliver Stone and Bruce Wagner. 278 minutes. Two videocassettes.

The X-files. 1993. Produced by 20th Century Fox Television and Ten Thirteen Productions. Misc. directors. 60 min.

John Brigham

6

BODIES OF LAW: THE SUPREME COURT, THE JUSTICES, AND DEATH[1]

Introduction

Life has special meaning when applied to bodies wrapped in the robes of justices on the United States Supreme Court. Laura Kalman, reviewing biographies of Thurgood Marshall in January of 1993, reported the justice lamenting his need to retire from the Supreme Court before a Democratic President could choose a replacement. Marshall said he couldn't wait, because he was "old and coming apart" (Kalman, 1993). A few months later, Justice Harry A. Blackmun, speaking after dinner at the New England School of Law, reported his own imminent departure from the Court. He wasn't suffering from any serious illnesses, but, he said of his fellow justices, "There's something physically wrong with all of us" (*NYT*, 1993). At the Court, law's timelessness is protected by corporal rather than political calendars.

Tenure for life was already an old idea in politics when it became the basis for judicial tenure in the American Constitution. In William Blackstone's view, tenure for life constituted a source of political stability. In this vision, the mortal body is subsumed in the agency of the State and presumably insulated from political temptation. One of the proponents of judicial life tenure, Alexander Hamilton, wrote in Federalist Number 78:

> The standard of good behavior for the continuance in office of the judicial magistracy is certainly one of the most valuable of the modern improvements in the practice of government . . . it

is the best expedient which can be devised in any government, to secure a steady, upright and impartial administration of the laws.

Hamilton argues that the "permanency in office" of judges is the *sine qua non* of a limited government. Life tenure is surely a key to the independent judiciary that Hamilton, sought. It constitutes a special place that we have come to accept for the American judiciary.

Death as a punishment draws from the same traditional expectations for law as the life tenure of justices and mirrors the tension between the law as transcendant and its connection to the human body. Capital punishment was more common in the *ancien regime*. It requires a sense that the state, law and authority is more than flesh and blood. Like the judge, the executioner traditionally wore a robe to cover his body, protecting the individual doing the deed and generalizing the punishment. In his much discussed article, "Violence and the Word," Robert Cover places the judge ordering the convicted person to prison and death at the heart of the law. He sees this order as revealing the corporal power of the law, its power to do violence. But, some contemporary scholarship (Young, 1996) questions the image of the judge at the center of the law and as constitutive of its violence. Cover's commentary may be more indicative of "legal liberalism" (Kalman, 1996) than the nature of law. Here, we explore law in the bodies of the judge and the condemned.

Today, we are being more candid about death and law. The decisions in death penalty cases occupy a special place in the Supreme Court's business and exemplify the institution in American legal culture (Prettyman, 1961). The justice as final arbiter has come to symbolize "the law" and the academic life of the law has become the words of its high court justices. While life tenure reflects our wish to be ruled by something other than flesh and bone, something that stands apart or above our bodies. The special place of our justices brings them to mind when the state imposes death. Consequently, death penalty jurisprudence has been preoccupied with delineating access to appellate judges in recent years. At the heart of law's body lies the exceptional cases of tenure for life—tenure until the body gives out—and capital punishment.

Judges, our only civilian policymakers with an official dress (Frank, 1949: 254), have traditionally gone to some lengths to hide their bodies. However, modern jurisprudence, positing a "cult of the robe," calls attention to the reality of interests represented by the human body and the Court has become much more candid about its human condition. Where traditionally the trials of the physical body have been played down as factors for jurisprudence and public policy, contemporary commentary is more open (Pusey, 1979). Once the Court's legitimacy came from the claim in law to transcend the flesh. Then the judicial body—its health, age, race or sex—had one set of implications. Now legitimacy is drawn from a Realist paradigm and the body has become central to law's place. An institutional life that turns on the mortality of its members provides a perspective on the state's claim of authority to put people to death. The Realist foundation for law has undercut judicial authority over life and constitutes one source of pressure on death penalty jurisprudence.

Legal Bodies

Scholarly fascination with the relation between our physical condition and our metaphysical aspirations is evident in contemporary thought about law. Some scholars are motivated by issues in interpretation (Goodrich, 1990), some by feminism (Eisenstein, 1985), and others have been motivated by both (Frug, 1992). Interpretive theory and feminism provide a basis for looking at a domain generally subject to neither post-modern nor feminist considerations, life on the Supreme Court, and they enliven the rhetorical correlation between the body of a justice, the body of the Court and the body of the law.[2]

Not too long ago, Michael Rogin juxtaposed celluloid images of the President as an actor with the actor as President drawing attention to the relationship between "two bodies," the physical and the ideal (Rogin, 1987). Rogin drew on Ernst Kantorowicz's influential 1957 book about the images of the King in the Middle Ages. Kantorowicz himself had quoted the Elizabethan Jurist, Edmund Plowden.

> The King has in him two Bodies . . . a Body natural, and a Body politic. His Body natural is a Body mortal, subject to all infirmities that come by Nature or Accident. But his Body politic is a Body that cannot be seen or handled . . . and this Body is utterly void of Infancy, and old Age, and other natural Defects and Imbecilities (Rogin, 1987: 82; Kantorowicz, 1957).

The doctrine separated the person from the office and made the kingdom independent of the body mortal that governed. Thus, politics could be subject to the rule of law. But, according to Rogin, the doctrine of the King's two bodies could also, "take the chief executive in the opposite direction . . . not separating physical person from office but absorbing the realm into the office holder's personal identity" (Rogin, 1987:82). While this second consideration may lead to more dramatic expressions of institutional aspiration on the part of officeholders, as in Nixon's uniforms for the White House police, the attempt to separate body from office says more about the ways our beliefs in government have developed.

In the Christian tradition, the spirit becomes material through eating. The practice that began with breaking bread at the last supper means "that what is present is always potentially a reference to some other order of being or to some other text" (Goodrich, 1990:54; 1 Corinthians 12). This Christian ritual is said by some to be a source for the authority in the Common Law. The theory of the Eucharist, over which much blood was shed during the development of the Christian religion, is a theory about social bonds taken on. Peter Goodrich holds that "the theory of presence in the Eucharist, becomes in law the question of the 'spirit of law'' or the law in our lives" and is related to community (Goodrich, 1990:55–57). In colonial New Mexico a similar imposition of eucharistic ideology was employed by Spain to bring Native Americans under the European yoke. As presented by Ramón Gutiérrez in *When Jesus Came the Corn Mothers Went Away,* Spanish rule is linked to the eucharist by the priesthood, authorities representing both the Lord and the State (Gutiérrez, 1992).

In the American legal pantheon, John Marshall was known for his ability to elevate his own opinion beyond the traditional seriatim judicial expression of individual interests into an "opinion of the Court." In this way, the Court itself gained stature. Marshall's most important opinion, *Marbury v. Madison* (1803), which claimed a special province for the judiciary in constitutional matters, also clarified the process by which governments made appointments. Marshall held that the acts of governing bodies, not paper, conferred official status thus placing the primacy of the law as institutional action over the individual acts of men (even in a case where he, Marshall, was the man himself).

Because we have taken the law into our lives, we often fail to see the embodiments. Indeed, since the Enlightenment, our demand for the separation of the secular from the sacred realm elevates the ideal of law above the flesh. Even in Realism we have trouble actually seeing the bodies in the law (Brigham and Harrington, 1989). However, various social movements in America have made the bodies in the law hard to ignore; the effort to abolish slavery, the move to regulate industrial capital, lynching and the anti-lynching league, and the anti-abortion movements are prime examples. The abolition of capital punishment is one of the most dramatic recent examples although in this regard it is similar to abortion.

Contemporary intellectuals have synthesized a number of these issues into new ways of seeing the body in law. Feminists have been attentive to the body and brought it into intellectual life (Cheah, 1996; Young, 1990; Eisenstein, 1985). Among the central concerns of feminism have been abortion rights and protection from rape and battery (Jacobus, *et al.*, 1990). Following Catharine MacKinnon (1983), Eisenstein (1985) described the constitution of reality in linguistic terms and charted the ways law constitutes male privilege. The methodological significance of this work is associated with the presence of men in the standard for equality. Whether as a basis for determining difference or sameness, the law has worked from a male standard. As such, law as an "authorized discourse" carries men into the world, or, as MacKinnon said about feminist critiques of male reality, "we always looked for the prick in the piece" (Leidholdt and Raymond, 1990: 4). In this way, male hegemony is constituted in law. In Mary Joe Frug's "postmodern" account law's power constructs a physical world in which "Differences between women and men are not biologically compelled, they are rather socially constructed" (Frug, 1992: 128). While acknowledging important changes in women's legal rights, Frug held that "there remains a common residue of meaning that seems affixed, as if by nature, to the female body" (1992: 129). She points to three aspects of that residue; a terror embodied in women facing rape or abuse, a picture of women as responsible for motherhood and child raising, and women as sexualized persons. In each aspect described by Frug, the law of the Supreme Court plays a role in constructing the body. But feminism, like contemporary law has also been constructed around a picture of the judicial body. In the case of feminism, the bodies of the Justices of the Supreme Court have usually been male. In the case of contemporary law, the justices are human.

Constitutive jurisprudence incorporates the post-structural and the feminist in a paradigm that makes us aware of the physical bodies of the law. The judicial body, like the Court itself, has been out of the public eye until recently. Powerful people often hide their physical condition, but in comparison with the President, there has been less access to, and certainly less interest in, the bodies of the justices (Gilmore, 1993). This is changing. In the sections that follow, this inquiry applies the political epistemology of body politics to the implications of old age, death and sex for the Supreme Court.

The Court's Bodies

Death, as a penalty, is expected to be reviewed with particular gravity at the Supreme Court because the Court is at the end of the line of legal appeal.[3] Life is how long justices get to keep their jobs. For students of the Court, mortality and incapacity arise over the possibility of openings or the ability of a sick justice to carry on. At the Court, even the sudden death of a healthy justice, like Chief Justice Stone's while reading an opinion in open court in 1946 (Stone, 1978), may be less disruptive than senility and the myriad incapacities of old age. Clearly the judicial body is a major determinant of Court policy. In the period 1972–87, from *Furman* v *Georgia* (1972) to *McCleskey* v *Keme* (1987), the Court went from tentative denial that execution is constitutional to affirmation that even where there is

Table 6.1   Court Majorities During the Metamorphosis on Death: 1972–1987 [*Furman* v. *Georgia* (1972) to *McCleskey* v. *Kemp* (1987)]

FURMAN MAJORITY	MCCLESKEY MAJORITY
Douglas 1939–75	Powell 1972–87
Brennan 1956–90	Rehnquist 1972–
Stewart 1958–81	O'Connor 1981–
White 1962–93	White 1962–93
Marshall 1967–91	Scalia 1986–

Furman 5 (White, Douglas, Stewart, Brennan, Marshall)
4 (Burger, Blackmun, Rehnquist and Powell)

McCleskey 5 (O'Connor, Powell, Rehnquist, Scalia, White)
4 (Blackmun, Brennan, Marshall, Stevens)

aggregate racial discrimination, the penalty of death may be imposed. During this time, the Court had 12 members whose appointments ran from William O. Douglas in 1939 to Antonin Scalia in 1986 (See table 6.1).[4] There was a metamorphosis in the corporate judicial body while the body of law on death was transformed. This section will outline some issues—leaving the Court, sickness and age as characteristics of justices, and the corporal presence of justices—and suggest their implications for judicial policy on the death penalty.

Leaving the Court

Most contemporary Supreme Court scholarship has a section on "Leaving the Court." Not too long ago, the conventional wisdom was that Justices of the Supreme Court, sort of like gunfighters, died with their robes on. Lawrence Baum notes the change in the last edition of his text (Baum, 1995: 74). According to Baum, the "problems" caused by aging justices have been alleviated somewhat since 1869 when Congress provided that the salaries of the justices be continued after they retired, but just in the last few years it has become evident that justices now usually retire before they are on their deathbed. Major attention was paid to an aging federal bench in the early twentieth century. Since 1937, justices who are 70 or over and who have served at least 10 years have been able to choose partial retirement with full pay and any subsequent salary increases. Judicial income is certainly a factor in retirement and helps to alleviate "the problem" of getting justices who are "old, ill, or not functioning effectively" to leave the bench.

This poignant situation has been a prominent feature of Court lore for some time, often invoked to encourage timely retirement before the current period. One of the first of many standard stories recounted about the Supreme Court tells how his brethren went to an aging Justice Oliver Wendall Holmes to get him to step down and reminded the justice of similar entreaties he had made to Justice Stephen Field nearly a half-century prior. Holmes is said to have responded to his younger colleagues that he had never himself done a dirtier day's work (Woodward and Armstrong, 1979: 161). Recently, physical problems have included Hugo Black's loss of memory, John Marshall Harlan's failing eyesight, and William O. Douglas' stroke.

Mortality as Opportunity

Health and the perception of vulnerability have a bearing on the pressure to retire that justices receive. This pressure comes in many forms, but usually there are policy consequence in the picture. Justice Felix Frankfurter was persuaded by John Kennedy to resign due to failing health. Justice Thurgood Marshall was pressured by both Richard Nixon and Jimmy Carter to resign. Marshall's health may have been the entre but the justice's resistance to such solicitations from Nixon should have been easy given their policy differences. The most famous issue around age and capacity was the Court packing plan of Franklin D. Roosevelt in which each justice over 70 was to lead to the appointment of an additional justice, "to help with the workload," Roosevelt argued. This battle, where age played a minor role, is central to Supreme Court lore and the premise that the Supreme Court is an institution where life tenure preserves the myth of impartiality.[5]

Age was the principle upon which Roosevelt's Attorney General, Homer S. Cummings, rested the court packing plan. Age was to be the neutral principle of reform that was supposed to allow the new administration, only months after coming into office in 1937, to change the make-up of the federal judiciary. Stimulated by an earlier Attorney General's role in providing decent retirement benefits in order to get rid of "worn-out judges," Cummings picked up the recommendation that James Clark McReynolds had made in 1913 that the President should appoint an extra federal judge whenever a judge carried on after the provided for age of retirement. Age was supposed to have become synonymous with being out of touch. However, with reverence for the institution stimulated by the plan's failure, the age of individual justices faded again into the background.

Youth and its implications for an extended term on the Court were promoted during the conservative administrations of Ronald Reagan and George Bush. The move to appoint younger judges in order extend their influence on the bench is conventionally associated with the Reagan presidency, but young judges like Joseph Story, who was 32 when he was appointed in 1811, Benjamin Curtis (42) appointed in 1851, and Douglas (41) in 1939 span nearly the entire history of the Court (Goldman, 1987). Goldman describes the process as one that evolved over the Reagan-Bush period. The average of 48.1 years during Bush's term is low and the proportion of judges appointed during the last two years of Bush's term who were under 45 was 44 percent while this average during Reagan's first term was a mere 26 percent. On the Supreme Court this sort of calculation is difficult because the numbers are so small. Yet, in the last few years all appointments have been relatively youthful with the most extreme case being Clarence Thomas at 43. With a life expectancy at the national average, Justice Thomas could serve on the Supreme Court until near the middle of the next century, through perhaps a dozen presidents.

Clarence Thomas embodied the process of turning man into justice to an unprecedented degree. From his initial introduction by the President while at his vacation home in Maine and the condescending attention to his laugh by his mentor Senator Danforth of Missouri, to the image he invoked of the nominee swinging from a video scaffold, Thomas was hounded about his body. Toni Morrison's treatment of the nomination in her 1992 collection *Race-ing Justice En-gendering Power* begins with his body. In her introduction to the collection, "Friday on the Potomac," Morrison equates Thomas with the slave in Daniel Defoe's *Robinson Crusoe* who put his head on the ground before Crusoe and place the white man's foot upon his head as a gesture of absolute servitude. She describes the hearings as "the site of the exorcism of critical national issues" which was "situated in the miasma of black life and inscribed on the bodies of black people" (1992:x). She drew attention to the "reassuring grin" that is for whites a "gesture of accommodation and obedience" (or, in a more linguistic sense a "metonym for racial accommodation"). She places the "spotlight on his body" in the initial articles on the nominee in *The New York Times* well before his body came "violently into view" with the charges of sexual harassment lodged by Anita Hill (1992: xii-xiii). Throughout, the body of this black man is treated symptomatically of a society that has had difficulty relating to the mind of a black person. Yet, what she calls "the fulcrum of the law" has Thomas' bulk tottering. On one side, a perverted African-American and on the other a justice of the Supreme Court. Thus, the politics of that nomination were both the presence and the absence of the body.

Decay beneath the Robes

Justice Douglas' health received widespread attention because his last years on the bench occurred in the period covered by *The Brethren* (1979). At 76, Douglas suffered a stroke while vacationing in the Bahamas December 31, 1974. His efforts to return to work and the impact of his incapacity on the Court is told in extraordinary detail. The Court's rules for proceeding with a sick justice are informal. Working around the incapacity of one of its most active members presented challenges throughout the Spring of 1975 which intensified when Justice Marshall was hospitalized with pneumonia in February. After 78 days away from the bench, Douglas returned to the Court in March. His wheelchair was rolled up to the bench for oral arguments on a ramp fashioned by the Court's carpenters. He had to leave in the middle of the session. Returning in the fall after a summer of struggle to regain his strength and entreaties from friends and former clerks to step down from the bench, *The Brethren* reported that Douglas was wheeled into the pre-term cert conference for the 1975 Term smelling from the "bag for his incontinence" and generally disrupting the traditional flow of work (Woodward and Armstrong, 1979: 464).

These reports on the incapacity of Justice Douglas and a few other indelicate references to decrepit bodies, were among the issues to which commentators took offense in reviewing *The Brethren*. Objections to intrusion by investigative reporters into the most intimate and private institution of the national government, ranged from subtle critiques of Legal Realism (Anastaplo, 1983) to extreme protectiveness (Lewis, 1980). George Anastaplo says, in his review, "What is novel in their accounts is not likely, by and large, to be accurate." He also notes that we don't need to know the politics much less the bodily functions of the justices to understand the Court and the Constitution. One of the authors of *The Brethren*, Scott Armstrong, justified reporting on Justice Douglas' physical breakdown at the conference "In order to show how difficult it was for the Justices to work together in one room" (Anastaplo, 1983: 1051). John P. Frank, in his review, attacked the sources relied on by Woodward and Armstrong, calling them "swine" for recounting incidents like one in which a justice, signing court papers on his death bed, signed the sheet instead of the paper (Frank, 1980: 162). The protectiveness of many authorities on the Court has caused this author to suggest that "the cult of the robe" has been replaced with "the cult of the Court".[6]

Death and Doctrine

The 15-year period between *Furman* and *McCleskey* was one of relative stability for the Court. The personnel changes of the Nixon Administration had already been put into place by the time *Furman* was decided. During this period, three justices left the Court, Douglas, Stewart, and Burger, while three came on, Stevens, O'Connor, and Scalia. The replacement of Stewart with O'Connor seems relatively insignificant in policy terms, at least on the death penalty. And while replacing Douglas with Stevens seems somewhat inconsequential in absolute policy terms, the subsequent replacement of Burger with Scalia intensified the consequences. Here, sickness, in the case of Douglas precipitated a change and made it more dramatic than the other more deliberate retirements. And, because death did not visit the Court during this time, opportunity presented itself in measured terms.

Epstein and Kobylka, in their book *The Supreme Court and Legal Change* (1992), find that legal argument has to join Court personnel, the climate of the times and the activity of interest groups to explain judicial outcomes. They hold that Stevens' replacement of Douglas was not crucial to the *Gregg v Georgia* (1976) majority, but that White and Stewart also defected from the *Furman* majority to produce *Gregg*.

> Having won their points in *Furman* and *Roe*, abolitionists and pro-choicers sought to maintain their legal and policy victories through reliance on the arguments that worked to give them their initial victories. This failed in the area of capital punishment because the LDF misread the doctrinal glue that held the *Furman* majority together . . . " (Epstein and Kobylka, 1992: 317).

After *Gregg*, the shift that goes beyond doctrine to the body of the law on death is to *McCleskey*. There, the Court fails to consider doctrinal and social scientifically relevant information in mitigation of the law's authority over death. In the shift from *Furman* to *McCleskey*, the Court moves from the relevance of statistical evidence on the corporate body of black men to the denial of that relevance.

Like all changes that involve the personnel at the Court, the beginning is a kind of judicial *habeas corpus*. The process for gaining Senate approval of a nomination to the Supreme Court puts forth the candidate's body for scrutiny by the legislators in an increasingly public spectacle. Louis Brandeis, a Jewish lawyer from Boston, appeared before a largely Protestant committee of Senators. Thurgood Marshall, a black man presented himself to the white political establishment represented by James O. Eastland of Mississippi, Strom Thurmond of South Carolina, and John McClellan of Arkansas. Justice O'Connor's audience was male and certainly unfamiliar with a feminine presence in authority on Capitol Hill.

The Court's bodies are human and their policy consequences are contained in the physical self. The Four Horseman were old and they were conservative. The present Court's conservatives are relatively young. Individual justices hang on to increase the likelihood of a policy continuity. Aging justices are pressured to leave, sometimes, but not usually to increase the efficiency of the institution. When we look at the justices and the Court, we turn the story of the Eucharist around. We are investigating not how the justices pass the law on binding us to their ideas but how the ideas that have bound us transform those who would give the law into its embodiment.

Until recently, high court decisions imposed significant obstacles to winning federal court review of second or successive habeas petitions. The justices require a prisoner to show "cause and prejudice" sufficient to overcome the failure to present a claim in the first federal habeas petition. If that fails the only remaining avenue for federal review is a showing that a lack of review would result in a "miscarriage of justice" which seems to mean execution of an innocent person. In *Schlup v. Delo*, (1995), the Court first indicated that the addition of Justices Stephen Breyer and Ruth Ginsburg to the bench has shifted the Court's death penalty propensity. In a decision written by John Paul Stevens, the Court rejected its own 1992 "clear and convincing evidence" standard which had required that no reasonable juror would have found him guilty. The new standard was to be a showing that "it is more likely than not that no reasonable juror would have found petitioner guilty beyond a reasonable doubt."

Late in the 1995–96 Term, the Supreme Court heard arguments in the case of Georgia death row inmate Ellis Wayne Felker over the federal law limiting appeals by death row inmates. The Anti-Terrorism and Effective Death Penalty Act, had been signed into law only a few months before. In it, Congress and the President assisted the Court in closing off appeals. The law limits those convicted of murder to one federal appeal unless an exception is made by a special three judge appellate panel. During arguments, Justices Breyer, Ginsburg and Sandra Day O'Connor focused on the Supreme Court's role in the new process and whether the Act was an unconstitutional restriction on the Court's jurisdiction or an unconstitutional suspension of *habeas corpus*. The decision, just three weeks after the case was argued, found no constitutional violation but simply a restraint on what the Court describes as "abuse of the writ."

Still, the Court's Term ended with some indication that the Justices might be staying the course of restricting death penalty appeals. Justice Breyer, writing for the Court, refused to set a time limit for state death-row inmates to file their first federal appeal. In an unanimous opinion, the Court set aside an order that would have allowed the execution of a Georgia triple killer, Larry Grant Lonchar. In the decision, Breyer wrote, "Dismissal of a first habeas petition is a particularly serious matter, for that dismissal denies the petitioner the protections of the Great Writ entirely, risking injury to an important interest in human liberty." While a prosecutor might show that a delay prejudiced the ability to respond, that issue would have to be argued in each case.

The Law's Bodies

Over a decade ago, Cover's "Violence and the Word" drew attention to the place where words and flesh join with the force of law. "Legal interpretation," he says,"takes place in a field of pain and death." To Cover, "interpretive acts signal and occasion the imposition of violence upon others . . . somebody loses his freedom, his property, his children . . . " (Cover, 1986: 1604). Considering the judge when sentencing a convicted defendant, he says, "is immensely revealing of the way in which interpretation is distinctively shaped by violence . . . " (1986: 1607). The law, in controlling the flesh, moves through the looking glass from ideal to real. Thus, "as the judge interprets, using the concept of punishment, she also acts—through others—to restrain, hurt, render helpless, even kill the prisoner" (1986: 1609).

Other contemporary manifestations of concern with the law's power to affect the material world includes Catharine MacKinnon's description of a "crunch" when bodies come up against the law. The crunch separates her view of law from liberalism (MacKinnon, 1993; 1987; 1983). Always with policy consequences, but always also with the jurisprudential significance this epistemological bridge possesses, the "crunch" is the point when the institutional machine smashes up against bodies. Most recently in *Only Words* where she belies the liberal separation between words and actions in the pornography debate, MacKinnon tracks a constitutive tradition. Critical Race Theorists wax autobiographical in order to show the constitutive force of the law (Williams, 1992) and *Words that Wound* makes the case for recognizing the explicit consequences that accompany hate speech (Matsuda, *et al.*, 1993).

There are historical antecedents for directing the jurisprudential gaze to the material in law through the connection between judges and doctrine. *Marbury v. Madison* (1803) was ultimately about whether an institutional decision or a piece of paper made one a judge. The great *habeas corpus* cases of the Civil War rested on the premise that the body could not be detained without justification in the law. And, while the *Lochner v New York* (1905) decision turned on perception of how much a baker could endure and *Muller v Oregon* (1908) rested on a perception of women's frailty, the famous turn away from this jurisprudence in *Brown* (1954) meant recognizing the social construction of the body of a segregated black person. New interests for the fetus and a new legal body was created in *Roe v. Wade* (1973). Ultimately, this interpretation of the physical in the gaze of the law is at the core of what law means.

In the case of the death penalty, *habeas corpus* to the Supreme Court places the institution at the end of the line in American legal culture. Retirement and the penalty of death are indelibly linked, for the shift from *Furman* to *McCleskey* when Justice Douglas retired. And rhetorically when Justice Blackmun stepped down. In a dissent to a denial of cert in the case of *Callins v. Collins* (1994), Justice Blackmun indicated "I no longer shall tinker with the machinery of death." This was March of 1994 the month before he announced his retirement. The opinion was a parting shot rich in the descriptions meant to "make execution personal" (Prejean, 1994) and establish that "the prospect of meaningful judicial oversight has diminished." Based in the jurisprudential shift from *Furman* to *McCleskey*, Blackmun's opinion also has the tone of one readying himself for an end to his judicial responsibilities.

> Rather than continue to coddle the Court's delusion that the desired level of fairness has been achieved and the need for regulation eviscerated, I feel morally and intellectually obligated simply to concede that the death penalty experiment has failed.

It also addresses an institution with a crying sense of loss over the doctrinal stance dominant as he writes and hope that a more enlightened path will eventually arrive, for, he says, "The path the Court has chosen lessens us all."

In order to complete the bridge between the ideal and the real, a number of scholars have followed Cover in suggesting the importance of communities that share the norms and narratives of the law—"interpretive" communities. The words and the people together give force to law. In interpretation, understood in this sense, the dichotomous relation between bodies and norms breaks down. For example, in *Palko v. Connecticut* (1937), the case that delineates the *ancien régime* in due process law, a presumably sensitive Benjamin Cardozo held that the execution of Palko after a second trial was reasonable and did not require the full array of federal procedural guarantees in the Constitution. Palko's life could be ended where the law was satisfied with his condition.[7] Today, the allegiance to law's structures in this case is hard to fathom, but we live under a jurisprudence where the logic and categories of the law give us the body as often as the opposite is true.

At the Supreme Court, institutional continuity and overlapping terms serve to mute the human quality of the place. As elaborated by Carol Greenhouse, the Court maintains a larger "cumulative and reversible" temporality against "temporal incongruities in that the incumbent of a legal office is mortal" (Greenhouse, 1989: 1648). We say, as the justices have taught us, that the Court decided *Marbury v. Madison* (1803) and that "it" decides various matters today. This continuity is most significant when linked to the resolution of new policy questions where the past weighs in to support decisions in the present. We speak of law as if a disembodied presence does the work. Some of the Court's authority lies here, but the tension relative to the mortal bodies of its members is not generally unsettling.

With the right perspective, the bridge may be made. In *Roe v. Wade*, the heartbeat and kicks of a child *in utero* become the takeoff for the second trimester of pregnancy where the states are informed they may begin to take account of that emerging life. Then again three months later the little bodies that can live outside of Mom, the potentially viable, carry the heavy hand of the law even further into a woman's body. Little Joshua DeShaney, battered and permanently injured stands as compelling testament to the present Supreme Court's refusal to obligate a state to protect wards its agents in the social welfare department do not have in custody. The *Sears Case* (1986) which raised sexual difference implications for the stature of women at work, split the women's movement, as did the *Cal Fed v Guerra* (1985) case at the same time. And of course, more recently the battery plant in *Automobile Workers v Johnson Controls* (1991), which took all too much account of women's bodies yet refused to protect them, epitomizes the situation of the conservative justices who now sit on the Supreme Court.

On the surface, greater attention to the mortality of the justices is always forthcoming when the Court is out of line with the dominant electoral majorities in the other branches of the American government. This has not been the case for some time. More generally, deeper perhaps, people who are mostly bodies and relatively insignificant jurisprudentially have been left out of this practice, certainly in the Anglo-American west and probably wherever there are lawyers. Drawing attention to the bodies at the pinnacle of American law is one way of letting the people back in. Another is recognizing their influence of doctrinal change.[8] In the end, jurisprudence comes full circle to reflect a conventional understanding that for a time was hard to find in the more august halls of justice, a government of laws is also a government of men, and some women.

Notes

1. Earlier presentations of this work were made at the 1996 American Political Science Association Meeting in San Francisco, the 1993 Law and Society Meeting in Chicago, and an Honors Seminar on Legal Bodies at the University of Massachusetts, Amherst in 1993. "Legal Bodies" concerned the Amherst Seminar in its meetings from 1991–93 and I have incorporated contributions from the Seminar into this chapter.

2. These relationships were alluded to by Chief Justice Earl Warren in his last comment in open court when he turned over his seat to Warren Burger. Reported in Bob Woodward and Scott Armstrong's probing investigation of the Court, *The Brethren*, the comments were directed at Richard Nixon who appeared before the Court for Burger's induction. The retiring Chief Justice said to the Chief Executive "I might point out to you, and you might not have looked into the matter, that it is a continuing body . . . the Court develops the eternal principles of our Constitution in accordance with the problems of the day." p. 24.

3. Barrett Prettyman, Jr. (1961), describes how the Supreme Court handled six death penalty cases. His summary argues that even death's "majestic presence" cannot guarantee that it will get the attention of the Court. The condemned must overcome such formidable constructions as the federal system which places the responsibility for criminal law with the states.

4. Serendipitously, the period coincides with some important studies of legal change (Epstein and Kobylka, 1992; Kennedy, 1988).

5. The four justices who drew the wrath of the President were described at the time in the following way. "McReynolds, a man of granite face and granite convictions, a hater who was unrestrained and furious in his hatreds; Butler, a bludgeon-minded railroad lawyer, pious, hearty, given to interminable anecdote and endlessly persistent with the persistence of a narrow man; Sutherland, gentle, simple, older seeming than his brethren; Van Devanter, genial, kindly, a man whom all men liked" (Alsop and Catledge, 1937: 4).

6. Brigham, 1987; See also Anastaplo, 1983 "We should take care, in our responses to the opinion-makers of our day, that we not permit a cheap realism to be substituted for a noble awareness." at p. 1074. In some sense the cheapest realism in this formulation is physical and we should wonder what sort of dichotomy this is. For another excellent discussion of the excesses of Realism see Fiscus, 1984.

7. "Is that kind of double jeopardy to which the statute has subjected him a hardship so acute and shocking that our polity will not endure it?" *Palko v. Connecticut*, 302 U.S. 328.

8. In 1970 48 percent of Americans approved of the Death Penalty. By 1991 it was 71 percent.

References

Alsop, Joseph, and Turner Catledge. (1937). *The 168 Days* (Garden City: Doubleday).

Anastaplo, George. (1983). "Legal realism, the new journalism and *The Brethren*," *Duke Law Journal* (Nov): 1045–1074.

Baum, Lawrence. (1995). *The Supreme Court, Fifth Edition* (Washington, D.C.: CQ Press).

Brigham, John. (1987). *The Cult of the Court* (Philadelphia: Temple University Press).

Brigham, John, and Christine B. Harrington. (1989). "Realism and its consequences," *International Journal of the Sociology of Law* 17: 41–63.

Cheah, Pheng, Fraser, David, and Judith Grbich. (1996). *Thinking Through the Body of the Law* (New York: New York University Press).

Cover, Robert. (1986). "Violence and the word," *The Yale Law Journal* 95: 1595–1629.

Eisenstein, Zillah R. (1985). *The Female Body and the Law* (Berkeley: University of California Press).

Epstein, Lee, and Joseph F. Kobylka. (1992). *The Supreme Court and Legal Change: Abortion and the Death Penalty* (Chapel Hill: UNC Press).

Fiscus, Ronald J. (1984). "Studying *The Brethren,* The legal-realist bias of investigative journalism," *ABF Research Journal* No. 2: 487–503.

Frank, Jerome. (1949). *Courts on Trial* (Princeton: Princeton University Press).

Frank, John P. (1980). "The Supreme Court: The muckrakers return," *A.B.A. Journal* 66:161–62.

Frug, Mary Joe. (1992). *Postmodern Legal Feminism* (New York: Routledge).

Gilmore, Robert E. (1993). *The Mortal Presidency* (New York: Basic Books).

Goldman, Sheldon. (1987). "The age of judges," *ABA Journal* 73:94–104.

Goodrich, Peter. (1990). *Languages of Law: From Logics of Memory to Nomadic Masks* (London: Weidenfeld and Nicolson).

Greenhouse, Carol J. (1989) "Just in time: Temporality and the cultural legitimation of law," *The Yale Law Journal* 98: 1631–51.

Gutiérrez, Ramón. (1992). *When Jesus Came the Corn Mothers Went Away* (Stanford: Stanford University Press).

Jacobus, Mary, Keller, Evelyn Fox, Sally Shuttleworth (eds.). (1990). *Body / Politics: Women and the Discourses of Science* (New York: Routledge).

Kalman, Laura. (1996). *The Strange Career of Legal Liberalism* (New Haven: Yale University Press).

Kalman, Laura. (1993). "Mr. civil rights," *The New York Times* (February 7).

Kantorowicz, Ernst H. (1957). *The King's Two Bodies* (Princeton: Princeton University Press).

Kennedy, Randall L. (1988). "*McCleskey v. Kemp*: Race, capital punishment, and the supreme court," *Harvard Law Review* 101: 1388–1443.

Leidholdt, Dorchen, and Janice G. Raymond (eds.). (1990). *The Sexual Liberals and the Attack on Feminism* (New York: Pergamon Press).

Lewis, Anthony. (1980). *The New York Review of Books* (Feb. 7): 3.

MacKinnon, Catharine. (1993). *Only Words* (Cambridge: Harvard University Press).

MacKinnon, Catharine. (1987). *Feminism Unmodified: Discourses on Life and Law* (Cambridge: Harvard University Press).

MacKinnon, Catharine. (1983). "Feminism, Marxism, method and the state: Toward feminist jurisprudence," *Signs* 8 (Summer): 645.

Matsuda, Mari J., Lawrence III, Charles R., Delgado, Richard, and Kimberle Williams Crenshaw. (1993). *Words That Wound* (Boulder: Westview Press).

Morrison, Toni. (1992). *Race-ing Justice, En-gendering Power* (New York: Pantheon).

Prejean, Sister Helen. (1994). *Dead Man Walking* (New York: Vintage).

Prettyman, Barrett, Jr. (1961). *Death and the Supreme Court* (New York: Harcourt, Brace and World).

Pusey, Merlo J. (1979). "The court copes with disability," *Yearbook* (Washington: The Supreme Court Historical Society).

Rogin, Michael. (1987). *Ronald Reagan, the Movie* (Berkeley: University of California Press).

Stone, Marshall. (1978). "My father the chief justice," *Yearbook* (Washington: The Supreme Court Historical Society).

The New York Times. (1993). "Blackmun sees retirement soon," (March 12).

Williams, Patricia. (1992). *Diary of a Law Professor* (Cambridge: Harvard University Press).

Woodward, Bob, and Scott Armstrong. (1979). *The Brethren* (New York: Simon and Schuster).

Young, Alison. (1990). *Feminity in Dissent* (London: Routledge).

Young, Alison. (1996). *Imagining Crime*. (London: Sage).

Cases

Brown v. Board of Education, 347 U.S. 483 (1954).

California Federal Savings v. Guerra, 758 F.2d 390 (9th Cir. 1985).

Callins v. Collins, 62 LW 3547 (1994)

EEOC v. Sears Roebuck 628 F. Supp. 1264 (N.D. Ill. 1986).

Furman v. Georgia, 408 U.S. 238 (1972).

Gregg v. Georgia, 428 U.S. 153 (1976).

Int. Union v. Johnson Controls, 59 U.S.L.W. 4209 (1991).

Lochner v. New York, 198 U.S. 45 (1905).

Marbury v. Madison, 1 Cr. 137 (1803).

McCleskey v. Kemp, 483 U.S. 776 (1987).

Muller v. Oregon, 208 U.S. 412 (1908).

Palko v. Connecticut, 302 U.S. 319 (1937).

Roe v. Wade, 410 U.S. 113 (1973).

Schlup v. Delo, 513 U.S. 298 (1995)

PART 3

SOCIETAL RESPONSES:
POLICING AND PENOLOGY

James W. Williams

7

TAKING IT TO THE STREETS: POLICING AND THE PRACTICE OF CONSTITUTIVE CRIMINOLOGY

Introduction

Despite the diversity of its faces and appearances, one of the uniting concerns of the constitutive paradigm (Henry and Milovanovic, 1996) lies within the nature of knowledge and the conditions of knowledgeability. More specifically, constitutive theorists are devoted to the conceptualization and interrogation of the modes through which subjects are transformed into objects of institutionalized knowledges through their own active participation. In setting the dynamics of social reproduction in this light, an irreducible relation is proffered between the constitution of subjects as known social agents, and the exercise of power on a local level according to the dialectics of translation, formalization, and codification as foundations for this knowledgeability. Immediately this resonates with the Foucauldian power-knowledge dialectic. In fact, much of constitutive theorizing is heavily dependent upon Foucault's fundamental insight that power and the forces of structuration must be understood in primarily epistemological, rather than political terms. Power is exercised in the production of subjects as knowable and known entities, and hence, in their reproduction as legitimate social types.

Regardless of this essential affinity, constitutive theorists ultimately diverge from an exclusively Foucauldian path in their ethnomethodologically inspired appreciation of the coproduction of subject and world. This viewpoint suggests that the discursive formations

identified by Foucault (1980) are themselves produced and reproduced through the interpretive practices and social interactions of subjects as they engage in their daily activities. The implication is that
power relations are not exercised independently of social agents, but
are themselves contingent upon the activities of individual subjects
and their reflexive efforts to make sense of their world.

In lieu of this dialectical stance, one of the fundamental insights
of the constitutive paradigm is its recognition that the knowledge-
power relation is irreducibly mediated according to local contexts
and conditions of knowledgeability, and consequently, the dynamics
of interpretation, sense-making, and social interaction that inhere
within these contexts. Accordingly, knowledge may not be essential-
ized as a medium of social reproduction, as its foundations within local
contexts and practical epistemologies introduces an element of contingency and ambiguity into its very nature. It is the recognition of
these unique, and to a large extent neglected, characteristics of knowledge that allows for an appreciation of both the objectification and
disempowerment of subjects at the hands of institutionalized knowledges, and the inevitable ambiguities and inconsistencies residing
within this dialectic given its necessary operationalization within
local sociohistorical contexts and intersubjective relations. Ironically
then, the potentials and possibilities for change and transcendence
may be seen to co-exist with the very social forms that contribute to
the objectification and disempowerment of the subject. The critical appreciation and conceptualization of this irony both constitutes the
groundwork for a dialectics of transcendence, and frames this dialectic in fundamentally epistemological terms.

Emerging from this brief exegesis of the principles and concerns
of constitutive criminology is the contention that the future development of the constitutive paradigm is dependent upon the establishment of a more extensive and sophisticated understanding of the nature of knowledge as a paradoxical site for both the dialectics of social
reproduction and the possibilities of transpraxis and social change.
Representing an initial step in this effort, this essay will explore the
unique characteristics of situated knowledges as a means of coming
to terms with the potentials for disempowerment and transcendence
that these qualities offer. The substantive context that will serve as
a foundation for this inquiry is that of policing.

Police work is ideal in this context given its existence as a crucial discursive site where lived events and particular subjects are

transformed into the dictates of formalized criminal justice based on the conceptual categories of criminality and deviance. These subjects and events, and the troubles that they represent, are thus rendered as the known property of the system of criminal justice. However, this constitutive dialectic stands in a critical and problematic relation to the necessary execution of the police function in relation to the ambiguity and uncertainty of the lived world, as well as its concurrent dependence upon a series of interpretive practices and intersubjective exchanges. Given this contextuality, police knowledge is neither constituted nor reproduced in an objective field, but is itself emergent within, and mediated by, a series of interpretive, intersubjective, and symbolic horizons. As such, police work provides a vantage point on the mediated nature of the power-knowledge dialectic, and thus a unique testimonial to the limits and boundaries of institutional discourses. Through an extension of this understanding of the police into the domain of constitutive theory, this article will attempt to present policing as a crucial medium for the articulation of the potentials and possibilities for transpraxis; consequently, it will represent an initial "statement concerning not only how coproduction takes place and how an alternative order (orderly disorder) can be envisioned, but how to progress from here to there" (Henry and Milovanovic, 1996: 64).

An essential theoretical component of this analysis will be provided by the dialectical phenomenology of Maurice Merleau-Ponty whose unique phenomenological interrogation of the situated and conditioned nature of knowledge will proffer a conceptual framework according to which the unique attributes of police work may be both understood, and related back to many of the phenomenological concerns of constitutive theorists themselves—that is, constitutive phenomenology, or critical postmodern phenomenology (Henry and Milovanovic, 1996: 64). In the end, it is hoped that the cross-fertilization of policing and constitutive literatures will provide a venue for the theoretical and substantive elaboration of the mediated nature of the knowledge-power dialectic and hence, given the contradictions and incongruencies revealed within this mediation, a flash point for the conceptualization of critical social change.

One of the defining features of the constitutive literature up to the present is its relative neglect of the police (a notable exception to which is Kappeler and Kraska in this volume). While it may be argued that the policing function is implicit within the more general references of constitutive theorists to the sense-making operations of criminal justice agents and their daily contributions to the discursive paradigms of social ordering, the unique and qualitatively distinct characteristics of police work as a situated, informal, and negotiated form of knowledge require that it not be equated with the other functionaries of criminal justice. However, it is just such a tendency which currently reigns within the constitutive literature which has tended to focus on the more formal dimensions of the criminal justice system—namely the courts—to the detriment of its frequently unseen operationalization.

From the perspective of the constitutive paradigm itself, this relative neglect is problematic on two fronts. First, the police represent a living embodiment of the discursive, interactional foundations of criminal justice, as well as an epitomization of the constitutive concern with the dialectical interrelation between agency and structure. It is through their functioning as a "front-line definitional coding system" (Manning, 1977: 101) that the police are constituted as a primordial site for the production and legitimation of the categorical distinctions underlying the discourses of criminality and social justice, and hence the perpetuation of "crime" as a system of social ordering and "criminals" as objectifications of the institutionalized knowledges upon which that system depends. Through these performances the police ultimately emerge as integral to the operationalization of law as a practiced mode of social ordering,

> As invokers of the criminal law, the police frequently act in practice as its chief interpreter. Thus, they are necessarily called on to test the limits of their legal authority. In so doing, they also shape the operative legality of the system of administering criminal law. That is, if the criminal law is especially salient to a population that has more or less recurrent interactions with the police, it is the police who define the system of order to this population (Skolnick, 1994: 14).

This sentiment is shared by a number of authors who identify the actions and interpretations of police as central not only to the public conception of law and order, but also the nature of specific cases as they proceed through the system of criminal justice (Ericson and Baranek, 1982; Manning, 1977; McBarnet, 1981). Further to this, it is the enactment of policing as an interpretive, socially organized activity which provides a living testimonial to the constitutive conceptualization of crime as a social process, rather than an objectifiable entity. This constitutive association between policing and crime is captured by Manning (1977) in his observation that,

> policing does not deal with a thing but a social object, crime, whose meanings, forms, and consequences vary considerably. "Crime" is not an unchanging, eternal reality unattached or unshaped by the meanings that people attribute to it. Quite the contrary. If people act in terms of their understandings of a phenomena, then it will not be surprising that their understandings shape and modify crime and the information out of which it emerges (1977: 256).

Police work, as a socially organized activity and interpretive practice, is constitutive of crime. In light of this association, the policing function must represent a central concern within constitutive criminology.

A second respect in which the constitutive paradigm's neglect of the police is problematic derives from the existence of police work as a qualitatively distinct mode of social organization. In opposition to the later stages of criminal justice where constituted knowledges have already become translated and codified in the form of institutionally legitimated renditions of particular individuals and events, and subsequently made impervious to competing interpretations and understandings, the policing function is played out within the context of the ambiguities and contingencies of lived events—it represents a transactional, contextual, and negotiated product of situated exchanges between officers and the public. As such, police work may be seen to embody the inconsistencies and incongruities of the systems of social control given the necessary operationalization of these systems within local contexts according to the interpretive practices of relatively autonomous social actors. Ultimately then, "the initial arrest stage where primordial sense data has not yet been completely captured within a linguistic coordinate system (rather it is lodged within competing ones)" (Milovanovic, 1988: 472) provides the greatest potential for resistance to the system of criminal justice, an observation that establishes policing as a starting point for the exploration and articulation of the nature and possibilities of transpraxis. Based on this unique framing of the police function, the following discussion will be devoted to the analysis of police work as a testimonial to the potential for subversion and resistance embodied within the specific nature and characteristics of situated knowledges—knowledges which both support and undermine institutional structures. Given the importance of not losing sight of this paradoxical quality of knowledge as a medium of both identification and resistance, the first step in this analysis will be to define the place of the police within the more general systems of structuration and social control. This will also allow for the identification of points of contact between the policing function and the interests of constitutive criminology, hence enacting a common framework according to which both literatures may be extended and elaborated.

The literature on policing over the past three decades has been primarily descriptive, atheoretical, essentializing, and reflective of an underlying tendency to reify police work as a socially necessary and relatively unproblematic mode of social control. However, this body of work does make one essential contribution to critical thought given its recognition of the ambiguities and limitations inherent within the traditional understanding of the police-crime-law relation. Contrary to the belief that the police are primarily engaged in the apprehension of "criminals" according to the dictates of "law," existing research suggests that daily police work infrequently involves contact with what is popularly understood as criminal (i.e. robbery, assault etc.), and that when decisions to act in an official capacity are made, these more often involve the invocation of the law as a means of legitimating police actions, rather than as a foundation for them (Ericson, 1982; Van Maanen, 1978; Pepinsky, 1975; Manning, 1977; Goodrich, 1984). According to this critical vision, the socially constructed nature of crime, combined with the contradictions of the policing mandate and the inadequacies of the police organization, suggest that policing represents more of a form of myth-making (Manning, 1977), rather than crime control. The police are dedicated to the presentation of an image of efficacy in the face of contradiction and uncertainty. It is in the management of this ambiguity that crime is constituted.

In a related vein, the law emerges from these studies as an indispensable resource in the task of image management as it is employed by officers on a daily basis to facilitate the misrecognition of the arbitrary and contingent nature of their actions, and hence to legitimate these interventions as responses to violations of law. This *post hoc*, legitimating function of law is epitomized by Black's (1980) observation that,

In sum, the written law seems to have limited value as a predictor of what the police will do from one case to the next. They nevertheless often make reference to the law, and use it to justify much of their behaviour. . . . Whether the police find that the written law has been violated apparently depends in many cases upon how they choose to exercise their authority, rather than the other way around. And this choice depends upon the social setting in which they find themselves (1980: 186).

A similar characterization of police work was shared by Pepinsky (1975) who argued that, "The law may impose limits on police decisions, but it surely does not determine the decisions. The frames of reference of legislators and legal scholars are simply too abstract to indicate to policemen how day-to-day decisions are to be made" (1975: 43). What emerges from this contextualization of police work is the notion that the characteristics of the policing function must be understood in critical juxtaposition to their assumed role in fighting crime and upholding the law. Thus, as Reiss and Bordua (1967) have noted, "Only in a superficial sense may the police be said to solve crimes or to enforce the law. The organization of society, the nature of violative activity, and the organization of the police department make it impossible to locate a population of subjects who have violated the law, or to solve most crime" (Reiss and Bordua, 1967: 41). This is not to say that crime and law are not significant to the police role; rather, it is to suggest that they perform to legitimize, rather than direct, daily police work. The foundations of policing must thus be sought elsewhere.

Bypassing traditional conceptions of policing, a more accurate indication of the nature of police work is supplied by a mountain of descriptive and ethnographic evidence. This suggests that the vast majority of police time is spent intervening in minor conflicts and disputes, managing indigent and "problem" populations such as the young, the unemployed, and the homeless, as well as engaging in a number of administrative and general social assistance duties (Manning, 1977; Ericson, 1982; Chambliss and Seidman, 1971). The impetus for police involvement in the majority of these instances is not evidence, or suspicion, of a violation of criminal law. Rather, police attention is seen to be demanded by the perception that particular acts, or types of individuals somehow constitute a threat to the social order. Policing thus comes to be defined in terms of a series of "situationally justified actions" (Manning, 1978: 71)—active interventions that "become rationalized after the fact because, from the police actors' perspective, certain situations literally demand intervention" (Manning and Van Maanen, 1978: 3). These observations have led a number of authors (Ericson, 1982; Chambliss and Seidman, 1971) to conclude that the police function primarily involves the reproduction of social order. Thus, its primary targets are "crimes" and "criminals" as perceived violations and violators of this order, rather than true sources of social harm. The end result of this ordering process is the constitution of crime as an autonomous and reified social reality.

In examining these operations more closely, it becomes clear that integral to the efforts of the police to intervene in situations constituting a perceived threat to the social order is the production and reproduction of a social field of difference and division (Bourdieu, 1977), one which forms the basis for the establishment and legitimation of relations of social power. Beyond their claims to safety and security, the police are constituted as a viable political force given their monopoly over the means of engendering authorized distinctions between subjects, distinctions which are enacted according to, and which ultimately reproduce, a binary logic of order and disorder. Deployed according to officers' interpretations and evaluations of situated exchanges between subjects, these enacted paradigms of orderliness, disorderliness, and symbolic distinction receive their legitimacy and significance through their affiliation with discourses of criminality, as segments of the population that are constituted as threats to the middle class conception of order are processed and disciplined through the categories of criminality and deviance. It is these labels, organized as linguistic typifications within the daily argot of the police officer and operationalized through self-fulfilling prophecies, which function to ensure the socially legitimated policing of these groups as criminogenic, rather than disordered. Herein crime itself is constituted.

Integral to the existence of the police as an interested mode of social differentiation is their implications in a series of functional homologies between discursive systems of symbolic distinction and the broader structures of social ordering. Once again drawing on the work of Bourdieu (1991), the police represent a foundation for the enactment and legitimation of disparities in social space through the identification of differences in physical space. Central to police work is the marking of social distances through the production and naturalization of specific categories of perception of the social world. As Bourdieu (1991) notes,

> The categories of perception of the social world are essentially the product of the incorporation of the objective structures of social space. Consequently, they incline agents to accept the world as it is, to take it for granted, rather than to rebel against it, to put forward opposed and even antagonistic possibilities. The sense of one's place, as the sense of what one can or cannot "allow oneself," implies a tacit acceptance of one's position, a sense of limits ("that's not meant for us") or—what amounts to the same thing—a sense of distances to be marked and maintained, respected and expected of others (1991: 235).

In this sense policing represents an epitomization of symbolic power as structural relations are reproduced through the enactment of conceptual distinctions which, in turn, are maintained and reinforced at the level of discursive practices. As the moderators of social space, the police come to play a potent role in the forces of hegemonic social reproduction and the power relations embodied therein,

> [The police] act in the interests of the powerful and authoritative against those without power and without access to the means of power. But not only do they serve this function, they serve to maintain the relative placement of social groups upon the political-moral ladder. By enforcing the law, they are always enforcing someone's interests against someone else's. This is given in the nature of the occupation (Manning, 1977: 6).

In sum, the police are concerned neither with "crime," nor "law" as conceived within public discourse. They operate to deploy a definitional coding system that provides, on a micro-level, for the entry of individuals into a network of instituted social control and, on a macro level, for the reproduction of the sociopolitical distinctions that these individuals—constituted as others—represent. The police, through their proclaimed efforts to maintain law and justice, thus embody "ceremonies that symbolize order, renew boundaries, and provide limits of acceptable social conduct" (Manning, 1977: 23). It is in accordance with these ceremonies, these dramatizations of order (Manning, 1977), that the police ultimately lay their claim to reality as an ordered system of symbolic distinction.

One of the defining features of this portrayal of police work is its synergy with the conceptual and theoretical foundations of the constitutive paradigm. In a manner similar to actors working within other areas of the criminal justice system, the police function on a daily basis to defend and reproduce extant social representations through their operationalization and deployment of an ordered system of discursive distinction. In this sense, they epitomize the constitutive understanding of control institutions, "From the perspective of constitutive criminology, then, control institutions are the relations among human agents acting to police the conceptual distinctions among discursively constructed social structures" (Henry and Milovanovic, 1991: 302). Beyond this general conceptual affinity, what is more revealing from the perspective of constitutive criminology is the centrality of discourse, language, and narrativity to the ordering functions of the police. In fact, it is through the socially organized medium of language that the micro-level interventions of police officers are translated into broader structures of social differentiation and control. Structural relations are thus produced and reproduced on a discursive and symbolic level according to the police officer's investment in linguistic typifications which organize and filter lived events and meanings in defense of extant social representations. Through language, social cognition and sense-making are ultimately rendered in sociopolitical terms, a link which is similarly drawn by constitutive theorists in their assertion that, "The principal means through which social structures are constituted is language and discursive practices that make conceptual distinctions through the play of differences" (Henry and Milovanovic, 1991: 299).

Police work is linguistically and symbolically ordered in two important ways. First, the officer's perception and interpretation of the physical and social world is structured according to linguistic typifications which operate to focus and organize attention. The common elements of the police argot provide the foundation for this linguistic structuring of perception and action as officers are socialized through their subculture to employ linguistic categories such as "the asshole" and "scum" as a basis for the typification of events and individuals, and hence the subsequent determination of legitimate courses of action (Van Maanen, 1978: 221; Cain, 1973). Through these organizational operations of language, subjects are constituted as others and, consequently, objectified through the discourses of impropriety and criminality; individuals are herein coerced into social categories. Once institutionalized within the occupational culture and worldview of the police, these linguistic categories become powerful means of social reproduction through their delimitation and naturalization of particular modes of thought and action,

> Sign and sign systems, once constituted, channel thought. Juridic linguistic workers . . . do not think by but think in language. Bounded signified material, connected with a signifier become the givens which, once incorporated within background horizons of subjects, preclude certain choices of thought and verbalizations. Non-justiciability is the fate that awaits juridical linguistic workers who engage in alternative semiotics (Milovanovic, 1986: 296).

Policing activities are also linguistically and symbolically mediated through the officer's construction and daily invocation of police narratives as a means of organizing and legitimating his/her actions and interpretations within particular situations. Intimating the generalizability of the story-telling foundations of the courts (Bennet and Feldman, 1981) to the activities of the police, the power and significance of police narratives derive from their ability to organize representations of individuals and events such that situational ambiguities and complexities are resolved (Manning, 1988; Cicourel, 1976; Goodrich, 1984). These lived events are subsequently rendered in the form of a coherent script that serves to legitimate police actions, and to organize a series of discrete and contestable circumstances into a factual account of "what happened." From the perspective of the constitutive paradigm, these narrative constructions are central to the ordering functions of criminal justice,

> Organizational agents, including control agents, must produce stable meanings in the very process of controlling deviance. Hence, human agents' semiotic work stabilizes the endless drift of signifieds under those signifiers, giving a particular meaning that is formalistic, rationalistic, and logical, and producing a stable and static semiotic grid that henceforth anchors the multiplicity of forces in movement (Henry and Milovanovic, 1991: 305).

Ultimately, it is through the codification and formalization of lived meanings that accompanies the process of translation and its editorial properties that situated subjects are disempowered at the hands of the police as they are forced to express and defend themselves according to a foreign system of meaning, and an abstracted and de-contextualized rendition of personal experience. In transforming individual troubles into the property of the state, police narratives come to epitomize and embody "linguistic oppression" (Arrigo, 1995: 458), as well as provide the foundation for the reproductive functions of the police as a misrecognized system of social ordering. The police emerge through these performances as a personification of the identitarian foundations of capitalist thought—they constitute a front line for the assimilation of the particular within the categories of the universal. Police activities thus operate not only in support of extant representations of the social order, but also the very logic upon which these divisions are based. Framed in this light, police work is revealed to embody many of the principles identified by constitutive criminologists as central to existing modes of alienation and disempowerment.

Despite its demonstrated affinities with the constitutive paradigm, as well as with other critical accounts of the police as an agent of coercive social control, the preceding characterization of police work is shortsighted in that it both essentializes and instrumentalizes policing as merely an appendage of a greater system of social ordering. The irreducible position of the officer as the sole interpreter of legal and social norms within the specific contexts of the policing field suggests that it is problematic to reduce police work to the mere execution of the principles of social ordering dictated at an organizational or societal level. Rather, police work must be understood within a more personal context wherein social imperatives and moral codes are translated into a personalized sense of rightness and wrongness as it applies to particular individuals and locations. It is these personal standards of judgment which, in turn, form the basis for the organization and exercise of police action as a specialized form of situational justice. Endorsing such a situated view of police work, Charles (1986) argues that,

> In reality officers concentrate on crimes that are important to them and ignore those violations which they consider unimportant. This is possible because street officers are assigned responsibility for enforcing all laws, are given no guidelines as to which laws are to receive priority in enforcement except that

felonies are more important than misdemeanours, and are not supervised. Consequently, the process of selective enforcement is largely decided by each individual officer, for no master plan is available. . . . What exists therefore is a system of random enforcement of the law, with only the most obvious criminal activity resulting in police action (Charles, 1986: 100).

As a result of this operational ambiguity, "Officers not only violate the intent and legal definitions of laws and departmental regulations from time to time, but various operational tactics and safeguards at the street level are developed to redefine, selectively interpret, and provide a practical means for officers to enforce the law in the streets" (Charles, 1986: 14). This sentiment is shared by a number of authors who draw attention to the relative autonomy of the police officer, and the consequent disjuncture between daily police work and the policies and dictates of the police organization (Manning, 1977; Pepinsky, 1975; Cain, 1973; Cicourel, 1976). A further testimonial to this conceptualization of police work as a situational, personalized, and qualitatively distinct mode of social ordering derives from the finding that deference and demeanor represent the foremost determinants of arrest (Chambliss and Seidman, 1971; Reiss, 1971; Chevigny, 1969). As Charles (1986), among others, has found: "Reluctance to comply with the police officer's perception of how the street encounter should progress dramatically increases the probability for violence and arrest" (1986: 66). Arrest thus emerges as a strategy designed to counter displays of disrespect to the officer according to a personalized standard of appropriate action and behavior. By extension, law enforcement comes to embody this individualized, interactional domain.

What this line of inquiry suggests is that policing proceeds according to a series of informal, situated, and personalized contexts that renders any accounts of the police as mere functionaries of the broader system of social control excessively simplistic and shortsighted (this is particularly a problem with positivistic Marxism). Instead, it is necessary through our efforts as constitutive theorists to appreciate police work as the embodiment of a particular, informal logic of social ordering that is enacted under specific sociohistorical contexts according to the guidelines of a specialized, practiced epistemology. Charles (1986), for example, has noted: "The decision process of the officer is a complicated labyrinth of value judgments, exigent circumstances, the officer's mood at the time of the encounter, the seriousness of the crime, and the attitude of the violator and significant others influencing the officer's judgment" (1986: 106). This tradition of "practical decision-making in a legalistic pattern" (Manning, 1978: 15) requires constitutive criminologists to focus attention on the ways in which officers form definitions of persons and situations as disordered or disruptive *in situ* according to the dialectical interactions between individual officers and the particular socio-historical contexts and circumstances within which they find themselves. Police work is performed neither unambiguously nor automatically, but is dependent upon particular conditions of knowledgeability.

It is the conditioned nature of police knowledge that constitutes a groundwork for appreciating the truly dialectical nature of social ordering as a process that transpires according to particular substantive contexts, and specific conditions of possibility. As such, it is constantly susceptible to inconsistency and disruption as these contexts themselves change and evolve, a possibility that is not an idiosyncrasy of policing but a defining characteristic of knowledge itself as it is produced and performed by human agents. However, before elaborating upon this formulation, it is necessary to explore in more detail the specific nature of police knowledge as a predecessor to these more general claims.

An ideal conceptual foundation for the analysis of policing as a contextual and situated form of knowledge is provided by Manning (1988) in his work on police communication systems. Adopting a distinctly phenomenological framework, Manning argues that it is essential to understand the processing of information that accompanies police work not as an objective process of registering, processing, and responding, but as a situated form of interpretive work organized in relation to practical contexts of social and organizational interaction. The definitions of situations and individuals that represent the foundation of police work are thus inseparable from a context of subjective meanings and practical action. As Manning notes, "The natural system of communication, the technology, the channels, the messages and the codes used must be seen within the context of human social definitions, actions, and subjectively intended meanings" (Manning, 1988: 234). This renders police work incongruous with an information-processing model as the majority of police responses,

> are not given in the level of information associated with the event but in the phenomenological meanings the police prospectively

attach to these kinds of events. By placing an informational model around these meaning-loaded events, one obviates the very features that officers responding to them use to set priorities, interest, and concern (Manning, 1977: 216).

Manning is not alone in this evaluation of the phenomenological, interpretive dimensions of police work. Cicourel (1976) and Sanders (1977) both make significant efforts to contextualize the "facts" of policing as products of socially organized, interpretive practices of individual officers, rather than autonomous objects of police knowledge:

> Information in an investigation is developed through interpretive practices, and a sense of a case is accomplished by the same practices. The typicality of any crime or criminal is not inherent in an objective set of conditions that take on certain forms but, rather, is a product of interpretive practices providing a sense of the typicality that is taken to be independent of the actor's doing (Sanders, 1977: 129).

Policing emerges from these accounts as the embodiment of a situated, localized, and phenomenologically mediated form of knowledge that is dependent upon specific contextual frames of reference and interpretive dynamics which are themselves organized in relation to the characteristics of the individual officer, the demands of the police subculture, and the various agendas of the police administration. To contemplate police work outside of this phenomenological mediation is to lapse into an abstract reductionism.

Manning's appreciation of the phenomenological foundations of police work may be extended and refined through a recognition of the dependence of the police upon the dimensions of space and time, as well as the dialectical referentiality enacted through the officer's body. In terms of the former, police actions and attributions are fundamentally organized according to a normative ecology which establishes implicit criteria for the proper use of place according to the normal distribution of individuals and events across particular locations at specific times (Sacks, 1978; Rubenstein, 1973; Charles, 1986; McGahan, 1984; Manning, 1977). The judgment of an act or individual to be "out of place" thus figures prominently in police suspicions, and decisions to act. Given this epistemological technique, the police emerge as specialists in the location of persons presenting improper appearances (Sacks, 1978). Rubenstein (1973) makes explicit reference to these unique features of police work in his observation that,

> [The officer] develops notions about what is the "normal" character of behaviour in different parts of his sector which he uses in deciding how to handle his assignment. . . . Whatever judgments he makes of the people, even if he holds them in low regard, he does not fail to account for the ways in which they use their places (or the places allowed them) on his tour. Behaviour tolerated in one place is disallowed in another because it violated his notions of what is right in that place (1973: 151).

Police work thus comes to rely upon a spatially and temporally ordered "history of recognizances" (Sacks, 1974: 194).

This perceptual order of space and time is complemented by the centrality of the officer's body both to the rendering of judgments concerning the actions and intentions of others, as well as the establishment of a sense of place within which other bodies are ordered. The symbolic and practical importance of what Holdaway (1983) refers to as "body territory" (1983: 46) is alluded to by Manning (1988) in his observation that police encounters,

> involve such matters as eye contact, constructing an order of speaking, positioning one's body in the setting, controlling the movements of the participants, listening to them without exchanges of order, anticipating the need for backup, sizing up the participants physically and psychologically, and knowing when to exit (1988: 134).

The body of the police officer thus emerges as a defining element of the police encounter, not only in terms of its role in accumulating knowledge concerning the intentions and acceptability of other bodies, but also given its constitution as a symbolic territory and standard of order which, if violated, will warrant immediate defensive action. In this respect, the body becomes associated with the dimensions of space and time as a fundamental constituent of the contextual and transactional nature of policing and the paradigms of order that it represents.

This discussion of the perceptual, temporal, spatial, and embodied characteristics of police work culminates in an appreciation of the inherently referential and perspectival nature of police knowledge as it is constituted within particular sociohistorical contexts. Following from this, police evaluations of persons and situations, and hence decisions to act, are dependent upon the constantly shifting relations between the background and foreground features of the officer's worldview. Drawing on Bittner (1967), Manning (1988) formulates this dialectical relation between the officer and his or her surrounding in terms of three fundamental horizons,

> The first horizon is temporal, the perceived relationship between the present problem and past and future events. The second horizon is scenic, the stable features of the background employed as a basis by which to handle the problem. The third horizon is manipulative, a consideration of the practicalities of the situation (Manning, 1988: 186).

The domain of mental imagery also emerges as central to the constitution of the officer's experiential horizons as it is his or her imaginative anticipation and reconstruction of events, based on past knowledge of the types of persons and places typically involved in these events, that represents an important foundation for police response as well as the retrospective legitimation of these actions (Manning, 1988). Mental imagery thus joins spatiality, temporality, and embodiment as a fundamental constituent of the background expectancies of officers as they engage in their daily work; consequently, it is integral to the enacted meaningfulness of the events and individuals with which the police come in contact.

The preceding discussion of police work highlights the contextualized and conditioned nature of knowledge as it is enacted within the policing context. As Manning notes, "Meaning and information interact and confound each other in a kind of reflexive reconfiguration. As a result, the message is not seen as a purely cognitive construction or as a mere physical thing but as a set of signifiers with ambiguous signifieds" (Manning, 1988: 215). From this perspective, the objectification of subjects that accompanies their integration into the system of criminal justice must not be conceptualized as an automatic and totalizing process. Instead, this constitutive dialectic is dependent upon interactions between a series of temporal, spatial, intersubjective, and linguistic horizons organized in relation to the perspective of the individual officer as an embodied observer. The result of this dependency is the introduction of ambiguity and contingency into the processes of social reproduction, hence making it susceptible to resistance and change.

Ultimately then, the police stand as an exemplification of both the processes of social ordering and the cracks and fissures embodied within this system of social control, indeterminacies which derive from the necessary foundation of institutionalized knowledges and discourses within the ambiguities of the lived world. A pathway is thus forged between the unique features of policing and police knowledge as irreducible modalities of social control, and transpraxis as a latent possibility of this very system of social reproduction. This is a link which draws heavily upon the dialectical phenomenology of Maurice Merleau-Ponty. Consequently, it must await further elaboration until the contours of Merleau-Ponty's position have been sufficiently illuminated.

Maurice Merleau-Ponty's dialectical phenomenology begins as an effort to critique and transcend the epistemological traditions of empiricism and intellectualism through an appreciation of the situatedness of the knowing subject within a series of temporal, spatial, and symbolic horizons which come to constitute the basic dimensions of its experience, and subsequently the organization of this experience in terms of a viewpoint on the world. Thus emerges Merleau-Ponty's conception of existence as "the movement through which man is in the world and involves himself in a physical and social situation which then becomes his point of view on the world" (Merleau-Ponty, 1964: 72). A defining feature of this philosophical vision is the centrality which Merleau-Ponty accords the body. In fact, for him it is our embodied position within the material and historical world that makes experience itself possible, "The body is the vehicle of being in the world, and having a body is, for a living creative being, to be involved in a definite environment, to identify oneself with certain projects and to be continually committed to them" (Merleau-Ponty, 1962: 82). Thus, it exists as a "fabric into which all objects are woven, and it is, at least in relation to the perceived world, the general instrument of my 'comprehension' " (Merleau-Ponty, 1962: 235).

Beyond its contribution to a materialist, dialectical, and referential conception of the subject, this treatment of the body is important to the extent that it brings to the fore the grounding of knowledge within an embodied, situated perspective on the world. It is a practical relation that both makes knowledge possible, and ensures its irreducible partiality and ambiguity,

To say that I have a visual field is to say that by reason of my
position I have access to and an opening upon a system of beings, that these are at the disposal of my gaze in virtue of a kind
of primordial contact and through a gift of nature, with no effort made on my part from which it follows that vision is pre-
personal. And it follows at the same time that it is always limited, that around what I am looking at a given moment is spread
a horizon of things which are not seen, or which are even invisible. Vision is a thought subordinated to a certain field, and this
is what is called a sense (Merleau-Ponty, 1962: 221).

One of the most significant and unique contributions of Merleau-
Ponty's thought lies in the articulation of this temporal, contextual,
and ambiguous quality of knowledge in socio-political terms as the
legitimating foundation for a politics of hope. For Merleau-Ponty, the
shifting series of spatial, temporal, and perceptual fields that constitutes our embodied relation to the world introduces an irreducible contingency and uncertainty into our existence—a radical indeterminacy
that, in his vision, is translatable into the dynamism of the sociopolitical realm. The result is the avoidance of essentialism and the establishment of transcendence as a real possibility. A return to the context of policing is necessary in order to both elucidate and substantiate
these claims.

Set in juxtaposition to Merleau-Ponty's dialectical phenomenology, police work comes to represent a living epitomization of the contextual, sociohistorical, and ambiguous nature of situated knowledges. The ultimate responsibility of the police is to survey and
evaluate individuals and lived events such that their deviance and/or
conformity to the values and dictates of law may be determined and,
subsequently, appropriate action taken to restore the threatened social order. Like the epistemological subjects of Merleau-Ponty's phenomenology, the police officer's execution of this function is dependent upon his or her embodied situatedness within a series of spatial,
temporal, and intersubjective horizons. It is this unique position with
the socio-historical world that constitutes a foundation for police
knowledge and, subsequently, their decisions to act and intervene.
Manning (1988) notes this contextual and spatial character of police
knowledge in his evaluation of calls to the police, "From a phenomenological perspective officer preferences shape the horizon within
which a given call is placed. This is, the present location of the offi-

cer in the spatiotemporal world and the structure of practical relevancies (Schutz, 1964) determine the definition of the calls. The preferences move in and out of relevance" (Manning, 1988: 138). The reliance of the police upon perceptually constituted normative ecologies itself represents a testimonial to the situated, embodied, and perspectival nature of police work. All of this stands in condemnation of the simplistic rendition of police work as a relatively unproblematic medium of social control. The police do not merely operate to impose a set of abstract principles and regulations upon the populace; rather, they are engaged in a process of negotiation between the institutional demands made of them and the situated ambiguity of lived events. Through these dependencies, the police are themselves subordinated to a field of contingencies and uncertainties.

Returning once again to Merleau-Ponty's lead—specifically to his association between the contextual and sociohistorical nature of knowledge, and ambiguity and contingency as irreducible characteristics of this knowledgeability—one can reasonably argue that the dependence of the police upon experiential, situated, and hence, ambiguous knowledges imposes serious limits upon their social ordering functions. These ambiguities, and their consequent delimitations, are uniquely accentuated by the intersubjective and dialogical nature of police work and its necessary execution within a field of negotiations and mutual dependencies. As Manning and Van Maanen (1978) note, "social control encounters, where an officer's response to perceived deviance is central, involve degrees of mutual dependency between participants. Therefore from this standpoint, all law enforcement is a matter of negotiation" (1978: 220). What this suggests is that the inevitable reliance of the police, and police knowledge, upon a phenomenological dimension of interaction and interpretation problematizes the instrumentalization of the police as agents of social control. This is not to say that subjects do not become objectified at the hands of the police as an effort in social reproduction; rather, it is to recognize the boundaries and limitations of this dialectic given its irreducible foundations within situated knowledges which are themselves ambiguous and uncertain. Ultimately, it is within the cracks and crevices of the phenomenological, socio-historical dimensions of police work that a space is created within which the dramas of resistance may be played out. The possibilities of transcendence and transpraxis are thus once again rendered in epistemological terms.

In generalizing this contextual understanding of knowledge and its relation to the dynamics of social reproduction to broader forms of structuration and social control, a warning is issued against essentializing this structural order. The social world does not exist as an impermeable social object that is reproduced without disruption, but is constituted and re-constituted within particular substantive and socio-historical contexts according to the interpretive practices and discursive commitments of individual subjects. While this conception of the dialectical coproduction of subject and world is a defining feature of constitutive thought, the preceding discussion advances upon existing constitutive theory through the recognition that this situated, contextual character of the dialectic introduces an irreducible element of ambiguity and contingency which, subsequently, problematize the process of social reproduction. The uniqueness of this understanding relates to its attribution of the limits of social ordering to the specific characteristics of knowledge itself, rather than to an abstract or tenuous political principle. Stated somewhat differently, the potentials for change and transcendence do not reside within the metaphors of chaos theory or a proactive politics, but within the situated knowledges and conditions of knowledgeability that, at previous points in time, constituted the very foundation for the processes of social reproduction. In this irony of the social world lies a space within which replacement discourses may be conceived, as well as the necessary avoidance of essentialism that is incumbent upon dialectical thought.

The preceding theoretical and substantive analyses bear a number of implications for the constitutive paradigm. First, they suggest that the conditions of, and potential for, transpraxis and replacement discourse must be sought within a critical interrogation of the very nature of knowledge itself. More specifically, they must be pursued within the irreducible contradictions between knowledge as it is revealed within the ambiguities of concrete circumstances and lived events, and knowledge as it is constituted according to the universalizing dictates of capitalist logic. Despite the relative successes of instrumental reason in appropriating the particular as its own, and subsequently, in enacting power relations in accordance with this function, the contextual and ambiguous character of situated knowledges upon which these forces are ultimately forced to rely, render this process necessarily contingent and tenuous. The context of police work has served as an epitomization of this contradictory nature of knowledge, and hence has been proffered as an essential field within which resistance to the dominant modes of social ordering may be enacted. Once again the work of Manning (1988) is of value here,

> It would appear that many of the basic assumptions of the managerial strata when viewed from the officers' perspective are inaccurate. They do not capture the meaningful dimensions of the ways in which information is defined by those on the ground; it does not capture their perspective of the work, and it does not adequately capture the intentionality of the participants. As such, the relationships between the system of control and the process of work come into radical, repeated, and occasionally disruptive contradiction (Manning, 1988: 241).

The proffering of police work as an inherently contradictory site within which the potentials for critical transcendence may be played out exists as a lasting testimonial to the necessary pursuit of constitutive concerns within the context of the particular; otherwise, constitutive analyses themselves will tend to lapse into abstractions and essentializations.

A second implication that emerges from this discussion is the need to develop constitutive criminology along phenomenological lines. While the importance of a phenomenological dimension has been recognized within constitutive theory, especially by Henry and Milovanovic (1996), there has been a noticeable absence of a theoretical framework according to which their allusions to a constitutive or critical postmodern phenomenology may be elaborated. It is my contention that the work of Merleau-Ponty may be of irreducible value to the constitutive paradigm given his efforts to recognize both the intentional subject and its perspectival relation to the world, and the inevitable boundedness and structuration of this subject in accordance with its location within a particular sociohistorical horizon. The uniqueness of this position is captured by Whiteside (1988) in her observation that, "[Merleau-Ponty] attempts to stake out a philosophical position with a conception of consciousness adequate to the comprehension of political phenomena" (Whiteside, 1988: 6). It will remain for future studies within the constitutive tradition to further explore the links between this notion of a dialectical or constitutive phenomenology, the contextual and mediated nature of the knowledge-power dialectic, and particular sites of resistance of which police work is but one. In relation to these concerns, the current effort has provided neither a cogent foundation for such an undertaking, nor a substantial indication of its nature or direction; it has merely indicated a point from which to begin.

References

Arrigo, Bruce. (1995). "The peripheral core of law and criminology: On postmodern social theory and conceptual integration." *Justice Quarterly*. 12(3): 447–472.

Bennet, L., and M. Feldman. (1981). *Reconstructing Reality in the Courtroom*. New Brunswick, NJ: Rutgers University Press.

Bittner, Egon. (1967). "The police on skid-row: A study of peace keeping." *American Sociological Review*. 32(5): 699–715.

Black, Donald. (1980). *The Manners and Customs of the Police*. New York: Academic Press.

Bourdieu, Pierre. (1977). *Outline of a Theory of Practice*. trans. Richard Nice. Cambridge: Cambridge Univ. Press.

Bourdieu, Pierre. (1991). *Language and Symbolic Power*. Cambridge, MA: Harvard University Press.

Cain, Maureen E. (1973). *Society and the Policeman's Role*. London: Routledge & Kegan Paul.

Chambliss, William J., and Robert B. Seidman. 1971. *Law, Order, and Power*. Reading, MA: Addison-Wesley Pub. Co.

Charles, Michael T. (1986). *Policing the Streets*. Springfield, IL: C. C. Thomas.

Chevigny, Paul. (1969). *Police Power: Police Abuses in New York City*. New York: Pantheon Books.

Cicourel, Aaron V. (1976). *The Social Organization of Policing*. London: Heinemann Educational.

Ericson, Richard V. (1982). *Re-Producing Order: A Study of Police Patrol Work*. Toronto: University of Toronto Press.

Ericson, Richard V., and Patricia Baranek. (1982). *The Ordering of Justice: A Study of the Accused Persons as Dependants in the Criminal Process*. Toronto: University of Toronto Press.

Foucault, Michel. (1980). *Power / Knowledge: Selected Interviews and Other Writings 1972–1977*. Ed. C. Gordon. Brighton: Harvester Press.

Goodrich, Peter. (1984). "Law and language: An historical and critical introduction." *Journal of Law and Society*. 11(2): 173–206.

Henry, Stuart, and Dragan Milovanovic. (1991). "Constitutive criminology: The maturation of critical theory." *Criminology.* 29(2): 293–315.

Henry, Stuart, and Dragan Milovanovic. (1996). *Constitutive Criminology: Beyond Postmodernism.* Thousand Oaks, CA: Sage Publications.

Holdaway, Simon. (1983). *Inside the British Police: A Force at Work.* Oxford, England: B. Blackwell.

Manning, Peter K. (1977). *Police Work.* Cambridge, MA: MIT Press.

Manning, Peter K. (1978). "The police: Mandate, strategies, and appearances" in Peter K. Manning and John Van Maanen, Eds. *Policing: A View from the Streets.* Santa Monica, CA: Goodyear Publishing Company Inc.

Manning, Peter K., and John Van Maanen. (1978). *Policing: A View from the Streets.* Santa Monica, CA: Goodyear Publishing Company Inc.

Manning, Peter K. (1988). *Symbolic Communication: Signifying Calls and the Police Response.* Cambridge, MA: MIT Press.

McBarnet, Doreen J. (1981). *Conviction: Law, the State, and the Construction of Justice.* London: Macmillan.

McGahan, Peter. (1984). *Police Images of a City.* New York: P. Lang.

Merleau-Ponty, Maurice. (1962). *Phenomenology of Perception.* Trans. Colin Smith. London: Routledge & Kegan Paul Ltd.

Merleau-Ponty, Maurice. (1964). *Sense and Non-Sense.* Evanston, IL: Northwestern University Press.

Milovanovic, Dragan. (1986). "Juridico-linguistic communicative markets: Towards a semiotic analysis." *Contemporary Crises.* 10: 281–304.

Milovanovic, Dragan. (1988). "Jailhouse lawyers and jailhouse lawyering." *International Journal of the Sociology of Law.* 16: 455–475.

Pepinsky, Harold E. (1975). "Police decision-making" in Don M. Gottfredson Ed. *Decision-Making in the Criminal Justice System: Reviews and Essays.* Rockville, MD: National Institute of Mental Health.

Reiss, Albert J. (1971). *The Police and the Public.* New Haven, CT: Yale University Press.

Reiss, Albert J., and David J. Bordua. (1967). "Environment and organization: A perspective on the police," in David J. Bordua, Ed. *The Police: Six Sociological Essays.* New York: Wiley.

Rubenstein, Jonathan. (1973). *City Police.* New York: Farrar, Straus, & Giroux.

Sacks, Harvey. (1978). "Notes on the assessment of moral Character," in Peter K. Manning and John Van Maanen Eds. *Policing: A View from the Streets.* Santa Monica, CA: Goodyear Publishing Company Inc.

Sanders, William B. (1977). *Detective Work: A Study of Criminal Investigations.* New York: Free Press.

Schutz, Alfred. (1964). *Collected Papers. Vol. 2, Studies in Social Theory.* Ed. M. Natanson. The Hague: Martinus Nijhoff.

Skolnick, Jerome H. (1994). *Justice Without Trial: Law Enforcement in a De-mocratic Society*. Toronto: Maxwell Macmillan Canada.

Van Maanen, John. (1978). "The Asshole" in Peter K. Manning and John Van Maanen Eds. *Policing: A View from the Streets*. Santa Monica, CA: Goodyear Publishing Company.

Whiteside, Kerry H. (1988). *Merleau-Ponty and the Foundation of an Existential Politics*. Princeton, NJ: Princeton University Press.

Victor E. Kappeler and Peter B. Kraska

8

POLICING MODERNITY: SCIENTIFIC- AND COMMUNITY-BASED VIOLENCE ON SYMBOLIC PLAYING FIELDS

In government it is order that matters.

—Lao Tzu

Introduction

The threat of crime, as evidenced by its myriad of constructed images and narratives, serves as the pretext for the installation of a growing system of formal social control. Deterrent efforts are aimed not only at crime but at ordering the full range of human relations, activities, and places as expanded control complements an emerging post-production economy. Crime is the mortar binding the historical use of state violence, its new and emerging forms, and the political economy. Social control, as practiced by police agencies, addresses the needs of an emerging and quite different economy. This economy has been described as one in which capital is detached from its tangible base of referent production (Baudrillard, 1993) and resituated in symbolic venues. We no longer live in an industrial society where capital is clearly attached to its labor or production signifier. As American society reaches the height of modernity and exhibits signs of the postmodern,[1] we should expect dramatic changes in both social control agencies and the patternings of social control. What was once the most visible institution of overt authoritative ordering, the police, now serves as a powerful mitigating medium for social and economic re-ordering through symbolic violence.[2]

The American police role in social ordering (Harring, 1983) and the institution's ability to manage its appearances effectively are certainly not new (Manning, 1971, 1988). What is new, however, is police use of corporate metaphors, community rhetoric, and the expansion of scientifically deployed social control. These changes are making the police institution even more valuable in the sociotechnics of a changing society. Policing seized the metaphors of market economics and rhetoric of community in an age where some have questioned the extent to which either of these traditional social forms still exist (Baudrillard, 1993, 1994; Strecher, 1991; Klockars, 1988). Shifts in the constructions of the rhetoric of policing as well as changes in the practices of policing are combining to allow dramatic transformation in the patterning of social control. Policing has been situated in the grand narrative of market economics; the practice of "scientific" problem solving (Goldstein, 1979, 1990); the responsiveness encoded in a localized narrative of community. Modern transformations in the police institution situate it as an ideal medium for expanding social order and masking symbolic violence from its political referent. Through the interplay of police rhetoric, scientifically justified practice, and the appearance of responsiveness, policing now serves as the premier institution for converging social control, symbolic violence, and self-deterrence.[3]

While scholars are aware of the importance of police use of symbolic violence (Manning, 1993a), the role of some forms of overt police violence may not be diminishing.[4] Police violence is being employed in well-imaged and better managed circumstances and highly defined social situations (Kraska and Kappeler, 1997). Indeed, overt police violence may be more refined, focused, and damaging than it has been in the past when one considers not only overt but symbolic violence. The normalization and universalization of the legitimacy of violence through scientific implementation enhances the effectiveness of symbolic violence as expressed in the circulation of its attendant imagery. Such a situation magnifies the social destructiveness of symbolic violence and bolsters the self-deterrence inherent in a hyper-rational society. This allows systemic regulation of both symbolic and institutional playing fields thereby expanding the social control of previously sheltered populations, places, and activities. Symbolic violence is more effectively implemented and resistance is more proficiently regulated through the mixing of community rhetoric, the circulation of overt violence, and the realignment of the constellation of social control agencies.[5] Some have referred to this discourse as the "quiet revolution" in policing (Kelling, 1988).

This article addresses narrative changes that have occurred in policing discourses as a result of the community policing movement. We analyze a model narrative of community policing and a police community survey. We deconstruct an oppositional representation of community policing that has circulated throughout the policing literature and has been positioned and reproduced in both academic and governmental circles. Text deconstruction illustrates the autonomous nature of control ideology as it underpins the community policing model. This illustration is made by sketching the internal dependencies and inconsistencies within and between traditional and community policing models. In keeping with the analytic approach used in constitutive criminology, text replacements are identified so movement can be detected and trajectories understood. The model's movement is illuminated by considering interpretive desires and linkages to global and textually external ideologies. We adopt a generative trajectory approach, but complement it with an enriched understanding of sensation as a source of ideas and means of reducing resistance to discourse. We conclude that policing as reconstituted by metaphoric and sensation replacement enabled the institution to expand targets of control and draw openly on a much larger array of control tactics.

Framing the Quiet Revolution: A Discourse of Control

Policing has undergone many changes in the past two decades. One of the most fundamental is the institution's adoption of community policing (Mastrofski, 1988). Community- and problem-solving policing have had a profound impact on the rhetoric of policing (Manning, 1993a). The rise of community policing has been accompanied by economic metaphors and a business strategy (Moore and Trojanowicz, 1988; Kelling and Moore, 1988) that contribute to the tone of policing discourses. Peter Manning (1992) has discussed in detail the transformation of police crime fighting rhetoric into economic rhetoric. This linguistic transformation occurred in a time when the general sentiment about economics was still production-distribution oriented and driven by retail and production metaphors. Police subsequently adopted the language of consumers, customers, and service providers (Manning, 1992, 1993a); some academicians advanced corporate strategies of policing (Moore and Trojanowicz, 1988) and others rewrote police history with a modernist gaze (Moore and Kelling, 1983; Kelling and Moore, 1988). This economically lagged rhetorical change and retro-history (Kappeler, 1996), suggests the new police rhetoric is grounded in a grand narrative structure of control ideology and advanced by bounded oppositional (Saussure, 1916) and substitutional (Eco, 1976) discourse. A deep structural transformation in the underlying ideology of policing is not evident.

So as not to mistake the certainty of this rhetorical transformation or its place in the grand narrative of crime control ideology, consider the following Bureau of Justice Assistance (1994a:41) advice to agencies implementing community policing.

Before implementing a community policing strategy, the agency should communicate the concept of community policing to its own personnel and to the community, including political and business leaders and the media. Different emphases and images may be appropriate for different audiences; however, a message to one group should not contradict or neutralize an equally valid message to another.

For example, messages to officers focusing on problem solving and arrests might conflict with images directed at the general public showing officers distributing teddy bears to preschoolers. Both messages and roles are valid; one emphasizes problem solving as a valuable anticrime tool, while the other shows the benefits of trust-building and partnerships with the community.

As police began projecting their image as merchants of governmental services, community policing advocates also facilitated a shift in the way police productivity was measured (Kelling and Moore, 1988). Police shifted the description of what they do and how well they do it away from crime toward controlling disorder and improving quality of life. Concern with the possibility of perceptual conflicts or resistance to how the new police productivity was to be understood is expressed in the same governmental instruction to police agencies.

The media must be included early in the implementation process to market successfully the idea of community policing. Media involvement ensures a wide dissemination of the community policing message and encourages the media to stay involved in future community policing efforts; the media also will be less apt to "derail" if there is a bump in the crime statistics or if some community policing policies are less effective than hoped. If the budget allows, media consultants can be useful. The agency's internal media relations unit should thoroughly understand the chief executive's vision of community policing and communicate it clearly in news releases and interviews. All who are marketing the concept must be careful not to claim more for community policing than it can deliver (BJA, 1994a: 42).[6]

Self-regulation and control of resistance during an institutional transformation are classic features of structural defense. Systems and structures must attempt to control adverse feedback while undergoing change (Piaget, 1968).

Changes in the language, marketing, and measure of policing may be the policy residual of liberal academic discourse, the rise of police science, and a renewed federal interest in repositioning policing within a more complex array of social controls.[7] Unlike the affirmative and liberalizing nature of replacement discourses often found in the practice of constitutive criminology we focus negative replacements that serve a control function. We have found no better evidence of the merger of police replacement metaphors, policy science, and federal repositioning than the following National Institute of Justice statement (1996:1).

More and more the Nation's police have come to be viewed as the central component in efforts to control crime and urban decay. Whether in the context of a call for more police involvement in communities or more police officers on the street, there is little doubt in the public mind of the importance of the police in controlling crime and crime-related problems of disorder. . . . In response to the need for information on "what works" in policing as well as public pressures to strengthen law enforcement responses to drug crimes, in 1990 the National Institute of Justice (NIJ) initiated the Drug Market Analysis Program (DMA). DMA sought to develop strategies for addressing street level drug problems and encourage technological innovations in the geographic analysis of crime. In Jersey City, New Jersey (one of five DMA demonstration sites) an evaluation was conducted in 1993 of an innovative drug enforcement strategy that focused on "hot spots" of drug activity. This study found consistent and strong effects of the experimental policing strategy on disorder-related emergency calls.

The discursive hue and cry of the quiet revolution replaced crime fighting with the scientific control of disorder to assure "quality of life" and "civility" as expressed in theses from "broken windows" (Wilson and Kelling, 1982) to "acquiring a taste for order" (Kelling, 1987). This radical transformation came at a time when the tools of law enforcement were changing. The rise of policy science gave the police institution a means by which to implement their derivative problem-solving desires. Even the former commissioner of the nation's largest police agency could not avoid the lure of redefining police work in terms of fear of crime, low-level drug dealing, teenage drinking, boomboxes and a host of other quality-of-life "crimes" (Bratton, 1995). Juveniles on the streets at night, music blaring from car stereos, graffiti artists' sprawling and uncontainable murals, panhandlers obstructing merchant doorways, and a lack of civility by skateboarders all became police concerns.[8]

While economically differentiated struggles, as expressed in "real" crime, were played out on institutional fields (Manning, 1994), police broadened the definition of what activities constitute social struggle and where these struggles were to occur. Perhaps policing needed to capture a lost "market share" of social control (Black, 1980; Manning, 1993b), or they needed a new avenue for institutional legitimization after the institution's "crime" control capabilities were called into question. In any case, the scientific identification of disorderly venues, deviant populations, and disorderly activities became the new policing (for examples see, Green, 1996; Sherman and Rogan, 1995a, 1995b; Sherman and Weisburd, 1995; Sherman, Gartin and Buerger, 1989; Koper, 1995). Police were no longer crime fighters, they became actively engaged in reordering social space, organizing social relations, and regulating disorder.

The quiet revolution allowed the police institution to be decoupled from its twin referents—government and law. Policing was seemingly purged of its overt political dimension by reattaching itself to policy science, problem-solving, and community desire rather than government or rule of law as both its source and limiting authority.

Policing appears a more responsive social institution by realigning itself as the signifier of community rather than by further forging its attachment to the increasingly demystified and limiting-enabling legalistic-professional model (see, Brodeur, 1981; Ericson, 1981; Murphy, 1988; Kappeler, Sluder and Alpert, 1994). In the new simulation of community desire by police, disorder was equated with crime and police practice was directed by those desires as well as liberal academic discourse and a federally sponsored policy science of value-neutral tone. This freed the police of some troublesome legal constraints limiting their authority and its own "impossible-improbable mandate" (Manning 1971, 1988; Williams and Wagoner, 1992). In turn, the new incarnation provided sufficient sterilization (through reliance on scientific legitimization) for the expansion and machination of policing. The replacement discourse of modern police executives was that disorderly activities, places, and people "create an atmosphere that frightens decent people and emboldens criminals" (Bratton, 1995:449). This form of replacement discourse fails to offer the affirmative and liberalizing characteristics often associated with constitutive criminology's use of local voices and narratives. In these discourses the emerging police enterprise was self-instructed by strategically placed prompts to scientifically identify and fix "broken windows," "uncivil people," and "decaying urban" places.

The police academic community[9] either remained silent or added to the quiet of the revolution. Even when academic voices of resistance were raised, they were mere whispers in the art of genteel oppositional discourse framed in the narrative of crime control ideology, legal accountability, and technical-operational policing. Early denunciations, like Carl Klockars' (1986) response to Gary Sykes' (1986) call for "street justice" as a means of more responsively addressing "community will," framed the discourse and its potentialities within legal rationality. The possibility of street justice through community policing became viable paradigmatic change that needed only attention to existing social arrangements to insure the new policing did not reverse civil rights progress. Appeals to civil rights and liberation ideology, however, have been understood as the death cry of both (Baudrillard, 1994). With government sponsorship, community policing texts within this narrative were mass produced and circulated in debate series form (see among others, Kelling, Wasserman and Williams, 1988; Kelling and Stewart, 1989). In this discursive exchange, police practitioners and academics reconstituted policing thereby reproducing and expanding patterns of social control and enhancing the police institution's power.[10]

Deconstructing a Community Policing Model Narrative

Here we deconstruct an oppositional representation of community policing. Model narratives, such as the one examined here, appear throughout the policing literature. While they vary, there is consistency among many of the surface facets of these models and their circulation (Peak, 1993; Trojanowicz and Bucqueroux, 1990; Walker, 1992; Wallace, Roberson and Steckler, 1995).[11] We selected this model among competing representations because of its positioning in terms of original publication, its subsequent repositioning by the Bureau of Justice Assistance (1994), and its widespread circulation and reproduction. The author and government's positioning of the model situate it squarely within the previously discussed quiet revolution discourse. A related motivation for selection of this particular model is the larger action narrative in which the BJA situated the text. The model appeared within a larger government document designed to guide police agencies in "making sense" of the reinvented package in action and utility terms. Understanding the socially situated text, its "discursive position," and how readers "make sense" of text are important aims of the postmodernist-constitutive project (Henry and Milovanovic, 1996).

Our deconstruction of the model narrative, presented below (see Table 8.1), is guided by several suppositions. First, text deconstruction illustrates the autonomous nature of control ideology as the underpinnings of policing. This illustration is best drawn by sketching the internal dependencies and inconsistencies (Hjelmslev, 1957) within and between dual model texts. Model narratives are not static. The identification of replacement metaphors and the illumination of dependencies and inconsistencies detect movement and identify trajectories.[12] Second, "structure has nothing to do with empirical reality but with models which are built after it" (Levi-Strauss, 1958: 279). As such, the policing model may say less about what is taking place in the action world of policing and more about the movement of ideas and images. Like positioning and making sense, a transpraxis of theory and action is an analytic preference (Henry and Milovanovic, 1996). Bolstering this second supposition are the findings in other re-

Table 8.1 Traditional versus Community Policing

QUESTION	TRADITIONAL POLICING (TPM)	COMMUNITY POLICING (CPM)
1. Who are the police?	A *government agency* principally responsible for law enforcement.	*Police are the public* and the public are the police; police officers are those who are paid to give full-time attention to the duties of every citizen.
2. What is the relationship of the police to other public service departments?	*Priorities often conflict.*	The police are *one department among many responsible* for improving the quality of life.
3. What is the role of the police?	Focusing on *solving crimes.*	A broader *problem-solving* approach.
4. How is police efficiency measured?	By detection and *arrest rates.*	By the *absence of crime and disorder.*
5. What are the highest priorities?	*Crimes* that are high value (e.g., bank robberies) and those involving violence.	Whatever *problems* disturb the community most.
6. What specifically do police deal with?	*Incidents.*	Citizens' *problems* and concerns.
7. What determines the effectiveness of police?	*Response* times.	*Public cooperation.*
8. What view do police take of service calls?	Deal with them only if there is no *real police work* to do.	Vital function and great *opportunity.*
9. What is police professionalism?	Swift/effective response to *serious crime.*	Keeping close to the *community.*
10. What kind of intelligence is most important?	*Crime intelligence* (study of particular crimes or series of crimes)	Criminal intelligence (*information about* activities of individuals or *groups*).
11. What is the essential nature of police accountability?	*Highly centralized*; governed by rules, regulations, and policy directives; accountable to the law.	Emphasis on *local accountability* to community needs.
12. What is the role of headquarters?	To provide the necessary *rules and policy* directives.	To preach organizational *values.*
13. What is the role of the press liaison department?	To *keep the "heat" off* operational officers so they can get on with the job.	To *coordinate* an essential channel of communication with the community.
14. How do the police regard prosecutions?	As an *important goal.*	As *one tool* among many.

Source: Malcolm K. Sparrow (1988) *Implementing Community Policing,* Perspectives on Policing 9, Washington, DC: NIJ and Harvard University, pp. 8-9. Italics, model labels, and numbers added.

search that police use of tactical violence quite naturally coexisted, even grew, with adoption of community policing ideology (Kraska and Kappeler, 1997).

Our analysis of this narrative model involves the identification and deconstruction of texts located in both the questions posed by the author and in the author's twin self-responses. Questions are physically located in the first column of the figure whereas self-responses are located under the traditional policing (TPM) and community policing (CPM) models. We leave it to the reader to determine the extent to which the traditional model represents simulation thereby focusing our attention on the movement of text and linguistic transformations between models rather than a deconstruction of the TPM. We have italicized terms and phrases that we feel represent basic replacements between the two models. Initially no distinction is made between metaphor and metonymy (see Jakobson, 1956; Eco, 1976) in the model as we focus attention on global ideological linkages and interpretive desires. A quick scan of the italicized replacements, however, shows the movement of desires back "into the unconscious where it remains connected to a long chain of signifiers" (Henry and Milovanovic, 1996: 9), which allows for the emergence and advance of the CPM.

Global Ideological Structures and Interpretive Desires

With these suppositions and distinctions in mind we use the term "cluster" to mark groupings of numbered text items into a thematic framework that illuminates linkages to metanarratives bounding crime-control ideology. The construction of these theme-question clusters sets the direction of the model's movement, illuminating both the author's interpretive desires and embedded linkages to textually external ideologies. At this phase in deconstruction, the model's trajectory is captured by highlighting "the organization of the discourse prior to its manifestation . . ." (see, Greimas and Courtés, 1979: 85). The author's method of presentation is viewed both in terms of the questions asked and the self-responses assigned to the two headings.

Reading the questions posed by the author reveals four transcendent thematic clusters. These clusters included preoccupation with the following generative and limitative themes: (1) how the police institution and its role should be interpreted and socially situated by the occupational-self and interested audience (items #1, 2, 3, 9); (2) how police products should be identified, measured, consumed, and evaluated (items #4, 5, 7); (3) what activities constitute police work as opposed to institutional products (items #6, 8, 10, 14); and (4) how police accountability is to be situated within existing social arrangements (items #11, 12, 13).

Question cluster 1 finds concern with practitioner and non-practitioner audiences. The author directs audience understanding of police identity by situating identity within the context of occupational role and interagency relationships. In posing these questions interpretation of police identity is limited to occupationally and bureaucratically generated self-conceptions. The non-practitioner audience is left to situate the police identity in the larger constructs of crime. Non-practitioner interpretations of police identity are often media based or driven by global understandings of external ideological structures tempered only by the reader's ability to situate police within dominate ideologies. The cluster limits interpretation of the institution's identity to the realm of relations and interactions between public service departments as opposed to the larger society. Such a limiting construction exposes an interpretive desire for police to be situated in an action rather than a theoretical paradigm. This cluster directs comparison of the police to other public service departments.

Question cluster 2 finds a concern with the manner in which the products of policing are understood by the audience. This cluster evidences both an interpretive desire and an attempt to situate the emerging model in the larger ideology of production economics. It also shows a linkage to applied science in the form of evaluation and outcome research, thereby linking it to a hyper-rational method of knowledge acquisition flourishing in the criminal justice enterprise and society (Kappeler, 1996).

Question cluster 3 evidences a desire to dichotomize police activity and institutional product. This delineation steers audience interpretation away from a political-economy-based understanding of policing to a scientific focus not on traditional legal actions or activities but on the imaged products. However, this construction also incorporates state-directed law enforcement activities in the advancing model. Thus, understanding of police activity by practitioners retains the TPM focus while simultaneously redirecting attention to the products thought to be produced by these activities.

Question cluster 4 links control of the police to the legalistic ideological structure by involving the notion of professionally-based accountability. Accountability and control are retained at the institutional level by situating evaluation within individual police agencies. Again, no mention or conception of society is introduced as an evaluating possibility. The movement toward a consumer based orientation to police accountability is limited not generated.

Collectively these clusters set the stage for the advancement of the model by linking the text to select external ideological structures (production-economic, positivistic-scientific, representative-democratic political, and authoritative-legalistic) and by limiting interpretive possibilities to neutralize resistant discursive responses. In this fashion the author "opens" and "closes" (Kristeva, 1969: 113–42) the many possibilities of reading the text before it manifests itself in the model. Eco (1968: 1620) explains this phenomenon as the method "by which the work fulfills its double function of stimulating interpretations and controlling free space of interpretations." While readers' beliefs and disbeliefs are suspended by the questions, the responses to be elicited have been directed by encoding interpretive desire to guide the construction of the relationship between policing and society. A level of reader comfort is secured for the new model before it is fully manifest.

With potential responses and reader interpretations limited, framed, and bounded by external ideological structures, a deconstruction of the self-responses in the advancing CPM finds at least seven clusters of interrelated and interdependent texts that further guide audience interpretation of the new policing. These instructional-response messages depend on juxtaposition of metaphoric counterparts in the TPM. As extracted from the CPM they cluster into: (1) a detachment of policing from government and political-legal accountability (items #1, 14); (2) a shifting of responsibility for crime control from police to citizen and other governmental agencies (items #1, 2); (3) a shifting of police orientation and public preoccupation from crime control to a broader range of human activities and directed desires (items #2, 3, 4, 5, 6); (4) an adoption of the high-rationality of policy science along with its attendant criterion of efficiency and effectiveness (items #3, 4, 5); (5) a retention of the enforcement core of policing (items #4, 10, 14); (6) adoption of the imagery of service provision and problem solving as institutional products with a hierarchical positioning of police as directors of community (items #1, 7, 8,

9, 13, 14); and, (7) a suggestion of community accountability, but an institutional situating of responsibility for police activities and values (items #8, 11, 12, 13). Understanding of the meaning of these self-responses is illustrated in a more detailed deconstruction of several of the specific texts in the CPM. Here we will turn our attention to such a deconstruction.

Textual Sensation and Sign Trajectories

For the sake of brevity we will limit our attention to a detailed deconstruction of the first four items that appear in the CPM. In deconstructing these items, we compare textual "sensations" and transformations in the "semantic" and "syntactic" progressions of the dual model narrative. We adopt, to a limited extent, Greimas and Courtés' (1979) generative trajectory but complement it with an understanding of sensation as both a source of ideas (Locke, 1690; Lambert, 1764) and a means of reducing resistance to change by emotionally situating the components of a semiotic triangle. Our use of sensation retains the fundamental characteristics of Greimas' (1966:69–101) "contextual semes" but emphasizes the role of idea-emotion in interpretive acceptance or resistance to discourse. In this scheme, idea and interpretative desire do not reside only with the author or text but also in the potential emotional properties of the seme as it influences the audience. In this fashion our deconstruction attempts to retain the essence of the text's broader humanistic properties by activating the reader.

In the TPM, the author's self-response to item #1 makes police the action signifier of government. The sensation of "authority" is actualized in the governmental practice of law enforcement and the discursive position of the police in this arrangement. The discursive position of the individual is absent or can only be conjured up as the recipient of law enforcement. No overt relational sign appears. In contrast, the CPM makes police the signifier of public and public the signifier of police. In this arrangement, policing is detached from government and reattached to the public in a obligatory relationship. This relationship does not fully unfold until the introduction of the phrases "full-time attention" and "duties of every citizen." The author does not respond in the CPM with any use of the term "community" in the simulation process, but rather selects among the possible paradigmatic signifiers the more expansive and less social term "public." Public is later replaced with the term "citizen." This chain of replacements takes on meaning when one considers the use of sensations.

At one semantic level, the political construction "participatory democracy" is embedded as a sensation in the first clause of the CPM. This sensation replaces the less removed "authority" sensation in the TPM. Yet, at a deeper semantic level the political construction, "public," is used as the actualization for the democratic sensation. This allows the CPM to retain its positioning of police by a double institutionalization of the newly introduced individual. The obligatory sign is based on a newly attached conception of the sovereign citizen. The individual, although not absent as in the TPM, becomes "dutiful citizen" in the CPM.

In the TPM, governmental authority is actualized in law enforcement. The CPM counterpart, however, modifies the syntactical relationship of actors by adopting the replacement "citizen duty." The use of "citizen duty" re-politicizes the authoritative ordering of the CPM, limits the police institution's exposure to responsibility for crime control, and expands its control beyond law enforcement to paying "attention" to citizens' duties. A sensation of product is introduced in the model in the form of an exchange relationship with the police positioned at the pinnacle of the production economy. This construction is clearly grounded in a blend of status and a sensation of production economics. Therefore the phrase, "police officers are those who are paid to give full-time attention to the duties of citizens" yields identification to a fading political economic order. The chronemic sign "full-time" is a metasign of second articulation where its difference refers to production status and thus back to a narrow economic code (see Hall, 1959; Koch, 1971, 1974). Collectively this response reduces resistance with the sensation of democracy, repositions the police at a higher level of authority seemingly outside the government-legal order, and takes policing to the level of simulacra.

The idea of shared responsibilities arises in item #2 of the CPM. Reading the movement from the TPM to the CPM finds the replacement of "conflict" in departmental priorities (no longer signifying government) with that of "responsibility" among departments. "Shared," with no connotation of democracy, serves as the resistance reducing sensation while government is re-introduced in the form of "departments" in the CPM. In this construction "citizen" and "public" are dropped from the signification leaving only departments as the actualizers of greater control by broadening their attentions to "quality of life." In this arrangement the term "conflict" and its negative sensation is replaced with the positive sensation "improving." This transformation allows resistance responses to be neutralized and power to be concentrated again in the governmentless signifier "departments" in a diversified risk-responsibility arrangement. The authority sensation is washed away in the model's progression and the police more fully share in the imagery of service providers. Government as a referent of department is missing and community is not to be found. The sensation of participatory democracy is suspended or pushed back in a vertical reading of the CPM.

Item #3 finds a replacement and juxtaposition of the phrases "solving crime" and "problem-solving." The ordering is changed to emphasize problems in the CPM rather than solutions in the TPM, further limiting the police institution's risk of failure or non-production. In this fashion, solutions are de-emphasized and products are expanded from "crime" to the production of "problems." Solutions are buried as a secondary concern. The sign "problem" is left detached until later constructions where it is ascribed with negative sensations like "concern" and "disturb."

The general iteration of the model is completed with the appearance of item #4 that suggests police productivity be understood and measured by the consumption of its de-politicized products rather than its imaged activities. "Arrest rates" are replaced with the "absence of crime" and the broader and less definable term "disorder." In this replacement chain, sensations associated with crime and arrest are attached to disorder. The CPM then confines evaluation to its problem-product not its activities. Since police produce both crime rates and arrests (Black, 1970, 1980) their presence or absence is an institutional artifact. The broader construction, "disorder," allows the police greater flexibility in the construction and evaluation of just what they do and how well they do it. In short, this section of the model's text allows for the retention of the core authoritative and discursive positioning of police as developed in the TPM, while the CPM repackages policing with positive sensations that modify role, product, and activity.

Postmodern Meaning of the Model Narrative

Policing reconstituted through metaphoric and sensation replacement enabled the institution to expand the applicable targets of control and to draw openly on a much larger array of tactics than were previously only covertly available within their legally restricted social role. The police became the image of responders to community needs and desires. They moved their appearances and rationality further away from citizen-controller toward a more comforting Norman Rockwell-like image—police as kind, community problemsolvers. As the language and imagery of community policing began to circulate free of its governmental referent, previous images like those found in the civil rights movement, the Watts riots, and the 1968 democratic convention faded. Policing, as we knew it, staged "its own murder to rediscover a glimmer of existence and legitimacy" (Baudrillard, 1994:19). The rhetorical and narrative death of police as the wielders of violence and coercion was so convincing that it bolstered some functionalist's notion that police violence was not a viable analytic tool (Reiss, 1993). Bittner's (1970) insight into the core role of policing as being violence and coercion was now banal and possibly invalid. In the fusion of policy science, police products, and the new rhetoric, extraordinary incidents like "Waco" and "Ruby Ridge" were not formal state-directed actions; they were operational mishaps outside the advancing community policing model.

Actualizing the Model Narrative: Reading and Writing Community

The preceding deconstruction might be viewed as cynical or misplaced if the resulting model was accompanied by reactive readings of community needs and proactive police responses to localized desires. Policing detached from government and signifying the public, however, was now free to read or write public will, present representational problems, and direct causal understanding. Even though the utility of police "community needs surveys" in developing policy and practice have been seriously called into question (Marenin, 1989; Skogan, 1975), police agencies are still admonished to read and assess community desire (BJA, 1994). Surveys of citizens, meetings with well positioned members of the community, discussions with media and political representatives were all viably restricted forums for police to discover needs, desires, and problems. Police executives began to scientifically read the community. Many, including the federal government, welcomed this reading as "democracy in action"

(BJA, 1994: 4). Framed as democratic action, this was at best represented democracy and at worst simulacra.

Supported by some police academics and the resources of the federal government, police agencies developed citizen surveys encoded with the external ideological structure of crime control and framed in the CPM. These instrumental messages elaborated for citizens their problems, advanced precoded causes, and directed law enforcement solutions. Consider the construction of questions in the following police survey (See Figure 8.1). The survey was reproduced, advocated, and circulated by the Bureau of Justice Assistance (BJA, 1994: 79–80).

Detailed consideration of the instrument as well as an inventory of other police instruments (see Tempe Police Department, 1993; Bradshaw, 1989; Henderson, 1995; NCCP, 1994), shows how the advancing CPM is encode into survey measures.[13] These constructions write for citizens, police as providers of solutions to police-generated problems. Encoded within the instrument are basic tenets of problemsolving as well as the elements necessary to measure the new police productivity. The instrument instructs citizens that fear of crime is a reality sensation whose signs are to be found among distinct populations and activities; that the easing of this sensation and manipulation of its signs are the measure of police productivity; and that solutions should be enforcement based. Citizens therefore are to interpret the causes of police-represented problems as stemming from local disorder, the circulation of drugs, violent gangs, unsupervised kids, and community outsiders. In essence the measure is the policing message—identify, ascribe, and control.

Police departments administered these encoded messages to "representative" members of the community. They then took their representational sample and re-represented it to the public. Simulation unfolds as the community learns[14] and localizes problems, causes, and solutions as the police re-replicate their former selves and their enforcement referent. In this fashion, the police reproduce the ideological structure of crime control while simultaneously producing a broader range and object of control—an arrangement of social control signs better tailored to an modern society. In this process the police circulate citizens' message-responses as verdicts for police action. What emerges from this second order simulation is an even more effective system of coordinated control where the politically and legally emancipated sign of police becomes the reader-writer of community

Figure 8.1 Bluegrass-Aspendale Community Survey

Please answer all of the following questions by circling the responses that best fit *your* opinions.

1. I often avoid going out during the daytime because I am afraid of crime.
2. The police department does the best job it can against crime in this neighborhood.
3. Bluegrass-Aspendale is a better place to live now than it was a year ago.
4. My fear of crime is very high.
5. Most of the crime problems around here are caused by drugs.
6. There is a good chance that I will be the victim of a property crime (theft, burglary) this year.
7. The police officers who patrol around here really know what's going on.
8. I often avoid going out after dark because I am afraid of crime.
9. Fear of crime is very high in this neighborhood.
10. There is a good chance that I will be the victim of a personal crime (rape, assault) this year.
11. Most of the crime problems around here are caused by gangs.
12. I regularly see police officers on patrol in this neighborhood.
13. I am more afraid of crime than I have ever been.
14. The police department hassles people too much in this neighborhood.
15. Most of the crime problems around here are caused by unsupervised kids.
16. The physical changes being made in Bluegrass-Aspendale will make it a safer place to live.
17. The police department is doing a better job in this neighborhood than it was a year ago.
18. The drug problem in this neighborhood is not as bad as it was a year ago.
19. Most of the crime problems around here are caused by people who don't even live in Bluegrass-Aspendale.
20. The police department should work closely with kids by organizing sports programs.

Source: Bureau of Justice Assistance (1994). *Neighborhood-Oriented Policing in Rural Communities: A Program Planning Guide*. Washington, DC: U.S. Department of Justice, pp. 79–80. Likert scale that accompanied questions and demographic items are omitted.

will and the purveyors or providers of enforcement solutions to highly representational problems and operationally modeled desires and activities.

A Closing Comment

The learned public desire for safety, fear of crime, resonance with community language, and the modern orientation to increasingly isolated social contact, allowed the police to expand their numbers and their influence into spheres of social life that once seemed beyond reach. Social indifference to police tactics was caused partially by pervasive images of crime projected by the media (Kappeler, Blumberg, and Potter, 1996) and by police promotion of responsiveness to community desires. Structural containment of symbolic violence eased and as society reached its height of hyper-rationality, operationality became policing. This resulted in the hyper-rational conquest of the intersections between people, activities, and space.

Within policing and academic circles, the language of policy science focused on urban space. Refinements in the mechanization of law enforcement were advanced with media crime talk, police disorder speech, and an emerging criminology of place (Sherman, Gartin, and Buerger, 1989). Targets of control became "hot spots" (Koper, 1995; Sherman and Weisburd, 1995) and intrusions into public and residential space were rationalized with talk of "crack houses" (Sherman and Rogan, 1995a) and "weeding and seeding." This high rationality found the intersection between territory, purpose, and politics. This transformation, of course, was within a larger social movement that expressed the high rationality of modernity.

Society had already begun to move in the direction of defensible social ordering. Walled bedroom communities (without sidewalks or space for social relations) and planned residential areas, isolated by the simulation of nature, punctuated the modern blend of people, place, and purpose. Individual-based suspicion (Skolnick, 1966), the cornerstone of police action, was replaced by surveillance (Murphy, 1988) and the control of populations and places threatening or defying the new rationality of place and purpose.   Residential and formerly private spaces became receptive to invasion by control agents[15] through the language of disorder, drug epidemics, and family violence. Through the language of problem solving and the zeal of solvers in search of problems, the expansive power and coercion of the state's detached signifier moved further into previously unregulated space and the daily lives of citizens. Such symbolic violence, of course, does not involve the obvious and brutal wielding of night sticks or unleashing of attack dogs. Rather, this invited intrusion involves the more subtle forms of control used by modern police forces—tactical raids accompanied by the news media, patrolling urban centers in combat uniforms, using directed-aggressive patrol techniques (Kraska and Kappeler, 1997; Kraska and Cubellis, 1996), electronic and visual surveillance (Manning, 1996), deceptive undercover investigations (Marx, 1992) and sexual violence (Kraska and Kappeler, 1995).

The social stage might well have been set with the "child-savers" movement and continued into what might be termed a "women-savers" movement (see Manning, 1993). Both social movements as well as the rise of technology in the earlier days of policing provided the impetus for the expansion of control into private places. Police adoption of technology changed both citizen expectations as well as invited the police into residential space (Walker, 1983). The child-savers movement allowed the police to inject state-sponsored control into the family relationships with the goal of acting on behalf of children. A similar but more scientificized movement occurred with the discovery and police operationality of responses to domestic violence. This further invitation of the police into homes gave the state greater latitude to reorder familial relations and power patterns. Similarly juvenile curfews swept the country and attached accountability and sanction to resistant guardians who failed to confine children's activities to the emerging residential prison.[16] The home became a focus of police concern, and social activities were directed back into residential space at the same time that space became economically meaningful. Power once generated within the family became regulated and its new patterning enforced. While it can be argued that state intervention into the family had a positive influence on balancing existing inequities, control systems are maximized in direct proportion to their liberating potentialities (Baudrillard, 1992, 1994).

The transformation of the police created expectations and complacency—a state-induced dependence and indifference. Police were now the social problem-solvers; the government's role in problem-solving created a generation of desire- or solution-dependent citizens unable to define or sort out the conflicts of social relations. Government succumbed to the power of police problem solving. Curfews, regulation, and enforcement all became solutions to social problems whether they reside in gender, social, economic or status inequity. Like other institutions, the police relied on the mass circulation of representational problems and the public's consumption of the new array of mechanically generated solutions. This high-production drama, encoded with the "conceit of prevention" (Manning, 1993), became the cornerstone for government intervention and police action at the new intersection of language, institution, rationality, and social-political space. Deterrence, the "black box" of crime control ideology, was repackaged for full symbolic deployment.

It is in the script of this "drama of control" (Manning, 1988) and its language and signs that the contradiction of individual and state takes backstage to universalized control. The police institution now merely serves as the backdrop and amplifier for the contradiction-confrontation between individual and state masked in terms of problems and community. This inherent conflict is merely more diffuse, more symbolic and more veiled at the current level of symbolic obfuscation. By staging its own death, the state and its seemingly decoupled institution of force emerge as a more responsive vehicle for administering community based violence and controlling the resistance of the non-obligatory and yet to be regulated sign.

Notes

1. We use the phrase "height of modernity" because in our opinion American society stands at the edge of the postmodern, sharing characteristics of both modernity and postmodernity.

2. The phrase symbolic violence spans various theoretical orientations and methods of analysis. For example at one end of the continuum, Manning (1996:3) defines symbolic violence as "maintaining the imagery of vertical and horizontal ordering consistent with conventional wisdom" where as Baudrillard (1993:36) notes that "symbolic violence is deduced from the logic of the symbolic: reversal, the incessant reversibility of the counter-gift and, conversely, the seizing of power by the unilateral exercise of the gift." We derive our definition of the phrase from a synthesis of these two perspectives. Therefore, symbolic violence is the unilateral appropriation of power, regardless of the mode of social action (language, image, practice) when such appropriation reverses the liberating potentiality of an action by reifying vertical and horizontal social order.

3. We use the term "self-deterrence" much in the same way as Henry and Milovanovic (1991) used the phrase "confinement by consent." Our use of self-deterrence, however, is best understood in a Baudrillardian (1994) sense as a product of the high rationality of modernity, where the social is imploded by both the ordering of human activity and the illusion of expanding choices.

4. Our national survey of American police departments found that in 1982, 59 percent of police departments had paramilitary units; by 1995 this percentage grew to 89. More disturbing was the finding that between 1980 and 1995 police use of these units increased by more than 500 percent and paramilitary activities had become normalized within policing (Kraska and Kappeler, 1997).

5. We offer as examples of this realignment the growing tendency of police organizations to develop crime/disorder control partnerships with business and other organized interest groups as well as police positioning themselves as the leaders of these collectives as evidence of the new constellation of social control (for governmental descriptions of these alliances see the collection of descriptive essays in the National Institute of Justice's *Journal* (August 1996).

6. The document from which this text was extracted is distributed by the Community Policing Consortium which is composed of the International Association of Chiefs of Police, the National Sheriffs' Association, the Police Executive Research Form and the Police Foundation. This consortium is funded by the United States Department of Justice, Bureau of Justice Assistance (see Gaffigan, 1994).

7. The first major federal intervention into policing occurred in 1968 with the advent of the Law Enforcement Assistance Administration (see Crime and Social Justice Associates, 1982). We use the term "renewed" to describe the current federal intervention in the form of funding community policing and policy science as well as increases in the number of police officers.

8. The contemporary language of urban disorder and decaying cities is reminiscent of the social pathology movement of decades ago. Lefebvre, in his book *The Production of Space* makes a similar observation and considers the viability of such a philosophy in the following remark.

> In connection with the city and its extensions (outskirts, suburbs), one occasionally hears talk of a "pathology of space," of "ailing neighborhoods," and so on. This kind of phraseology makes it easy for people who use it—architects, urbanists or planners—to suggest the idea that they are, in effect, "doctors of space." This is to promote the spread of some particularly mystifying notions, and

especially the idea that the modern city is a product not of the capitalist or neocapitalist system but rather of some putative "sickness" of society. Such formulations serve to divert attention from the criticism of space and to replace critical analysis by schemata that are at once not very rational and very reactionary. Taken to their logical limits, these theses can deem society as a whole and "man" as a social being to be sicknesses of nature. Not that such a position is utterly indefensible from a strictly philosophical viewpoint: one is at liberty to hold that "man" is a monster, a mistake, a failed species on a failed planet (Lefebvre, 1991:99).

9. For support of this contention in both text and image forms, see August 1996 issues of the *National Institute of Justice Journal*. (View images presented in this government publication on pages 30 and 35 together and/or read any essay in the issue).

10. We use the phrase "academic community" with the same implications as Kuhn's (1962) use of the phrase "scientific community."

11. Henry and Milovanovic (1991, 1996) provide an excellent discussion of the ability of oppositional discourse to reproduce the ideology of crime control.

12. Viewing community policing as the "drama of control," Manning (1988:36–37) provides one of the most comprehensive listings of ideological components in this act of policing. The model narrative considered here is reprinted in texts (Peak, 1993; Walker, 1992; Wallace, Roberson and Steckler, 1995) and its components can be found in other narrative forms (Trojanowicz and Bucqueroux, 1990).

13. In traditional-critical semiotics this is done by a rather strict distinction between semantic and the syntactic (see, Greimas and Courtés, 1979). In radical (or what some refer to as skeptical) postmodernism, the distinction is not as clearly delineated (see Baudrillard, 1992, 1993, 1994). We adopt the traditional-critical distinction to the extent that it provides some standardization but enter the realm of radical postmodernism when meaning suffers from standardized or linear analysis.

14. Consider the following BJA message to police agencies for developing community surveys:

> Citizen surveys do not have to be lengthy or complicated to provide the planning team with useful information. A survey of all residents in a very small community or a sample of residents in a larger community can be done

quickly and inexpensively; so can surveys of special groups such as businesses or students. Police officers often have been used to conduct surveys—an approach that also contributes to greater police-citizen contact. Local colleges are frequently willing to assist as well. Topics that should be explored in citizen surveys include:

Crime victimization experiences.

Observations of drug dealing, crime, and disorder.

Perceptions of neighborhood conditions and quality of life.

Fear of crime.

Experiences with police.

Attitudes toward police and other government agencies.

Priorities given to various community problems.

Participation in various community activities.

Demographic information (BJA, 1994:25).

15. Accounts of the police teaching citizens how to identify problems and problematic populations abound. For example Lakewood, Colorado police teach citizens, community leaders, and educators how to identify gang members, their behaviors and ways to prevent and control their "criminality" (Stedman, 1992); the DARE program is a classic example of police teaching misinformation to children about drug abuse (Manning, 1992). The GREAT gang-education program serves as a most recent example of this practice.

16. In a national study of small city police departments, Kraska and Cubellis (1996) found that there was a 1,588 percent increase police use of SWAT teams between 1980 and 1985. During this same time period, they found that the percentage of activities by these SWAT teams classified as warrant work increased from 30 to 94 percent.

References

Baudrillard, J. (1992 Eng. Trans.). *The Illusion of the End*. Stanford, CA: Stanford University Press.

Baudrillard, J. (1993 Eng. Trans.). *Symbolic Exchange and Death*. London: Sage.

Baudrillard, J. (1994 Eng. Trans.). *Simulacra and Simulation*. Ann Arbor, MI: The University of Michigan Press.

Bittner, E. (1970). *The Functions of the Police in Modern Society*. Washington, D.C.: National Institute of Mental Health.

Black, D. (1970). "Production of crime rates." *American Sociological Review*, 35: 733–48.

Black, D. (1980). *Manners and Customs of the Police*. New York: Academic Press.

Bradshaw, R. V. (1989). *Reno Police Department's Community Oriented Policing-Plus*. Reno, NV: City of Reno.

Bratton, W. J. (1995). "The New York City Police Department's civil enforcement of quality-of-life crimes." *Journal of Law and Policy*, 3: 447–464.

Brodeur, J. (1981). "Legitimizing police deviance." In C. D. Shearing, (ed.), *Organizational Police Deviance*. Toronto: Butterworths and Company.

Bureau of Justice Assistance (1994). *Neighborhood-Oriented Policing in Rural Communities: A Program Planning Guide*. Washington, D.C.: U.S. Department of Justice.

Bureau of Justice Assistance (1994a). *Understanding Community Policing: A Framework for Action*. Washington, D.C.: U.S. Department of Justice.

Crime and Social Justice Associates (1982 [1995]). "The iron fist and the velvet glove." In V. E. Kappeler (ed.), *Police and Society: Touchstone Readings*. Prospect Heights, IL: Waveland Press.

Eck, J. E. (1990 [draft]). *Implementing a Problem-Oriented Approach: A Management Guide*. Washington, D.C.: Police Executive Research Forum.

Eco, U. (1968). *Das offene Kunswerk*. Frankfort: Suhrkamp.

Eco, U. (1976). *A Theory of Semiotics*. Bloomington: Indiana University Press.

Eco, U. (1979). *The Role of the Reader*. Bloomington: Indiana University Press.

Ericson, R. V. (1981). "Rules for police deviance." In C. D. Shearing (ed.), *Organizational Police Deviance*. Toronto: Butterworths and Company.

Gaffigan, S. (1994). "The community policing consortium announces availability of practical primer on community policing." *New Release* (October, 3): 1–2.

Goldstein, H. (1979). "Improving the police: A problem-oriented approach." *Crime and Delinquency*, 25: 236–258.

Goldstein, H. (1990). *Problem-Oriented Policing*. New York: McGraw-Hill.

Green, L. (1996). *Policing Places with Drug Problems*. London: Sage.

Greimas, A. J. (1966). *Structural Semantics*. Lincoln: University of Nebraska Press.

Greimas, A. J., and J. Courtés. (1979). *Semiotics and Language*. Bloomington: Indiana University Press.

Hall, E. T. (1959). *The Silent Language*. Greenwich: Fawcett.

Harring, S. L. (1983). *Policing a Class Society: The Experience of American Cities, 1865–1915*. New Brunswick, NJ: Rutgers University Press.

Henderson, C. (1995). *Community Resource Areas: A Residential Survey.* Hillsborough County, FL: Sheriff's Office.

Henry, S., and D. Milovanovic. (1991). "Constitutive criminology: The maturation of critical theory." *Criminology* 29: 293–315.

Henry, S., and D. Milovanovic. (1996). *Constitutive Criminology.* London: Sage.

Hjelmslev, L. (1957). "Pour une semantique structurale." In L. Hjelmslev (ed.), *Essais Linguistiques.* Copenhagen: Nordisk Sprog-og Kulturforlag.

Jakobson, R. (1956). "Two aspects of language and two types of aphasic disturbances. In R. Jakobson (ed.), *Selected Writings II.* The Hague: Mouton.

Kappeler, V. E. (1996). "Making police history in light of modernity: A sign of the times?" *Police Forum,* 6: 1–6.

Kappeler, V. E., Blumberg, M., and G. W. Potter. (1996). *The Mythology of Crime and Criminal Justice, 2nd Ed.* Prospect Heights, IL: Waveland Press.

Kappeler, V. E., Sluder, R., and G. P. Alpert. (1994). *Forces of Deviance: Understanding the Dark Side of Policing.* Prospect Heights, IL: Waveland.

Kelling, G. L. (1987)." Acquiring a taste for order: The community and the police." *Crime and Delinquency,* 33: 90–102.

Kelling, G. L. (1988). *Police and Communities: The Quiet Revolution.* Washington, D.C.: U.S. Department of Justice.

Kelling, G. L., and M. H. Moore (1988 [1995]). "The evolving strategy of policing." In , V. E. Kappeler (ed.), *Police and Society: Touchstone Readings.* Prospect Heights, IL: Waveland Press.

Kelling, G. L., and J. K. Stewart, J. (1989). *Neighborhood and Police: The Maintenance of Civil Authority.* Washington, D.C.: U.S. Department of Justice.

Kelling, G. L., Wasserman, R., and H. Williams (1988). *Police Accountability and Community Policing.* Washington, D.C.: U.S. Department of Justice.

Klockars, C. B. (1986 [1995]). "Street justice: Some micro-moral reservations. Comment on Sykes." In V. E. Kappeler (ed.), *Police and Society: Touchstone Readings.* Prospect Heights, IL: Waveland.

Klockars, C. B. (1988). "The rhetoric of community policing." In J. R. Green, and S. D. Mastrofski (eds.), *Community Policing Rhetoric or Reality.* New York: Praeger.

Koch, W. A. (1971). *Varia Semiotica.* Hildesheim: Olms.

Koch, W. A. (1974). "Tendenzen der Linguistik." In W. A. Koch (ed.), *Perspektiven der Linguistik II.* Stuttgart: Kroner.

Koper, C. S. (1995). "Just enough police presence: Reducing crime and disorderly behavior by optimizing patrol time in crime hot spots." *Justice Quarterly,* 12: 649–72.

Kraska, P. B., and L. Cubellis. (1996). "Paramilitary policing in small town USA: A national study." A paper presented at the annual meeting of the American Society of Criminology in Chicago, IL.

Kraska, P. B., and V. E. Kappeler. (1997). "Militarizing American police: The rise and normalization of paramilitary units." *Social Problems,* 44: 1–18.

Kraska, P. B., and V. E. Kappeler. (1995)." To serve and pursue: Exploring police sexual violence against women." *Justice Quarterly*, 12(1): 85–112.

Kristeva, J. (1969). *Le langage, cet inconnu*. Paris: Seuil.

Kuhn, T. S. (1962). *The Structure of Scientific Revolutions*. Chicago: The University of Chicago Press.

Lambert, J. H. (1764). *Neues Organon oder Gedanken uber die Erforschung und Bezeichnug des Wahren und dessen Unterscheidung vom Irrthum und Schein*. Hildesheim: Olms.

Lefebvre, H. (1991 Eng. Trans.) *The Production of Space*. Oxford: Blackwell.

Levi-Strauss, C. (1958). *Structural Anthropology*. New York: Basic Books.

Locke, J. (1690). *An Essay Concerning Human Understanding*. London: Collins.

Manning, P. K. (1971 [1995]). "The police: Mandate, strategies and appearances." In V. E. Kappeler (ed.) *Police and Society: Touchstone Readings*. Prospect Heights, IL: Waveland Press, pp. 97–126.

Manning, P. K. (1988). "Community policing as a drama of control." In J. R. Green and S. D. Mastrofski (eds) *Community Policing Rhetoric or Reality*. New York: Praeger.

Manning, P. K. (1992 [1995]). "Economic rhetoric and policing reform." In V. E. Kappeler (ed.) *Police and Society: Touchstone Readings*. Prospect Heights, IL: Waveland, pp. 375–92.

Manning, P. K. (1993a). "The preventive conceit: The black box in market context." *American Behavioral Scientist*, 36(5): 639–50.

Manning, P. K. (1993b [1995]). "Violence and symbolic violence." In V. E. Kappeler (ed.) *Police and Society: Touchstone Readings*. Prospect Heights, IL: Waveland.

Manning, P. K. (1994). "The police: Symbolic capital, class and control." In G. S. Bridges and M. A. Myers's (eds.) *Inequity, Crime and Social Control*. Boulder, CO: Westview Press.

Manning, P. K. (1996). "Policing and reflection." *Police Forum*, 7:1–6.

Marenin, O. (1989). "The utility of community needs surveys in community policing." *Police Studies*, 12: 73–81.

Marx, G. T. (1992). "Under-the-covers investigations: Some reflections on the state's use of sex and deception in law enforcement." *Criminal Justice Ethics*, Winter/Spring: 13–24.

Mastrofski, S. (1988). "Community policing reform." In J. Green and S. Mastrofski (eds.) *Community Policing*. New York: Praeger.

Moore, M. H., and G. L. Kelling. (1983). "To serve and protect: learning from police history." *The Public Interest*, 70:49–65.

Moore, M. H., and R. C. Trojanowicz. (1988). *Corporate Strategies for Policing*. Washington, D.C.: U.S. Department of Justice.

Murphy, C. (1988). "The development, impact, and implications of community policing in Canada." In J. R. Green and S. D. Mastrofski (eds.) *Community Policing Rhetoric or Reality*. New York: Praeger.

National Center for Community Policing (1994). *Police Department Community Survey.* East Lansing, MI: Michigan State University.

National Institute of Justice (1996). "Policing drug hot spots." *Research Preview.* Washington, D.C.: National Institute of Justice.

National Institute of Justice (1996a). "Communities: Mobilizing against crime making partnerships work." *National Institute of Justice Journal* (August): 1–56.

Peak, K. (1993). *Policing America: Methods, Issues, Challenges.* Englewood Cliffs, NJ: Prentice Hall.

Piaget, J. (1968). *Structuralism.* London: Routledge and Kegan.

Reiss, A. J. (1993). *A Theory of Police.* Paper presented at the annual meetings of the American Society of Criminology, Phoenix, AZ.

Saussure, F. (1916). *Course in General Linguistics.* New York: McGraw-Hill.

Sherman, L. W., and D. P. Rogan. (1995a). "Effects of gun seizures on gun violence: "Hot spots" patrol in Kansas City." *Justice Quarterly*, 12: 673–710.

Sherman, L. W., and D. P. Rogan. (1995b)." Deterrent effects of police raids on crack houses: A Randomized, controlled experiment." *Justice Quarterly*, 12: 755–81.

Sherman, L. W., and D. Weisburd. (1995). "General deterrent effects of police patrol in crime "hot spots": A randomized control trial." *Justice Quarterly*, 12: 625–48.

Sherman, L. W., Gartin, P. R., and M. E. Buerger. (1989). "Hot spots of predatory crime: Routine activities and the criminology of police." *Criminology*, 27: 27–55.

Skogan, W. (1975). "Public policy and public evaluations of criminal justice system performance." In J. A. Gardiner, and M. A. Mulkey (eds.) *Crime and Criminal Justice.* Lexington, MA: D.C. Heath.

Skolnick, J. H. (1966). *Justice Without Trial: Law Enforcement In A Democratic Society.* New York: John Wiley and Sons.

Sparrow, M. K. (1988) *Implementing Community Policing,* Perspectives on Policing 9, Washington, D.C.: National Institute of Justice and Harvard University.

Stedman, J. (1992). "Taking a closer look at gangs." *Problem Solving Quarterly*, 5(1): 11–17.

Strecher, V. G. (1991 [1995]). "Revising the histories and futures of policing." In V. E. Kappeler. (ed.) *Police and Society: Touchstone Readings.* Prospect Heights, IL: Waveland Press, pp. 69–82.

Sykes, G. (1986 [1995]). "Street justice: A moral defense of order maintenance policing." In V. E. Kappeler (ed.) *Police and Society: Touchstone Readings.* Prospect Heights, IL: Waveland.

Tempe Police Department (1993). *Innovative Neighborhood Oriented Policing Program.* Tempe, AZ: City of Tempe.

Trojanowicz, R. C., and B. Bucqueroux. (1990). *Community Policing.* Cincinnati, OH: Anderson.

Tzu, L. (1963 Eng. Trans.) *Tao Te Ching*. London: Penguin Books.

Walker, S. (1983 [1995]). "Broken windows and fractured history: The use and misuse of history in recent police patrol analysis." In V. E. Kappeler (ed.) *Police and Society: Touchstone Readings*. Prospect Heights, IL: Waveland Press.

Walker, S. (1992). *The Police in America, (2nd Ed.)*. New York: McGraw-Hill.

Wallace, H., Roberson, C., and C. Steckler. (1995). *Fundamentals of Police Administration*. Englewood Cliffs, NJ: Prentice Hall.

Williams, F. P., and C. P. Wagoner. (1992). "Making the police proactive: An impossible task for improbable reasons." In V. E. Kappeler (ed.) *Police and Society: Touchstone Readings*. Prospect Heights, IL: Waveland Press, pp. 365–74.

Wilson, J. Q., and G. L. Kelling. (1982). "Broken windows: Police and neighborhood safety." *Atlantic Monthly*, 249 (March):29–38.

Mary Bosworth

9

AGENCY AND CHOICE IN WOMEN'S PRISONS: TOWARD A CONSTITUTIVE PENOLOGY[1]

> We need to make a space for an understanding of self-identity and
> autonomy which will not clash with our conviction that individu-
> als must be understood as embedded, embodied, localized, consti-
> tuted, and fragmented, as well as subject to forces beyond our con-
> trol. We need to understand ourselves clearly as actors capable of
> learning, of changing, of making the world and ourselves better
> (Weir, 1995: 263).

Introduction

Issues of agency and choice have long been central to discussions in
critical and social theory (Carr, 1961; Berlin, 1969; Bourdieu, 1977;
Giddens, 1984; 1991). Such literature seeks to understand the paradox that individuals constantly produce and reproduce the social
world, despite being profoundly restricted by large-scale inequalities
in power relations and in the distribution of economic, educational
and health resources. In the words of Anthony Giddens, "human
agents never passively accept external conditions of action, but more
or less continuously reflect upon them and reconstitute them in light
of their particular circumstances" (Giddens, 1991: 175). That is to say,
power relations are rarely entirely fixed, and instead there is often
some potential for resistance. Most recently, agency, identity and
choice have been the focus of feminist theory and identity politics, as

scholars working in these overlapping fields have sought to identify the specific ways in which gender and race define both the choices and the evaluative framework open to individuals (I. M. Young, 1990; Calhoun, 1994; 1995; Benhabib, 1992; Bordo, 1993; Braidotti, 1994). According to this contemporary literature, our identity is formed as a result both of expressions of individual agency, and in reaction to various forms of social control. The reflexive relationship between who we are and the choices we have is contingent upon our evaluation of those choices. It is, therefore, possible to fashion acts of resistance, from positions of weakness.

Clearly, such questions about the capacity of individuals to act, and their ability to enact power, while simultaneously being disempowered and vulnerable, may shed much light on the experience of imprisonment. Yet, traditionally—and despite the theoretical work of Michel Foucault (1979), David Garland (1990) and Adrian Howe (1994)—such questions of power and agency have been under-theorized within criminological studies of the prison (Sparks, Bottoms and Hay, 1996: Chapter 2).[2] Instead, there has been a marked distinction between theoretical, historical studies of punishment, and contemporary, empirical studies of imprisonment. In this essay I shall attempt to bridge this gap by outlining elements of what could be thought of as a "constitutive penology" (Milovanovic and Henry, 1991). Specifically, I shall analyse the ways in which incarcerated women perceive themselves to be "agents" and the values which they attach to this self-image. While much of women's energy in prison is directed at maintaining their self-identity as active and participating agents, there is inevitable erosion of the women's sense of self by institutional constraints. As I shall demonstrate, such changes to the women's sense of self are related to diffuse "regimes of femininity" operating within the establishments which are reinforced by the women's life experiences of poverty, violence and abuse. Thus, my analysis builds on what has largely been a theoretical inquiry in the emerging field of constitutive criminology (Milovanovic and Henry, 1991; Arrigo, 1993; Henry and Milovanovic, 1994; 1996), through an exploration of the practical implications of a "constitutive view [that] sees human subjects as active agents producing a dynamic social world which simultaneously produces them as both social and individual agents and as both active and passive identities" (Henry and Milovanovic, 1996: 36–37). By exploring the contingent nature of women's agency in the context of broader societal discourses of femininity and gender, I hope to suggest directions for the development of a transformative critique of the role and effect of prisons today.

Drawing on research conducted in three women's prisons in England during 1995–96, I shall discuss how power is negotiated by women in prison. As is well documented in sociological studies of women's imprisonment, the regulation of female prisoners takes a specific, gendered form which relies upon the employment of conventional ideals of passive, feminine behavior (Carlen, 1983, 1985; Eaton, 1993; Faith, 1993; Worrall, 1990; Sommers, 1995). Traditional ideals of femininity are clearly inherent in the employment and education offered in women's prisons. Such activities typically include sewing, cooking, cleaning, and "mothercraft". The women's capacity for autonomy is further regulated or reduced by high levels of medication[3] and by frequent punishment for petty infractions of prison rules and regulations (Genders and Player, 1987; Carlen, 1990; Sim, 1990: chapter 7; Player, 1994). Femininity thus appears as both the goal and the form of women's imprisonment.

Nonetheless, most women strive to resist, subverting and challenging aspects of the hegemonic notion of passive femininity promoted by the institution. Their resistance occurs in a variety of ways, including religious, cultural or ethnic practices, lesbian activity, education, and the idealization of motherhood. Although each of these approaches cannot free women from the prison—as the women remain restricted by the boundaries of the daily regimes and by the prison walls—they are each an expression of agency, and one which is possible despite the rigours of confinement. They illustrate that the ability to be an agent transcends the range of choices available, and rests on other, more diffuse, elements which are embedded in the material and symbolic world of the community in which the prison is situated.

In order to highlight the specificity of women's experiences of imprisonment, I shall draw on contemporary feminist theory for an appreciation of the gendered nature of agency and choice. Despite numerous divisions within the literature, most commonly represented in the debates for and against "difference" or "essentialism" (hooks, 1980; Gilligan, 1982; Eisenstein and Jardine, 1985; Irigaray, 1985a; 1985b; Spivak, 1994; Fuss, 1989; Wittig, 1978; Benhabib, 1992; Schor and Weed, 1994; Weir, 1995, 1996; I. M.Young, 1990), feminist accounts of identity politics and agency are unified by a conception of power as gendered, contextualised and relational rather than universal. According to many feminists, a subject is not a fixed *a priori* "being," but is rather "a process of material (institutional) and discursive (symbolic) practices" (Braidotti, 1994: 99). Who we are is a result of practical lived experiences, such as wealth and education, which interact with complex, dispersed, ideas and "stories" or narratives (which are both told to us and which we tell to ourselves) about masculinity, femininity, ethnicity and sexuality. I contend that this literature on identity enables criminologists to discuss the prisoners both as "women," who are subject to restrictive expectations of appropriate feminine behavior, and as "women in prison," who are circumscribed by a particular context which itself is influenced by beliefs about punishment, responsibility, agency and choice.

Considering the relationship between choice and agency through an appreciation of identity politics demonstrates the effects of difference upon women's experience of imprisonment. For women in prison are not a unified group. They divide among themselves according to ethnicity, nationality, crime, sexuality and age. Little research has documented the effect of these elements upon the configuration of power in prison. In particular, although it has been made clear that "race" impacts significantly upon the likelihood of being sentenced to imprisonment (Irwin and Austin, 1994: 4–5), and that it has an effect on the relationships formed inside prison (Carroll, 1974; Genders and Player, 1989), it remains somewhat marginalised in prison studies (although see Richie, 1996: Introduction; Díaz-Cotto, 1996).[4] Not only does a consideration of difference problematize prison studies, it may introduce new life into a field which has been increasingly hijacked in popular discourse by a simplistic and reactionary concern with law and order (DiIulio, 1987). A discussion of agency, that can take into account socio-economic and cultural experiences should enable critical criminologists to challenge the dominant instrumental approach to prison studies. By focusing on the relationship between the symbolic and material effects of imprisonment, rather than re-working questions of its "failure" or "success" we may move beyond a concern with "what works," in which prison studies have been mired since the 1970s (Martinson, 1974). As a result, it may become possible to articulate the numerous ways in which the prison reinforces unequal (gender and race) power relations throughout society.

Methodology: Doing Time

The three English penal institutions included in my research differed significantly in their security levels and in their inmate[5] population, yet each offered similar work and education. HMP/YOI Drake Hall, which was the first prison visited, holds up to 250 women of all ages from 16 years old, with a majority of the women serving first time, short sentences. It is an "open prison," with minimum security, large grounds, spacious new accommodation, and ample resources. In contrast, HM Remand Centre Pucklechurch—which has since been closed—held 88 women, either unconvicted and awaiting trial, or convicted and awaiting sentence. At the time of this research the women were regularly locked in their cells for 23 hours a day. None of the cells had integral sanitation, and as a result there was much complaint and high tension levels among those incarcerated.[6] The third prison included in the study, was the Women's Annex at HMP Winchester. It is a small high-security "privilege" unit attached to a local men's prison[7] with a capacity for 66 adult women serving long sentences. Women are supposed to be screened before being sent to Winchester since it is not meant to accept prisoners on medication, or with a history of drugs or violence in prison. It had only been in operation for nine months when I went there and it held a disproportionate number of drug offenders and foreign national prisoners.

During the prison fieldwork, each component of which lasted from three to six weeks, I combined semi-structured questionnaires with participant observation to develop a feminist, qualitative-research style. Feminists perceive a relationship between knowledge and power in which knowledge is both gendered and potentially transformative (Cain, 1986; Smart, 1989; Fine, 1992; Griffiths, 1995). Moreover, feminists from all disciplines have been particularly vocal in their criticism of traditional modes of positivistic research in the social and natural sciences and have proposed the development of new and specifically feminist methods which would be less hierarchical and more gender sensitive (see Cain, 1986, Gelsthorpe, 1990, 1992; Harding, 1987; Reinharz, 1992; Stanley and Wise, 1993). Yet, because of the diversity of solutions offered, it remains controversial whether it is even possible to speak of such a phenomenon as "feminist methodology," or whether instead there are as many methodologies as feminists.[8]

Overall I formally interviewed 52 women using a semi-structured questionnaire. The interviews were conversational rather than formal, to encourage the prisoners' input. The women ranged in age from 18 to 58, and their sentences from six months to life imprisonment. Interviews varied in time, from 45 minutes to three hours, with some women interviewed more than once. The qualitative methods I used reflected a combination of theoretical reading and reflexive, situation-based reaction. Interviewing was easiest in Drake Hall, where I was present in the prison for the longest period of time, and managed to build the greatest rapport with staff and prisoners alike. Because it was an "open" prison, the women had much more freedom to come to meetings and group discussions. As a result I was able to pursue a greater variety of techniques for gathering information there, than at either of the two other institutions. In contrast, research in Pucklechurch was extremely restricted because I could only talk to the women for the brief periods of time in which they were out of their cells. Individual tape-recorded interviews were impossible since there was no private space to interview the women and so I had to rely on note taking. Finally, in Winchester, all discussions were conducted in just one wing of the prison, on the education block, due to the difficulty of maneuvering within a high security prison without possession of keys.

Agency and Choice in Women's Prisons

Despite a number of material differences between the establishments, which were generally related to security classification and inmate population, in each prison the women were all trenchant in their criticism of the range of choices available to them in education and work activities. Paid work was limited to industrial sewing, cleaning, gardens and kitchens, and education was focused mainly upon remedial skills, typing, sewing, cooking, and hairdressing. There were almost no opportunities for gaining any qualifications outside of the hairdressing and typing courses, and so most women left prison as unskilled as they arrived. Eleanor[9] thus spoke for many when she bleakly said "Because I am in prison, I have no choices."

Although they complained most commonly about their lack of choices, the women in prison were also quick to criticize those choices that were made available on the basis of race and gender, indicating that choice was valued not simply because of quantity, but also in terms of quality. They were concerned with what kinds of activity and opportunities the prison could provide. Thus, groups of women bemoaned the fact aspects of "choice":

> **Eleanor:**   The choice is so old-fashioned, you know what I mean . . .
>
> **Zora:** Yeah, yeah . . .
>
> **Eleanor:**   As if all women just want to sew, cook and clean . . .
>
> **Bell:**   Iron, wash clothes, why can't they have mechanical, or carpentry . . . I'd do that.
>
> **Eleanor:**   Do some silk painting . . . !
>
> **Mary:**   Although do some of the women like it?
>
> **Eleanor:**   Of course some of the women like it! But, . . .
>
> **Zora:**   The majority don't.
>
> **Eleanor:**   A lot of women like different things as well.

There was sustained criticism of the scope of choices for inmates from minority ethnic groups, as the activities offered neglected to differentiate between needs and expectations of women from different backgrounds. The absence of minority staff members, and the failure of any of the prisons to provide work and education options designed to meet specific needs and desires of inmates from different ethnic groups were particularly resented. Thus, an Afro-Caribbean woman in Drake Hall argued that the already limited choices were compounded for women of color, who made up a significant proportion of the prison population. For, according to Zora:

> The only thing you could possibly say that you could come out of here and get a job with is possibly hairdressing and in there they don't cater for Afro-Caribbean hair. So basically, there's no point of anyone from an ethnic group even trying.

However, the effect of ethnicity on the women's experience of imprisonment was far from uniform (see Rice, 1990: 63). The intersection of race, class and nationality prevents any simple discussion of choice and oppression for minority women in prison, since they did not constitute a homogenous group (see Schwartz and Milovanovic,

1996, especially Chapter 3). In fact, prisoners often formed intimate friendships among themselves based on age and region rather than just on race, as women from the same housing estates or urban areas often already knew each other or had shared similar experiences on the outside. As a result, among the British born women, the significance of racial difference appeared to be more dependent upon class relations, rather than on a unitary sense of shared racial oppression. Indeed, women of different ethnic groups, from similar areas in London, were more likely to share horizons of evaluation than a group of Black women from different classes and nations. Thus, for example, I witnessed a heated discussion between a group of black women from Nigeria, Jamaica and Britain who were disputing the propriety of a Nigerian woman to curtsey to the officers. While Maya explained her actions as a form of self-affirmation, because, as she said, it "shows my identity," the other women felt that her actions were dangerous as they were generalised by the officers to reinforce racist stereotypes about "uncivilized," "simple" black women. In this instance, many elements were apparent in the women's evaluation of their prison experience, and in their condemnation of Maya's actions. Most importantly, the dispute cannot be interpreted without consideration of the women's lives outside the prison. For Maya not only belonged to a different nationality, she also belonged to a different class. Thus, her frame of evaluation, the reasons she gave for her actions, and her perceptions of her choices, were drawn from a life extremely unlike those of the other three women.

Another group of black women who held very different evaluative frameworks from the black British women, were the foreign nationals who were imprisoned for importation of drugs. As the "war on drugs" expands across the Western world, an increasing number of foreign women—who are typically from developing nations—are incarcerated in the prisons of England and Wales (Rice, 1990: 61; Hudson, 1993: 17). They are often arrested at the airport when they enter Britain, and are typically given long sentences, which may be supplemented once they are deported home again. Typically, their cases are tragic and their crimes often in response to dire economic need, or to threats of violence. For example, I was introduced to a woman from Colombia who had agreed to smuggle cocaine into Britain in a bid to prevent the execution of her son by the militia. According to the Roman Catholic chaplain, Julia failed in her attempt, and as a result, her son was killed.[10] Another woman, from Nigeria, was facing an eight year sentence. Recently widowed, Audre had been coerced into smuggling by a money lender, to support her seven children. The children ranged in age from two years to 18, and now had no adult to provide for or look after them. Clearly, these women—who are further disabled by limited language ability in English—have other needs, and would thus like to make different choices from the majority of the prison population. Thus, for example, despite objectively having much better material benefits at her disposal in English prisons, Audre was seeking to be deported to Lagos so that she could be visited by her children. In particular, these women from developing nations require financial assistance in order to send money back to their families. Yet, to my knowledge, only one prison—HMP/YOI Styal near Manchester—recognizes this need, and employs many of its foreign nationals in higher paying piecework, encouraging them to continue to support their families in their country of origin.[11]

Thus, while choice clearly is curtailed in prison, opportunities are not restricted evenly. For women of color and other "minority" groups, including lesbians and the religiously devout, choices are further restricted. While some conservatives may argue that prison ought to reduce opportunities on the basis of retribution or managerialism (Di-Iulio, 1987), few would be entirely sanguine about inconsistency in such choice reduction. Moreover, if there are familiar axes along which opportunities diminish—such as class, race and sexuality—then it may be possible to use literature outside of criminology to appreciate the negotiation of power in prisons. In the words of Milovanovic and Henry, criminologists may then hope to show that the "discursively structured routine of prison life, and the meaning of being in prison, must be understood in relation to various and often contradictory discursive practices that sustain, oppose, and attempt to replace them" (Milovanovic and Henry, 1991: 205). In other words, an appreciation of difference may reveal greater oppression as well as new possibilities for resistance.

According to the women, lesbian relationships were fairly common among the inmate community, yet there was no official recognition of them. Although potentially a form of resistance—since lesbian relationships were an infringement of prison rules, sexuality divides the inmate community. Some prisoners, like Luce, enjoyed the opportunity to form intimate relationships with other women: "I would say that in all my life I have never been as close to anyone as I have been in here, because I've never lived with a girl before." Yet, many heterosexual women were extremely critical of any lesbian activity, either because of prejudice or for the more "everyday" reasons that lovers quarrel or are affectionate in ways which impinge on the privacy of others. While the prisons formally condemned any sexual intimacy between the women, more commonly officers "turned a blind eye," unless they felt that an older woman was "enticing" young offenders. Thus, lesbianism in prison was met with an official silence analogous to that in the broader community (Wittig, 1992). As a mode of public resistance, lesbianism was, therefore, muted. However, in terms of facilitating the construction of a private realm of emotions and sexual intimacy, it may have been more successful.

A final quality which divided the inmate community, but which also provided the possibility of resistance, was religion. Women from religious groups other than the three official ones of the prison service—Catholic, Anglican, and Methodist—often found it difficult to practice their faith. Such restrictions were somewhat dependent upon race and ethnicity. Thus, for example, Hester, who was a white convert to Islam, was treated with cynical disbelief, yet was largely left alone to practice her faith as she wished. In contrast, an Egyptian Muslim, Nawal, was characterized by the staff as a "fundamentalist" and a "troublemaker." Despite being a soft-spoken, educated, and thoroughly conservative woman, Nawal was perceived as a threat to the good order and discipline of the unit. Hester managed to negotiate a relatively uncontroversial expression of her religion as long as she was prepared to accept the patronizing attitude of staff, while Nawal was in a weakened physical condition because the prison was refusing her Halal meals. Rather than accept Kosher food as did Hester, Nawal was engaged in a protracted, direct confrontation to obtain all the elements she required to practice her faith.

Difference in sexuality, religion, ethnicity, and nationality, has little place in prison. Yet, women in prison constantly endeavored to resist the restrictions placed upon them by their limited choices. They rarely endorsed or practiced the *passive* feminine behavior encouraged by the establishment. They did not aspire to homogeneity. They did valorize aspects of an idealized femininity. Very few of these women wished to break with a binary gender order (Butler, 1990). Indeed, they drew much of their strength, agency, resistance and sense of self, from their roles outside as mothers, wives, girlfriends and daughters. Consequently, in their bid for autonomy and control, women often did not radically challenge the goals encouraged by the prison. Rather, they reinterpreted the goals of femininity as positive attributes of the women's lives in the community. For as Olympia and Patricia complained:

Olympia: They treat us like children.

Patricia: But the thing is, they don't realize that the majority of us have got children out there. You know, we cook and we clean, we run homes when we're out there, we've got families, we live just the same as everybody else. You know, it just happens to be unfortunate that we are in this position. For some of us yeah, for others no. You know? It's like they treat us like we don't know anything. Like we didn't go to school. Like we don't know how to do this or that.

This slippage, between the goals of the institution, and the self-identity of the women, reveals a contradictory effect of the idealized femininity which underpins much of the daily routine of women's prisons. Discourses of femininity produce the possibility of resistance, at the same time as they firmly bind women in a position of weakness.[12] As a result, a central "effect"[13] of women's imprisonment is the construction of not just a "disciplined," "docile" or "law-abiding" self, but a *feminine identity* (Carlen, 1983; Howe, 1994). However, a single, uniform representation of femininity was not produced. Rather, in a manner akin to that proposed by Judith Butler (1990) in her work on the subversion of gender identity, women were able to construct competing feminine identities, or "gender performativity," through which they resisted some of the disempowering effects of imprisonment.

Central to much of their resistance, yet also integrally tied to an idealization of femininity, was a valorization of "motherhood." Thus, for example, Patricia who is cited above, was a young Black woman, very critical of imprisonment. While the separation from her child clearly brought Patricia much pain, being able to identify herself as a "mother" appeared to give her strength as it provided an identity which was embedded both materially and symbolically outside the prison. However, women's appeal to the symbolic power of femininity through the idealization of motherhood could not stand alone as a form of resistance. Rather, their success in resistance was dependant upon socio-economic factors. For example, Audre's identity as "mother," with seven children back in Nigeria, was almost entirely defined by her limited economic and geographical circumstances.

LIVERPOOL JOHN MOORES UNIVERSITY
LEARNING SERVICES

Therefore, their identity as "woman" intersected with many other factors, including nationality, race, class, sexual orientation and age. As a result, the women did not represent a uniform image of hegemonic femininity. Rather, they displayed many variations on a theme and, in their variety, managed to challenge some of the restrictions of the universalizing effects of imprisonment. While their identity as "women in prison" was constituted by the closed walls of the prison, their alternative interpretations of the meaning of the material and symbolic choices open to them provided the possibility of resistance. Consequently, their potential for "agency" was located within the possibility of a variation in their repeated performance of their identity as "women in prison" (Butler, 1990: 145). Despite the numerous and apparently overwhelming limitations which were fundamental to their prison sentences, the women I spoke to typically saw themselves as interacting and shaping their daily lives in prison. As Sylvia said: "I mean you know what girls in prison are like—they will go and have their say. Sometimes it gets them somewhere, and sometimes it don't."

The women generally were not afraid to make demands on the staff, particularly if the demands related to life-style issues in prison. Despite the undeniable restrictions they faced, most women saw themselves as rational, responsible agents. Accordingly, in their public negotiation of power, they often endeavored to present themselves as individuals with rights and deserving of justice and fair play. Thus, for example, Angela—who was typical of a number of the women in prison, in that she had never finished high school,[14] and had been in frequent contact with the law—claimed that: "I don't wrong them, or hate no officer . . . but there are certain times when they try to take their little liberties with you, and I don't care, I will stand up for myself to the fullness, even if I have to go down to the block if I believe in something."

In this instance, Angela appealed to an ideal of the active, autonomous subject, who is self-sufficient and strong. She believed that she was the bearer of rights, and so should not have to endure officers "taking liberties" with her. She also perceived herself to be fair and just, since she did not "wrong" or "hate" the staff. Her words were echoed by many other women in diverse situations. Like Angela, Simone presented herself as a fair and sober judge of character. However, her example demonstrates the limited success of such a presentation of self. Thus, she spoke of a time when, having arrived at a new prison, she was located on a wing which she found unacceptable:

LIVERPOOL JOHN MOORES UNIVERSITY
LEARNING SERVICES

I said to one of the officers, I said—how I felt basically was that I was dying inside, literally dying inside, and I thought if this goes on for any substantial time I'll die. I might be there in the flesh, but I certainly wouldn't be there in spirit. And it was frightening, to think it was going to destroy me, and that's when I told an officer that "I've got to get put off this house, if I get put down the block, if I have to hit an officer, I will put myself down a block and be isolated, rather than put up with this." And so I said that to her, "I am dying inside, and you must get me off this house."

Simone's example demonstrates the women's limited ability to rely on a rights-based idea of justice in prison. Although initially appealing to a spirit of humanity, and good will in the officer, Simone ultimately invoked the "spirit of Leviathan" and the stereotype of prisoners being menacing, potentially violent individuals. Notwithstanding women's desire to be perceived as responsible individuals with all the rights that entails, their identity as "inmates" constantly worked against them. Ultimately, therefore, they often invoked other self-images to achieve their ends. In particular, they often provided relief on stereotypes of femininity.

Issues of femininity played an important role in the a dispute in the last prison I visited, where the women complained about the distribution of extremely rough toilet paper—which they likened to tracing paper—until it was replaced with more acceptable material. This small-scale dispute is perhaps typical of the types of problems in many prisons. In their dispute, the women utilized a series of different approaches, each of which represented a diverse mode of resistance. First they complained about their "rights": they were entitled to appropriate toilet paper. However, the staff ignored this approach. Then, the women attempted to steal the remaining provisions, which the staff were using. Yet, this approach was risky, since being caught with toilet paper resulted in extra days on their sentences. Then, a number of prisoners attempted to incite a collective demonstration against the authorities. This attempt was also unsuccessful, because too few women agreed to participate. Finally, the women mobilized the medicalized and pathologized image of women as biologically dependent, in order to challenge authority (Sim, 1990: Chapter 6; Ussher, 1991). Specifically, they complained about the inadequacy of the paper for menstruating women, or for women with thrush, or women with hemorrhoids. In this, successful bid for change, women confronted the

LIVERPOOL JOHN MOORES UNIVERSITY
Aldham Robarts L.R.C.
TEL 051 231 3701/2624

senior staff directly, thereby taking control of images which are typically seen to oppress women. Thus, as Sylvia said:

> The governor's away at the moment, but when he comes back I'm going straight into his office, and I'm going to say: "I don't know if anyone's put it to you Sir, with you being a man, but when girls have got piles, thrush, and are on their period, they can't use this hard toilet paper. So you're going to have to do something about it." And hopefully he will understand.

Clearly the women value and promote self-images of control and participation. These images are used to combat the "pains of imprisonment" and to structure relationships with other prisoners. Yet, the prisoners' images of themselves as active, reasoning agents is constantly under assault from institutional constraints which encourage them to exhibit traditional, passive, feminine behavior at the same time as denying them independent identities and responsibilities as real mothers, wives, girlfriends, and sisters. They must, therefore, negotiate discourses which valorize traditional, passive forms of femininity—epitomized by the work and education typically offered by establishments—as well as those which encourage autonomy, agency, responsibility—found, for instance, in the valorization of motherhood. As we have seen the women evaluate their choices through a framework which is embedded in their social relationships and in their ethnic and cultural identities outside the prison. Consequently, the women's ability to resist the strains of imprisonment do not rest entirely upon the choices which prison makes available to them. Rather, women resist through enacting diverse images of femininity that, in their variety, subvert the dominant image of white heterosexuality advocated by the prison and idealized in the community. The diversity of the women in prison, "implies that ["women in prison" are] open to formations that are not fully constrained in advance" (Butler, 1995: 135) and, thus, that there is the possibility of change and resistance.

Conclusion: Beyond a Community of Victims

That incarceration limits choices and opportunities for self-expression is obvious. For many proponents of incarceration, such restrictions are undoubtedly endorsed. It is part of the meaning and expectation of a sentence of imprisonment that certain elements of social life—most obviously, freedom of movement, freedom of choice and liberty—are curtailed. Indeed, the rhetorical power of components of the notion "freedom" is clearly acknowledged, and frequently invoked, by the inmate community, through such claims as: *"they can take my liberty, but they can't take my smile"* (Christobel, HM Remand Centre Pucklechurch, November 1995), or *"they can take my freedom of speech, but they can't stop me thinking"* (Olympia, HM Winchester, February 1996).[15] Thus, it is to be expected that imprisonment undermines people's capacity for autonomy and disqualifies individuals from making decisions about how to conduct their own lives.[16] Such reduction of choice and autonomy has long been understood as one of the key "pains of imprisonment" (Sykes, 1958; Morris and Morris, 1963). The complaints made by women in my research echo many other voices of the confined:

> **Eleanor:**   I didn't realize when I come into prison exactly what it meant having your freedom taken away from you. Now I realize what it means, . . . and that's what happens here. Everything is out of your control, when you eat, when you sleep, what you can buy, what you can wear, . . .
>
> **Virginia:**   Who you can see.
>
> **Eleanor:**   Who you can see
>
> **Virginia:**   When you can see them . . .
>
> **Eleanor:**   Yeah. It's all taken out of your hands, having no money in your pocket, restricted to this little area. You know, only having women to talk to. I didn't realize what it meant until you're here, and then you realize what it means. And the worst thing about it, is that it's out of your control.

However, as this essay has revealed, the limitation of choices and the restrictions of autonomy in prison are not absolute, nor are they distributed equally. Rather, power relations are constantly negotiated in prisons as women are not always compliant, nor are they uniformly passive. Like most prisoners, their non-compliance typically takes the form of low-level verbal challenges to the authority of the officers and to the validity of the regime. More specifically, a number of complex symbolic acts and representations, which constitute an alternative self-identity to the *passive* femininity encouraged by the institution, intersect with and enable the practical, verbal, resistance of women in prison. As a consequence, much of their energy is directed at maintaining a self-image as active and participating agents. As Germaine said to me:

> Women are women. Women will never go along with a rule or regulation at all. They question everything. If they can't have something, it's "why can't I have it?" "What do you mean I can't have it?" Then they come back—"can I have it?" No. Women will always question life in general, really.

Examining women's testimonies about how prison has changed their sense of identity helps to destablize the seeming immutability of the treatment of women in prison. It restores agency to a community of women who have traditionally been described in universalizing, pathologizing terms as "mad," "bad," or just sexually deviant (Ward and Kassebaum, 1965; Giallombardo, 1966). It also helps to show the finer details of the effects of imprisonment, and to demonstrate the conflicting ways that regimes of femininity both undermine and bolster the women's sense of identity. In this way, "constitutive penology" may encourage suggestions for reconstructive, or transformative ways of understanding women's imprisonment (Milovanovic and Henry, 1991). According to such an approach, the women are crucially involved in the construction of daily prison life, and thus are able to subvert it. By focusing on the relationship between identity and agency, the constitutive criminologist may be better placed to imagine alternatives to the current arrangements. For, as the women themselves recognized, there were many more alternative possible choices and expressions of agency than those which are commonly conceptualized in penal practice and analysis, if only the women were to be considered as agents:

> **Eleanor:**   I don't think the choices are broad enough, and I don't think the choices are in the right things . . . you know, when you look at the facts at what type of women are in prison, a lot of the women who are in prison, about 99 percent of them have been sexually abused—either raped or sexually abused . . .
>
> **Zora:**   Mentally unstable basically . . .

Eleanor: But not mentally unstable. It's women who, through their experience, what's happened to them they could become counselors. They could become drug counselors, rape counselors . . .

Bell: It's true, it's true . . .

Eleanor: Child abuse counselors . . .

Betty: Something that they know about . . . turn the tables on their bad experiences . . .

Bell: Cos judges, they've never had any experience of offending, they all come from well-off families, they've never been skint, so if someone . . .

Eleanor: . . . Probation officers, all of those types of jobs. A lot of the women would be more than capable of doing them.

Notes

1. An earlier version of this article was presented at the American Society of Criminology Meeting at Chicago, November 1996. I would like to thank Anthony Gerbino and Richard and Michal Bosworth for their comments on earlier drafts of this article.

2. Although see Cohen and Taylor, 1972 and more recently Sparks, Bottoms, and Hay, 1996 for studies of male imprisonment which have explored the contingency of negotiations of power in maximum secure establishments using social theory.

3. The women interviewed condemned the actions and practices of the prison medical service and provided multiple examples both of the enforcement of abrupt "cold turkey" from illicit drugs, and described much unnecessary prescription of a variety of pharmaceutical drugs in favor of treatment or counseling. For more discussion of the medicalization of women in prison, see Carlen, 1985; Padel and Stevenson, 1988 and Sim, 1990: Chapter 6. See Maden, 1996 for an opposing point of view.

4. See more generally, Cook and Hudson, 1993 for a discussion of "racism and criminology," and Schwartz and Milovanovic, 1996 for a recent criminological analysis of the intersection between race, gender and class.

5. I use this word advisedly, despite its pejorative and paternalist implications, as it was a term by which the women designated themselves.

6. At least one of the reasons for the frequent "bang-up" was an extremely high staff sickness rate which was perceived by many to be related to the fact that no jobs were guaranteed once Pucklechurch was relocated to the new, purpose built facility, nearby Eastwood Park. As it happens, the new facility—which was designed to service the South-West Region of England and Wales for convicted women and those on remand—has been dogged by bad publicity as it has been found to have under-size beds on which many women cannot fit, and cramped cells (HMCIP, 1996).

7. In the prison system of England and Wales, local men's prisons function as points of entry to the male penal estate. Here men are classified and then sent out to other prisons depending on their security classification. Each local prison also houses some inmates for longer periods in order to fulfill essential tasks like kitchen duties and grounds. The only women's prison which approximates a local prison is Holloway Prison in London which acts as a sorting pool for large parts of Southern England and Wales.

8. See the debate in *Sociology*, 1992, between Hammersley, Ramanazoglu and Gelsthorpe, for a concise summary of the debate over the constitution of a feminist methodology.

9. The women have all been renamed in order to protect their anonymity. They have been given names of famous feminist authors. This choice is purely polemical on my part, and is not meant to imply that all of the women described themselves as feminists—although some did. In order to reflect the racial and ethnic mix of the respondents, the women of color have been allocated names of feminists of color.

10. This interview was conducted through the priest, since Julia spoke extremely limited English and I do not speak Spanish.

11. I understand from my interviews that HMP Cookham Wood in the South-East also runs special programs for its foreign national women.

12. In terms of traditional prison sociology, the women were more akin to Mathiesen's "disrupted" inmate population (1965: 122–136) than Sykes' (1958) "cohesively oriented" one.

13. Here I am referring to Foucault's notion of "effect" and the disciplined self (Foucault, 1979, 1991), both of which are issues which need to be considered in terms of gender (Howe, 1994).

14. Due in large part to a learning difficulty which was only belatedly identified in prison.

15. See Foucault, 1979: 231–256 for a discussion of the symbolic role played by the prison in reinforcing the ideal of liberty. See Brown, 1995 for

analysis of the profound symbolic and material power of "freedom" in modern consciousness and social organisation.

16. This paradox, in which this denial of individual agency then places the prison, was famously described by penal reformer Alexander Patterson when he declaimed "It is impossible to train men for freedom in a condition of captivity" (cited in King and Morgan, 1980: 2).

References

Arrigo, B. (1993). *Madness, Language and the Law*. Albany, NY: Harrow and Heston.

Benhabib, S. (1992). *Situating the Self: Gender, Community and Postmodernism in Contemporary Ethics*. Cambridge, UK: Polity Press.

Berlin, I. (1969). *Four Essays on Liberty*. Oxford: Oxford University Press.

Bordo, S. (1993). *Unbearable Weight: Feminism, Western Culture and the Body*. Berkeley, CA: University of California Press.

Bourdieu, P. (1977). *Outline of a Theory of Practice*. Cambridge: Cambridge University Press.

Braidotti, R. (1994). *Nomadic Subjects: Embodiment and Sexual Difference in Contemporary Feminist Theory*. New York: Columbia University Press.

Brown, W. (1995). *States of Injury: Power and Freedom in Late Modernity*. Princeton, NJ: Princeton University Press.

Butler, J. (1990). *Gender Trouble: Feminism and the Subversion of Identity*. New York: Routledge.

Butler, J. (1995). "Contingent foundations: Feminism and the question of 'postmodernism.'" In L. Nicholson (Ed.), *Feminist Contentions: A Philosophical Exchange*. New York: Routledge.

Cain, M. (1986). "Realism, feminism, methodology and law," *International Journal of the Sociology of Law*, 14: 255–267.

Calhoun, C. (Ed.). (1994). *Social Theory and the Politics of Identity*. New York: Blackwell.

Calhoun, C. (1995). *Critical Social Theory: Culture, History and the Challenge of Difference*. Oxford: Blackwell.

Carlen, P. (1983). *Women's Imprisonment: A Study in Social Control*. London: Routledge and Kegan Paul.

Carlen, P. (Ed.). (1985). *Criminal Women: Autobiographical Accounts*. Cambridge, U.K.: Polity Press.

Carlen, P. (1990). *Alternatives to Women's Imprisonment*. Milton Keynes, U.K.: Open University Press.

Carr, E. H. (1961). *What is History?* Harmondsworth, U.K.: Penguin.

Carroll, L. (1974). *Hacks, Blacks and Cons*. Lexington, KY: D.C. Heath and Company.

Cook, D., and B. Hudson. (Eds.), (1993). *Racism and Criminology*. London: Sage Publications.

Diaz-Cotto, J. (1996). *Gender, Ethnicity and the State: Latina and Latino Prison Politics*. Albany, NY: SUNY Press.

DiIulio, Jr., J. J. (1987). *Governing Prisons: A Comparative Study of Correctional Management*. New York: Free Press.

Eaton, M. (1993). *Women After Prison*. Buckingham: Open University Press.

Eisenstein, H., and A. Jardine. (Eds.), (1985). *The Future of Difference*. New Brunswick, NJ: Rutgers University Press.

Faith, K. (1993). *Unruly Women: The Politics of Confinement and Resistance*. Vancouver: Press Gang Publishers.

Fine, M. (1992). *Disruptive Voices: The Possibility of Feminist Research*. Ann Arbor: The University of Michigan Press.

Foucault, M. (1979). *Discipline and Punish: The Birth of the Prison*. Harmondsworth, UK: Penguin Books.

Foucault, M. (1991). "Governmentality". In G. Burchell, C. Gordon, and P. Miller (Eds.), *The Foucault Effect: Studies in Governmentality*. Chicago: The University of Chicago Press.

Fuss, D. (1989). *Essentially Speaking: Feminism, Nature and Difference*. London: Routledge.

Garland, D. (1990). *Punishment and Modern Society: A Study in Social Theory*. Oxford: Clarendon Press.

Gelsthorpe, L. (1992). "Response to Martyn Hammersley's paper 'On Feminist Methodology.'" *Sociology*, 26: 213–218.

Gelsthorpe, L., and A. Morris. (Eds.), (1990). *Feminist Perspectives in Criminology*. Milton Keynes, U.K.: Open University Press.

Genders, E., and E. Player. (1987). "Women in Prison: The treatment, the control and the experience." In P. Carlen and A. Worrall (Eds.), *Gender, Crime and Justice*. Milton Keynes, U.K.: Open University Press.

Genders, E., and E. Player. (1989). *Race Relations in Prisons*. Oxford: Clarendon Press.

Giallombardo, R. (1966). *Society of Women: A Study of a Women's Prison*. New York: John Wiley & Sons, Inc.

Giddens, A. (1984). *The Constitution of Society: Outline of the Theory of Structuration*. Cambridge, UK: Polity Press.

Giddens, A. (1991). *Modernity and Self-Identity: Self and Society in the Late Modern Age*. Cambridge, UK: Polity Press.

Gilligan, C. (1982; 1993). *In a Different Voice: Psychological Theory and Women's Development*. Cambridge MA: Harvard University Press.

Griffiths, M. (1995). *Feminisms and the Self: The Web of Identity*. London: Routledge.

Hammersley, M. (1992). "On feminist methodology." *Sociology*, 26, 187–206.

Harding, S. (Ed.). (1987). *Feminism and Methodology: Social Science Issues.* Milton Keynes, U.K.: Open University Press.

Henry, S., and D. Milovanovic. (1994). "The constitution of constitutive criminology: A postmodern approach to criminological theory." In D. Nelken (Ed.), *The Futures of Criminology.* London: Sage Publications.

Henry, S., and D. Milovanovic. (1996). *Constitutive Criminology: Beyond Postmodernism.* London: Sage Publications.

HMCIP (1996). *HM Prison Eastwood Park: Report of an Unannounced Short Inspection.* London: HMSO.

hooks, b. (1982). *Ain't I A Woman? Black Women and Feminism.* London: Pluto Press.

Howe, A. (1994). *Punish and Critique: Towards a Feminist Analysis of Penality.* London: Routledge.

Hudson, B. A. (1993). *Penal Policy and Social Justice.* London: The Macmillan Press Ltd.

Irigaray, L. (1985a). *Speculum of the Other Woman.* Ithaca: Cornell University Press.

Irigaray, L. (1985b). *This Sex Which is Not One.* Ithaca: Cornell University Press.

Irwin, J., and J. Austin. (1994). *It's About Time: America's Imprisonment Binge.* Belmont, CA: Wandsworth.

King, R., and R. Morgan. (1980). *The Future of the Prison System.* Aldershot: Gower.

Maden, T. (1996). *Women, Prisons and Psychiatry: Mental Disorder Behind Bars.* Oxford: Butterworth-Heinemann Ltd.

Martinson, R. (1974). "What works? Questions and answers about prison reform." *The Public Interest*: 35, 22–54.

Milovanovic, D., and S. Henry. (1991). "Constitutive penology." *Social Justice*, 18: 204–224.

Morris, T., Morris, P., and B. Barer. (1963). *Pentonville: A Sociological Study Of An English Prison.* London: Routledge and Kegan Paul.

Padel, U., and P. Stevenson. (1988). *Insiders: Women's Experience of Prison.* London: Virago Press.

Player, E. (1994). "Women's prisons after Woolf." In E. Player and M. Jenkins (Eds.), *Prisons After Woolf: Reform Through Riot.* London: Routledge.

Ramazanoglu, C. (1992). "On feminist methodology: Male reason versus female empowerment." *Sociology*, 26: 207–212.

Reinharz, S. (1992). *Feminist Methods in Social Research.* New York: Oxford University Press.

Rice, M. (1990). "Challenging orthodoxies in feminist theory: A black feminist account." In L. Gelsthorpe and A. Morris (Eds.), *Feminist Perspectives in Criminology.* Milton Keynes, U.K.: Open University Press.

Richards, M., McWilliams, B., Batten N., Cameron, C., and J. Cutler. (1995a). "Foreign nationals in English prisons: I. Family ties and their maintenance." *The Howard Journal*, 34: 158–175.

Richards, M., McWilliams, B., Batten N., Cameron, C., and J. Cutler. (1995b). "Foreign nationals in English prisons: II. Some policy issues." *The Howard Journal*, 34: 195–208.

Richie, B. E. (1996). *Compelled to Crime: The Gender Entrapment of Battered Black Women*. New York: Routledge.

Schor, N., and E. Weed. (Eds.). (1994). *The Essential Difference*. Bloomington: Indiana University Press.

Schwartz, M., and D. Milovanovic. (Eds.). (1996). *Race, Gender, and Class in Criminology: The Intersection*. New York: Garland Publishing, Inc.

Sim, J. (1990). *Medical Power in Prisons: The Prison Medical Service in England 1774–1989*. Milton Keynes, U.K.: Open University Press.

Smart, C. (1989). *Feminism and the Power of the Law*. London: Routledge.

Sommers, E. K. (1995). *Voices from Within: Women Who Have Broken the Law*. Toronto: University of Toronto Press.

Sparks, R., Bottoms, A., and W. Hay. (1996). *Prisons and the Problem of Order*. Oxford: Clarendon Press.

Spivak, G., with E. Rooney. (1994). "In a word." In N. Schor and E. Weed (Eds.), *The Essential Difference*. Bloomington: Indiana University Press.

Stanley, L., and S. Wise. (1993). *Breaking Out Again: Feminist Ontology and Epistemology*. London: Routledge.

Sykes, G. (1958). *The Society of Captives: A Study of Maximum Security Prisons*. Princeton, NJ: Princeton University Press.

Ussher, J. (1991). *Women's Madness: Misogyny or Mental Illness?* London: Harvester Wheatsheaf.

Ward, D., and G. Kassebaum. (1965). *Women's Prison: Sex and Social Structure*. Chicago: Aldine Publishing Company.

Weir, A. (1995). "Towards a model of self-identity: Habermas and Kristeva." In J. Meehan (Ed.), *Feminists Read Habermas: Gendering the Subject of Discourse*. London: Routledge.

Weir, A. (1996). *Sacrificial Logics: Feminist Theory and the Critique of Identity*. New York: Routledge.

Wittig, M. (1978). "One is not born a woman." *Feminist Issues*, 1.

Wittig, M. (1992). *The Straight Mind and Other Essays*. London: Harvester Wheatsheaf.

Worrall, A. (1990). *Offending Women: Female Lawbreakers and the Criminal Justice System*. London: Routledge.

Young, I. M. (1990). *Justice and the Politics of Difference*. Princeton, NJ: Princeton University Press.

Jim Thomas and Dragan Milovanovic

10

REVISITING JAILHOUSE LAWYERS:
AN EXCURSION INTO
CONSTITUTIVE CRIMINOLOGY

A frequent mistake, and one which is moreover hardly justifiable,
is to try to find cultural expressions for and to give new values to
native culture within the framework of colonial domination (Fanon,
1968: 244).

Introduction

When it was discovered that prison guards in California's Corcoran
prison had been staging deadly fights between inmates and wager-
ing on the outcomes, it helped explain why 50 prisoners were shot by
staff between 1988–96, the highest rate of prison shootings in the
country (Holding, 1996). Something was dreadfully wrong with a
prison system once considered one of the nation's best. When a "get-
tough" prison warden in Georgia was accused of torturing unresist-
ing inmates, it was portrayed by media as an extreme anomaly
(*Chicago Tribune*, 1997a). When New York City police officers were
arrested for choking and brutally sodomizing a prisoner with a toilet plunger and other officers chose not to intervene (Cooper, 1997),
media attention made visible treatment of prisoners that normally
remains concealed. When a prisoner in Brazoria County Jail in Texas
filed a civil rights lawsuit against his captors for being kicked by
guards and bitten by a jail dog, which provoked national outrage
when a video tape of the incident was broadcast by the major media

in summer of 1997 (e.g., *Chicago Tribune*, 1997b), the dramatic bru-
tality of guards on prisoners reminds us that despite prisoners attempts to use the courts to improve prison conditions and reduce
abuses by staff, much remains as it was when staff at Arkansas'
Tucker Farm routinely tortured and murdered prisoners nearly three
decades ago (e.g., Bronstein, 1979: 20). These current events also
raise questions about how prisons, prison reform, and prison culture
should be studied. Prisons and prison culture have received little attention from scholars in the past decade (but see Bosworth, this volume), and conventional approaches to studying prisons and prison culture ask few satisfying questions and provide even fewer insights that
would allow us to understand the impermeability of prisons to reform.
Because we find it disappointing that nothing of a theoretical nature
on jailhouse lawyers has materialized since our own work in 1989
(Milovanovic and Thomas, 1997 [1989]), our discussion here reflects
an exploratory assessment of how constitutive criminology might be
developed to advance analysis of prison culture and the jailhouse
lawyer (JHL). We draw from our collective three decades experiences
of research on prisons, prisoner litigation, and prisoner reform to
offer in brief outline form our thinking on preliminary issues that we
will be developing in an on-going project.

An Excursion into Constitutive Criminology

The organization of the production and dissemination of academic
knowledge into rather narrow compartments that we call "disciplines"
imposes a type of violence on scholarship, and these disciplinary rup-
tures reflect a type of territorial dominance of and competition between knowledge colonies. To borrow from Raskin (1971), this "colo-
nized knowledge" creates a culture in which ideas are routinely ripped
from their contexts and forced, Procrustean style, into disciplinary
niches by those certified to act in the name of the discipline as determined by their location in the departmental pantheon and the appearance of their works in journals deemed as "within the discipline."

Most often, the results of knowledge colonization appear benign,
and our cultural blinders obscure how even the most accurate data
and sophisticated analyses distort the researcher's gaze upon a topic,
resulting in partial understandings. There is, of course, no doubt that
many partial understandings can be useful, but sometimes we want

something more. We want something that is not bound by arbitrary disciplinary barriers. We want something that totalizes inquiry by recognizing the complexity and dynamic properties of the topic itself, and also by recognizing how the production of knowledge interweaves with the social, political, and historical context that directs attention to worthwhile questions and shapes how those questions will be asked and answered.

One way to begin subverting disciplinary colonization in criminal justice is through constitutive criminology. Here, we suggest one way it might be applied by focusing on the topic of prisons in general and jailhouse lawyers (JHLs) in particular. Our essay is exploratory rather than exhaustive; the intent is to illustrate with broad brush-strokes the ways in which constitutive criminology can guide research.

Constitutive criminology is a bridge-building perspective and a method of conceptualizing, interpreting, and communicating research questions and data. The goal is to display and challenge how social interaction, social structure, and culture create unnecessary and debilitating forms of social domination in systems of social control, including legal or normative practices. The utility of constitutive criminology lies not only in its capacity for integrating ideas across disciplines but also in its heuristic power to push scholars to dig below the realm of conventional assumptions and appearances.

Constitutive criminology, unlike much of more conventional criminology, offers alternative conceptualizations. First, it allows for infusion of cross-disciplinary concepts, theories, and ideas. Second, it provides a conceptual framework for placing the development of ideas in historical and social context as a way of displaying the constructionist underpinnings of knowledge. Third, by privileging neither quantitative nor qualitative research, it avoids the internecine methodological battles that continue to plague the social sciences.

Scholars guided by constitutive criminology attempt to provide a re-orientation to conventional perspectives that tends toward an overly-structural emphasis on crime and state responses to it on the one hand, or slide toward nihilistic relativism and radical subjectivity, which characterized much of the earlier, nihilistic forms of semiotically-related postmodernist analyses, on the other. Constitutive criminology draws attention to the social, political and historical context that creates systems of privilege, oppression, and control that benefits some people while putting others at a disadvantage.

Borrowing from semiotics and deconstruction, constitutive criminology directs the researcher's gaze to the discursive practices that
shape how we conceptualize our science, frame public policies and legislation, and establish the rhetorical terrain on which public dialogues occur.

A constitutive penology critically analyzes discursive practices
whose invocation constitutes penology and the "reality" of prison life.
It focuses on the coproduction of a prison "reality" in discursive forms
which then take on reifactory dimensions. Constitutive penology advocates a replacement discourse, a transpraxis:

> is a non reificatory connection of the way we speak with our so-
> cial relations and institutions, such that through its use we are
> continuously aware of the interrelatedness of our agency and the
> structures it reproduces through the constitutively productive
> work of our talking, perceiving, conceptualizing and theorizing"
> (Milovanovic and Henry, 1997 [1991]:154).

We want to now examine the contemporary scene of the jailhouse
lawyer in this light.

Gazing into Prisons

Constitutive criminology suggests several tenets relevant to the study
of prisons and JHLs that we will elaborate throughout this essay.
First, although people are active producers of, and often rebel against,
penal policy and practice (Milovanovic and Thomas, 1997 [1989]), the
manner in which these productions occur is often obscured or reified.

As an example, one of the authors was a radio talk show guest a
few years ago, and the host asked: "How can we reduce the prison population?" Our guest replied, "Tear down the walls!" The phone banks
lit up with irate callers who demanded to know how any society could
survive without prisons. Our point was that prisons, as a carceral for
offenders, are a recent historical development dating to the early
nineteenth century. Yet, our laws, public policies, and public discourse
about crime and punishment expunges our collective cultural mem-
ories with the result that we believe prisons have always existed and
must therefore continue to exist in order to reduce crime and protect
the commonweal. We forget that prisons are a social construct, cre-

ated by the state and implemented not only by controlling the body of the offender, but also by imposing a sign system that confers upon the offender a demonizing stigma that reduces human value. It is within this sedimented, relatively stabilized discursive structure that ongoing dialogue and narratives about "social problems" are constituted.

A second tenet requires that we suspend our belief in and acceptance of the legitimacy of the "social constructions" proffered by conventional theorists that underlie theories, concepts, and models of prison or prison culture. For example, prison violence is routinely perceived as a symptom of the anti-social character of prisoners or the disregard some prisoners have for authority. However, an alternative view might be that prison violence reflects a form of self-help by prisoners who, lacking a discursive platform to air complaints or challenge conditions of confinement, find the language of violence both cathartic and instrumental in expressing their needs (Thomas, 1997). This is not to necessarily advocate these discourses; rather, what is needed is a more holistic, constitutive perspective which better conceptualizes the narrative constructions that become dominant and how others are rendered irrelevant or are marginalized.

Third, the discourse by which media, scholars, and others depict prisoners in general and jailhouse lawyers in particular creates and reinforces, and thus gives credibility to, the memes, or cultural replicators, that shape social policy and public dialogue. Put more simply, penal policy is:

> less the outcome of implementing new ideas than of a discursive process through which aspects of existing practices are selected, emphasized, refined, and formally discussed, while other aspects are ignored, subordinated, dispersed, and relegated to the informal (Milovanovic and Henry, 1997 [1991]: 154; see also Hudson, 1993: 8).

This in turn provides the narrative framework in which those in opposition situate themselves. This coproduction constitutes the reality we call "the prison experience."

The demonizing of prisoners, a rhetorical ploy used especially by politicians in playing on public fears of crime, must be re-examined to dispel the inaccuracies on which the image is based. After all, over half of the new court commitments to US prisons are incarcerations for non-violent crimes (BJS, 1996: 568), prisoners dramatically differ in backgrounds, personality, and lifestyle (BJS, 1996: 567), and most important, over three-quarters of the nation's prisoners will be back on the streets in less than four years (BJS, 1996: 572–3).

The holistic nature of constitutive criminology creates a comprehensive perspective, a way of sorting through the intertwining, intersecting and interrelated nature of the tension between social offenses and social control. Given this, we want to briefly summarize some trends in prisoner litigation and legislative responses, describe some of the legal backlash, and then return to the work of jailhouse lawyers in the contemporary prison situation.

Prisoner Litigation: A Short Background

In the past three decades, state prisoners have increasingly turned to federal courts in attempts to resolve private troubles in public forums. This is called prisoner litigation. A jailhouse lawyer is a prisoner knowledgeable in law who helps other prisoners with their legal problems. These legal problems are diverse, and can include preincarceration problems (with landlords, employers), family problems (divorce, child custody) or postconviction complaints. There are two basic types of prisoner litigation. The first are habeas corpus petitions, which are challenges to the original conviction or to continued incarceration. The second are civil rights suits, which are challenges to prison conditions. Our concern here is primarily with civil rights litigation, because these are attempts to challenge the excesses of punishment and debilitating environment. Through civil rights litigation, jailhouse lawyers find law an occasionally effective way of restoring meaning and order to chaos.

In an earlier study of jailhouse lawyers (Milovanovic and Thomas, 1997 [1989]), we suggested that prisoner litigation cannot be understood in isolation from broader social, political, and carceral issues. We argued that when conditions of existence become unsatisfactory, people may attempt to change them. We also showed that JHLs play out an ironic form of praxis—activity intended to impact their existence—in that they reaffirm the powers of control even as they try to alter those powers.

Milovanovic and Henry (1997 [1991]) have observed that this occurs because the jailhouse lawyers often reinforce a dominant law-

and-order discourse by translating everyday contextualized inmate understandings into legalistic versions, cleansed of interconnectedness and potential articulations of system-centered injustices. However, informal discourses also circulate. Characteristically, some inmates oppose, some acquiesce, some become fatalistic; but, in each case, a discourse already abounds providing meaningful resources from which "reality" can be constructed, albeit with its own unique turn, which simultaneously and substantially remakes the discursive form (Milovanovic and Henry, 1997 [1991]).

(Re)Constituting the Jailhouse Lawyer

Because constitutive criminology entails a holistic approach unrestricted by disciplinary borders, understanding the activity and practice of the JHL requires placing their enterprise in the broader context of law, corrections, and socio-historical background. Analysis of the JHL's world often tells us as much about the researcher as it does about the subject of discourse. Hence, while our own analytic foci below are not arbitrary, they do reflect the intellectual and practical relationship between ourselves and our topic, which—for constitutive criminology—itself becomes part of the analytic narrative. The following is intended to be illustrative of some contemporary movements in prison litigation rather than exhaustive, and it forms the basis of our broader inquiry into a neglected topic to be reported at a later date.

Historical Background

The recent roots date to post-Civil War reconstruction legislation, especially the "Ku Klux Klan Act" and the Fourteenth Amendment. The former Act, which became Title 42 USC Section 1983, was intended to protect freed slaves and prohibited deprivation of rights by any official acting "under color of law." The latter, often considered a shorthand summary of the Bill of Rights, extended to all citizens equal protection of Constitutional rights. Section 1983 fell dormant by the end of the nineteenth century, but the emergence of the civil rights movement in the 1950s created the social conditions amenable to recognizing the rights of marginalized groups. In 1960, Chicago police officers improperly arrested and detained a Black citizen, who resurrected the old "Ku Klux Klan" statute to charge the police with civil rights violations (*Monroe v. Pape*, 365 U.S. 167, 1961). In recognizing the legitimacy of the nineteenth century statute as a cause of action by which a citizen could challenge the action of state officials, the Supreme Court provided the grounds for state prisoners to challenge the conditions of their confinement in federal courts. Since then, Section 1983 challenges by prisoners to their conditions of confinement grew dramatically through the 1970s, peaking in the mid-1980s (Thomas, 1988).

Since the mid-1980s, politicians, legislators, and media pundits have argued that the pendulum has swung too far in favor of prisoners' rights. The courts, too, have aggressively curtailed the expansion of rights, and have even reversed them. Especially since 1990, courts and legislatures have combined to curtail prisoners' rights, including access to law and limitations on challenging improper convictions, especially in capital cases.

Discursive Production and Jailhouse Lawyering: Case Law

A good part of an understanding of jailhouse lawyers and jailhouse lawyering is gained by an understanding of discursive production. We need to look at how discursive production entails making distinctions, drawing contrasts and constructing categories of difference. This is a coproductive activity. Often neglected in discussions of prison is how, in the process of deconstructing, the form is taken for granted, and, hence, reconstituted anew by liberal as well as radical commentary. The "reality," of prisons, then, is constantly reasserted as if it had an objective existence. Jailhouse lawyers face a dilemma that is most often not recognized; in the misrecognition, hegemony is maintained. The dilemma is that oppressed subjects often make use of the supposed machinery of oppression in redressing their grievances, and in this way reconstitute the form.

Legal discourse is a case in point. Jailhouse lawyers who have incorporated the discursive categories of law to petition the courts inadvertently reconstitute the categorical distinctions embedded in it. Words and legal concepts such as "frivolous," "standing," "substantial burden," "deliberate indifference," and "qualified immunity," for example, having originally been given stable semiotic form during the stage of juridico-semiotic production (see Milovanovic, 1994: 147–49) are used as the very narrative constructions of jailhouse lawyers, tantamount to an investment in decontextualized, alienated forms. Thus both the defendant as well as the litigant coproduce a reality which is but one version of what had taken place. Together this coproduction maintains a reality that provides data for the criminologists who investigate penal questions. In the process, the conventional criminologists take as a given that which needs to be explained as a coproduced activity. We are the poorer for it. Moreover, the complexity of being human in a society where repressive and dominating tendencies prevail is denied; rather, the polyvocal, multifarious nature of desire and its expression is placed in bureaucratic categories for easy, "rational" processing.

Take for example case law from *Farmer v. Brennan* (510 US 941, 1974), where the court faced with an Eighth Amendment cruel and unusual prison issue among others, noted a distinction: "The Eighth Amendment does not outlaw cruel and unusual "conditions"; it outlaws cruel and unusual "punishments." In its haste to dismiss inmate's claims, the court created categorical distinctions which thereafter took on a life of their own; in the process, the problematic nature of the distinction has been neutralized. Henceforth, when inmate litigants make use this distinction, they too coproduce a reality that further suppresses domains of potential inquiry.

Prisons function to punish, and punishment includes conditions and culture that punish not only by deprivation, but also by debilitation and repression. However, prison goals and policies are established by state and federal statutes and must conform both to legislative proscriptions and Constitutional prescriptions. JHLs litigate in an attempt to make their keepers conform to statute and case law. The language of their petitions, while conforming to the discourse common in legal petitions, describes the explicit existential despair and repression of the conditions experienced by prisoners.

Case law dissolves these experiences into the generic linguistic formula of legal documents, and substitutes for the lived experience of pain, the sanitized images of legal concepts. Especially since the early 1990s, the courts have consistently reversed the gains of the previous three decades, not so much by advocating reversing the trend in prisoners' rights (although this has emerged on occasion) as by using legal discourse as a means to redefine the conceptual terrain. For example, instead of ruling on whether a prisoner's rights were violated by a beating, the legal issue becomes "who has standing to be sued." Instead of determining whether staff was negligent for placing a transsexual in the general population, the issue becomes a debate over whether courts should establish an "absolute standard" of negligence.

Legislation

Not trusting to the courts to restrict that which can be done more visibly and ruthlessly by fiat, legislators in the past few years have capitalized on the fear of crime, the demonization of offenders, and demagogic rhetoric in attempts to reduce prisoners rights while simultaneously restricting basic amenities such as education and increasing the debilitating nature of prisons. Legislation was driven more by rhetoric than by coherent policy analysis, but hyperbole such as the following was effective in swaying legislators:

> I'm sick and tired of these people getting by with murder and rape and child molestation and just being allowed to be in jail . . . I say let them out in the rock pile to pay their penalty. No more mollycoddling! (Illinois State Senator Adeline Geo-Karis, cited in Parsons, 1996: 1).

Between 1994 and 1997, several of Bills were either passed by or introduced in Congress that would turn back many of the gains JHLs made in previous decades. A few examples typify the language of legislation proposed or enacted that would subvert prison conditions.

One "get-tough" Bill, the "No-Frills Prison Act" (1997), amended the Violent Crime Control and Law Enforcement Act of 1994 to withhold federal funds from states unless they demonstrated that the state prison system:

1. provides living conditions and opportunities within its prisons that are not more luxurious than those that the average prisoner would have experienced if not incarcerated;

2. does not provide to any such prisoner specified benefits or privileges, including earned good time credits, less than 40

hours a week of work that either offsets or reduces the expenses of keeping the prisoner or provides resources toward restitution of victims, unmonitored phone calls (with exceptions), in-cell television viewing, possession of pornographic materials, instruction or training equipment for any martial art or bodybuilding or weightlifting equipment, or dress or hygiene other than as is uniform or standard in the prison; and

3. in the case of a prisoner serving a sentence for a crime of violence which resulted in serious bodily injury to another, does not provide housing other than in separate cell blocks intended for violent prisoners, less than nine hours a day of physical labor (with exceptions), any release from the prison for any purpose unless under physical.

Other federal legislation includes: the "100 Percent Truth-in-Sentencing Act" (1997), which would reduce all good time credits for prisoners convicted of a violent crime; an Amendment to the Religious Freedom Restoration Act of 1993, which would restrict the Religious freedoms of incarcerated persons; the "Prison Security Enhancement Act" (1997), which would prohibit prisoners from engaging in activities designed to increase their physical strength or fighting ability, as well as prohibit related equipment. Other legislation would require prisoners to pay for health care, eliminate grants and other resources for higher education, restrict filings of habeas corpus petitions, and limit the number of appeals and range of issues in capital convictions.

Perhaps the most restrictive legislation is the "Prisoner Litigation Reform Act" (1997), which not only curtails prisoner filings, but also imposes a loss of good time (or an extended sentence) on prisoners deemed to file "frivolous" suits. Although the Act pertains only to "frivolous" federal filings, some states have followed suit and passed similar legislation. In Illinois, for example, the governor in 1997 signed a Bill that allows reduction of prisoners' good time credits by state officials if a federal judge deems a prisoner petition "frivolous."

There is little opposition by either critics or advocates of prisoner litigation to excessively trivial petitions. JHLs are among the strongest opponents of trivial or malicious litigation, because such filings not only make their own jobs harder and subvert their credibility, but also run the risk of leading to "bad law," which can undo gains in prisoners' rights (Thomas, 1988). Extremely outrageous cases, such as the Illinois prisoner who sued a warden for employing electronic technology to monitor his thoughts, or the prisoner who challenged his continued incarceration in the belief that he was the son of the Queen of England are obviously trivial. They are also quickly weeded out in the preliminary screening through which all prisoner civil rights petitions go prior to review by a judge.

The danger of legislation that would penalize prisoners for filing "frivolous suits" lies in the very real potential of creating a chilling effect for those who would present legitimate complaints. As Thomas (1989) argued, the belief that prisoner civil rights petitions are "exploding" is false. Further, using Illinois as an example, prisoner civil rights petitions have remained fairly stable at between 900 to 1,000 filings each year for the past decade, despite the near doubling of the prison population (Office of Prisoner Correspondence, 1997). Hence, laws that would extend a prisoner's incarceration would not seem to be driven by a pressing problem, but rather by symbolizing "get tough" policies.

Another serious problem with anti-litigation legislation lies in the discourse of the law and how the meanings of that discourse may not be shared identically across audiences. For example, "frivolousness" connotes a lay meaning of "silly" or "trivial." At law, the term means "without legal merit." As a consequence, a prisoner who is severely injured by staff negligence, for example, would likely not have a silly or trivial case. The substance of the legal complaint could reflect serious problems in prison policy or behavior of staff. Yet, there might not be legal recourse for the problem. Because the case lacks legal merit, it would, at law, be deemed frivolous. The problem, of course, is that prisoners risk an extension of their prison stay for such "frivolousness." Further, because judges do not share identical discursive frameworks, judicial interpretation becomes a lottery in that what one judge or jurisdiction finds "frivolous" may be interpreted differently before another.

In the aggregate, legislation and case law, combined with public and media hostility, have created obstacles for JHLs. Will the obstacles be an effective gatekeeping mechanism to reduce prisoners' ability to use the law as a form of praxis in changing the conditions of their existence? There is no simple answer, but it is possible to provide some insights by examining how JHLs do what they do.

Jailhouse Lawyers, Transpraxis, and Replacement Discourses

In previous work on jailhouse lawyers we have identified various discursive adaptations by the jailhouse lawyer (Milovanovic and Thomas, 1997 [1989]: 127). We conceptualized the jailhouse lawyer more as a "primitive rebel," an existential rebel responding to conditions of absurdity and disempowerment. We noted that "a prison rebel is not a revolutionary" and more often, that he (our study concerned male jailhouse lawyers) is not driven by a coherent philosophical or political discourse (Milovanovic and Thomas, 1997 [1989]: 127). Milovanovic and Henry (1997 [1991]: 161,164–66) have argued that imprisonment brings with it an engagement with at least four discourses: conforming, alienated, instrumental, and oppositional. In neither case do we find a full-fledged politicized narrative construction. The task before us is to suggest a possible direction for the development of a replacement discourse by way of a transpraxis.

Several commentators have begun to address the issue, but we find their positions inadequate for explaining how a possible alternative discourse could evolve and attain a relative stability, one that provides master signifiers which are more reflective of existential conditions in confinement as they relate to the "outside" and political economy. The question becomes: how "can the subaltern speak?" (Spivak, 1988; see also Howe, 1994: 210).

Preliminary answers emerge from Foucault's involvement with prisoners and his theoretical reflection on his experience. He noted that "only those directly concerned can speak in a practical way on their own behalf" (1977: 206–209) and that the role of the interventionist intellectual was one in which s/he provides "instruments of analysis" (1980: 62). Notwithstanding the feminist critique that these "instruments" may be phallocentric to begin with (Howe, 1994: 209), we question whether "standpoint epistemology" by itself provides the grounding for a transpraxis, for (1) the embraced discourses always already are ideologically laden, (2) various and often diverging "standpoints" exist, (3) the role of the cultural revolutionary (e.g., the supposed change agent) remains untransparent to those affected, and (4) little if anything is being provided as to how precisely a new discourse may evolve within which more contextualized narratives may be constructed, narratives that reflect polyvocality.

We would like to suggest a possible direction. This draws from earlier work (Henry and Milovanovic, 1996: 203–211; Milovanovic, 1996) which developed a constitutive perspective of replacement discourses. This built on the work of Paulo Freire's (1985) dialogical pedagogy which recognized the dialogical nature of the construction of replacement discourses, and on Jacques Lacan (1991). Lacan's "discourse of the hysteric" (to be read as oppositional subject), notes the hegemonic tendencies of those who merely make use of dominant discourse, and, that alternatively, the "discourse of the analyst" provides a way of creating new master signifiers, signifiers that better reflect the dynamic state of being in context. The integration of the ideas of Freire and Lacan, offers one potential direction for a transpraxis, for it responds to the four critiques levied against the use of employing a strictly standpoint epistemology.

The question now becomes: How do we incorporate components of this integrated approach into the prison situation? Put another way, how does a movement from the oppositional subject to the revolutionary subject take place within the context of prison? We are not arguing for the development of a discourse that rationalizes or justifies many of the harms inflicted by convicted felons. Rather, we recognize that inmates are often relegated to discourses that are conforming, alienated, instrumental, or oppositional. And hence, the form of resistance is at best reactive-negative, not reconstructive.

Even in the oppositional discourse embraced by the primitive rebel, dominant legal discursive forms are "willingly" being imposed on existential situations of despair. In this situation we are not in the position of understanding, but more in the position of attributing causality and responsibility. With better understanding procured through giving form to inmate's desires in more open narrative construction (replacement discourses), we suggest that interventionist strategies for reducing harm may take a more innovative form. After all, inmates will eventually return to society, and lacking education, motivation, or marketable skills, crime often seems a seductively normal activity. And as we learn more about the problems of crime and the offender, we also learn more about ourselves and configurations of unhealthy social conditions.

In explaining a form of "rebellious lawyering" (Lopez, 1992; Milovanovic, 1996) it was indicated that the interaction between a lawyer and a client involves at least three identifications. These identifications can be ranged against each other to locate various loci. Each can be listed along continuums. First, identification with language whereby on the one pole is an identification with formal language such as law-speak, the other end with the language of the body whereby the person identifies more with an amorphous form of utterances that are dynamic, unstructured, elusive (e.g., often presented by the poet, novelist, and insane) (see, for example, Kristeva, 1980). Second, identification with master signifiers whereby on the one end the subject strongly identifies with dominant signifiers and symbolic forms, and on the other disidentifies with these same forms even as s/he uses them (see also Pecheux, 1982). And third, identification with discursive subject-positions whereby on the one end, the person identifies with the juridic subject in law, and on the other with the revolutionary subject (see also JanMohamed, 1994). The first two identifications are symbolic, the third, imaginary. Building on Lopez's sensitive argument, which offered a dialogical problem solving form rooted in Freire's (1985) work, by incorporating dimensions of Lacan's (1991) analysis of the discourse of the analyst, we indicated how movement within this three-dimensional grid could take place (Milovanovic, 1992).

We showed how the development of new master signifiers and new identifications by the revolutionary subject could materialize in which empowerment and new forms of narrative constructions could materialize. In other words, this analysis indicates how alternative replacement discourses may emerge, discourses that offer identifications whereby the existential despair of inmates could be contextualized. These are not "objective" truths; rather, as Butler (1992) informs us, more in the form of "contingent universalities."

This suggests that building on the work of Foucault (1980), Spivak (1988), Carlen (1990) and Howe (1994), the "subaltern" may begin to speak. Needed, however, is the explanation of how the cultural revolutionary would emerge in the prison context. In all probability, many encounters with the more sensitive workers within the prison environment already introduces the inmate to alternative constructions and hence alternative identifications. We already have examples of those who taught themselves while incarcerated and who became revolutionaries or revolutionaries in the making (e.g., Malcolm X; see also Martin Sostre, who, when pardoned by the Governor of New York State after an active effort by Amnesty International, began organizing "squatters" on the lower East Side of New York City).

Our own (Jim Thomas, Dragan Milovanovic) ongoing work with jailhouse lawyers has indicated that the rudiments of a more revolutionary subject are often already at play. But more commonly often fleeting and unstable. And this is how "corrections" would have it; for, as long as the inmate presents an incoherent narrative, the status quo remains.

However, with the emergence of a more revolutionary discursive subject-position, alternative readings will emerge. In other words, with movement along the three identificatory axes, away from reified abstracted forms, new forms of narrative constructions may emerge. Thus, while the cultural revolutionary within the context of the prison cannot, in a unilateral way, provide "instruments of analysis" (Foucault, 1980: 62), because doing so entails the imposition of a discourse of the master, it is yet possible to "help create the conditions which permit prisoners to speak for themselves" (Howe, 1994: 170).

Foucault (1977), assumes that collapsing theory into practices and privileging the prisoner and his/her "counter-discourse" would be a more revolutionary practice. Without more, however, this rehearses many standpoint epistemology themes which assume what should be problematized (for a related position, in part, see Howe, 1994: 210). The challenge, then, becomes how the cultural revolutionary will emerge in the prison context who actively contributes to these conditions in dialogical encounters. This then also posses questions to the "outside" revolutionary in her/his commitment for social change. The two are indeed connected. The challenge for future work will be to push ahead with this thesis. Here, we have only been modestly suggestive.

Conclusion

Although our discussion was intended primarily as an opportunity to begin identifying significant foci and conceptual themes for a more ambitious study of jailhouse lawyers, we also attempt to provide sufficient background and data to allow readers to understand the complexity of the JHL's experience. If we have been successful in our exploratory application of constitutive criminology or penology to JHLs, we have suggested several themes on which to build.

First, we have provided a broad outline for how constitutive criminology can be refined and developed for a more ambitious study that bridges paradigms and disciplines. Our approach proceeds from a conceptual framework that incorporates historical, ideological, phenomenological, and semiotic analysis on narrower topics that rarely integrate these issues.

Second, we hope to have provided a few insights into prisons and prison culture by directing attention to the legitimate problems facing prisoners and how some attempt to resolve these problems. Using JHLs as a window into prison culture, the debilitating nature of prison culture becomes more evident. By illustrating the obstacles to and backlash against prisoners' legitimate use of the legal system to peacefully redress grievances, it becomes easier to appreciate the efforts of JHLs in challenging their conditions of confinement. We also noted that JHLs co-produce their narratives: dominant discursive legal forms are often elements in legal narrative constructions and hence the legal form is often inadvertently reconstituted.

Third, by examining the tension between those who would curtail prisoners' rights and unnecessarily increase punishment, and those who see the protection of civil rights and the expansion of privileges as a significant component in rehabilitation and post-release success, we direct attention to several issues. First is the ideological division between the "punishment" and "treatment" purpose of prisons. Second is the theoretical question of sorting out the implications of the "just desserts" and deterrence models of punishment, derived largely from principles of classical and neo-classical criminology, and the more critical theoretical orientations suggested by conflict, interactionist, and postmodern perspectives. Third is the issue of the question of the effectiveness of "get-tough" policies focused on retribution rather than redemption. Although we have not pursued these issues here, our perspective requires that they be integrated into a more ambitious project.

Fourth, we suggested that the political hyperbole and lack of critical media attention to political claims does a disservice to the public by substituting informed debate with demonizing rhetoric. The rhetoric influences legislation, and the legislation in turn shapes the formation of legal issues and discourse of case law. In providing a few brief illustrations, we contend that understanding discursive formation of policy, law, and media is essential to understanding prison policy in the United States.

Fifth, we suggest a direction of analysis concerning the role of a cultural revolutionary in a prison context and the possible coproduction of alternative master signifiers and narrative forms. In short, we suggest a line of analysis whereby the oppositional subject may become a revolutionary subject.

We reconfirm our earlier works where we claimed that the activities of JHLs could be understood as a type of primitive rebellion. We erred, however, in believing that efforts to reform prisons by challenging conditions that did not comply with existing legal or humanitarian standards would become accepted by politicians. We did not anticipate the backlash, even in a period of decreasing crime and increasing tolerance of "deviance" and even of "difference." Within our previous framework, we had no ready way of sorting out the issues we raised. Thus, our gaze was partially obscured from the complexities of prisons, policy, law, and society. Constitutive criminology provides an antidote to such intellectual myopia.

References

BJS (Bureau of Justice Statistics). (1996). *Sourcebook of Criminal Justice Statistics*, 1995. Washington, D.C.: U.S. Department of Justice.

Bronstein, A. (1979). "Reform without change: The future of prisoners' rights." In A. J. Bronstein and P. J. Hirshkopf (Eds.), *Prisoners' Rights*. New York: Practising Law Institute, pp. 19–33.

Butler, Judith. (1992). "Contingent foundations: Feminism and the question of 'postmodernism.'" In J. Butler and J. Scott (Eds.), *Feminists Theorize the Political*. New York: Routledge, pp. 3–21.

Carlen, P. (1990). *Alternatives to Women's Imprisonment*. Milton Keynes: Open University Press.

Chicago Tribune. "Guard ties warden to inmate torture." (1997a), July 2: A-8.

Chicago Tribune. "Tales of abuse in Texas jails begin to surface." (1997b), August 22: 9.

Cooper, Michael. (1997). "2d Police officer gives account of sexual assault of Haitian." *The New York Times*, August 18, A:14.

Fanon, Frantz. (1968). *The Wretched of the Earth*. New York: Grove Press.

Foucault, Michel. (1997). "Intellectuals and power," In D. F. Bouchard (Ed.), *Language, Counter-Memory, Practice*. Ithaca: Cornell University Press.

Foucault, Michel. (1980). "Body/Power," In C. Gordon (Ed.) *Michel Foucault: Power/Knowledge, Selected Interviews and Other Writings, 1972–77*. Brighton: Harvester Press.

Freire, Paulo. (1985). *The Politics of Education*. South Hadley, MA: Bergin and Garvey.

Henry, Stuart, and Dragan Milovanovic. (1997 [1991]). "Constitutive criminology," In D. Milovanovic (Ed.). *Postmodern Criminology*. New York: Garland Publishing, pp. 77–92.

Henry, Stuart, and Dragan Milovanovic. (1996). *Constitutive Criminology: Beyond Postmodernism*. London: Sage.

Holding, Reynolds. (1996). "Officials accused of trying to block FBI investigation." *The San Francisco Chronicle*, October 28:A1.

Howe, Adrian. (1994). *Punish and Critique: Towards a Feminist Analysis of Penalty*. New York: Routledge.

Hudson, Barbara. (1993). *Penal Policy and Social Justice*. Toronto: University of Toronto Press.

JanMohamed, A. R. (1994). "Some implications of Paulo Freire's Border Pedagogy." In H. Giroux and P. McLaren (Eds.), *Between Borders*. New York: Routledge.

Kristeva, J. (1980). *Desire in Language*. New York: Columbia University Press.

Lacan, Jacques. (1991). *L'Envers de la Psychanalyse*. Paris: Editions du Seuil.

Lopez, G. (1992). *Rebellious Lawyering: One Chicano's Vision of Progressive Law Practice*. San Francisco: Westview Press.

Milovanovic, Dragan. (1997 [1988]). "Jailhouse lawyers and jailhouse lawyering," In D. Milovanovic (Ed.), *Postmodern Criminology*. New York: Garland Publishing, pp. 95–114.

Milovanovic, Dragan. (1994). *Sociology of Law*. Albany, NY: Harrow and Heston.

Milovanovic, Dragan. (1996). " 'Rebellious lawyering': Lacan, chaos, and the development of alternative juridico-semiotic forms," *Legal Studies Forum* 20(3): 295–321.

Milovanovic, Dragan, and Stuart Henry. (1997 [1991]). "Constitutive penology," In D. Milovanovic (Ed.), *Postmodern Criminology*. New York: Garland Publishing, pp. 153–69.

Milovanovic, Dragan, and Jim Thomas. (1997 [1989]). "Overcoming the absurd: Prisoner litigation as primitive rebellion," In D. Milovanovic (ed.) *Postmodern Criminology*. New York: Garland Publishing, pp. 115–31.

Office of Prisoner Correspondence. (1997). Northern Federal District Court (Illinois), Chicago. Personal Communication.

Parsons, Christi. (1996). "Lawmakers want to make prison even harder time." *Chicago Tribune*, April 7: Sect 4, pp 1–2.

Pecheux, M. (1982). *Language, Semantics and Ideology*. New York: St. Martin's Press.

Raskin, Marcus. (1971). *Being and Doing*. New York: Random House.

Spivak, G. (1988). "Can the subaltern speak," In C. Nelson and L. Grossberg (Eds.), *Marxism and the Interpretation of Culture*. London: Macmillan.

Thomas, Jim. (1988). *Prisoner Litigation: The Paradox of the Jailhouse Lawyer*. Totowa, NJ: Rowman and Littlefield.

Thomas, Jim. (1989). "Repackaging the data." *New England Journal of Civil and Criminal Confinement*, 15(1): 27–53.

Thomas, Jim. (1997). "Some functions of prison violence." Unpublished manuscript, Northern Illinois University.

PART 4

INSTITUTIONAL TRANSFORMATION AND CONSTITUTIVE JUSTICE

Robert C. Schehr

11

INTENTIONAL COMMUNITIES, THE FOURTH WAY: A CONSTITUTIVE INTEGRATION

Introduction

This chapter illustrates applications of chaos theory to the study of social movements. I contend that contemporary theorizing on social movements limits recognition of subaltern modes of resistance (i.e. resistance to oppression by political, economic, and cultural subordinates through their silent redefinition of the conventional social world's constitutive elements).[1] It restricts resistance to rare historical eruptions colloquially recognized as revolutions, or mass mobilizations typically directed at political and/or economic transformations. In contrast, I argue that social theorists must pay closer attention to subaltern modes of resistance since, following chaos theory, small changes at the level of the lifeworld can lead to unanticipated changes in social systems. To make this point, I discuss intentional communities (ICs) and their members' creative appropriation of mythistory, and innovative techniques for managing interpersonal and group dynamics, which demonstrate their signification of alternatives to contemporary modes of living. I conclude by locating ICs within chaos theory's strange attractor bifurcation diagram based on their appropriation of nostalgic utopia and dangerous-memory.

The Limits of Traditional Social Movements Theory

In his most recent effort to identify the interstices of contemporary collective behavior, Alberto Melucci comes to a surprising and refreshing realization:

> This paradox of small interventions producing big effects has to be incorporated in our understanding of how complex societies function. Proceeding in this direction, social sciences would draw closer to the new paradigm emerging in natural sciences, particularly manifest in systems theory and quantum physics (1996a: 185).

This exciting recognition of the creative energy inherent in what chaologists refer to as "perturbations," or micrological flux, unfortunately goes no further than this brief statement. But there appears to be growing awareness among social scientists of the efficacy of privileging the perpetual intersection of identity consciousness, and multitudinous encounters with power knowledge regimes, symbols systems, and economic and political steering mechanisms (e.g., Boggs, 1985; Fantasia and Hirsch, 1995; Gusfield, 1994; Gyani, 1993; Ingelhart, 1990; Johnston and Klandermans, 1995; Snow and Benford, 1992; Touraine, 1988).

That Melucci (1996a) stops short of making a case for a theory of social movements based on a combination of chaos and postmodern theory signifies his desire to retain some components of classical interpretations of social movement and collective behavior. Indeed, group activities hovering within the lifeworld that resist political, economic, and cultural expressions of oppression through silence by redefining dominant cultural symbols, codes, and values are viewed by Melucci (1996a: 183) as offering a potentially new mode of collective action. The product, Melucci reveals, is "no longer the sum total of individuals but a different relationship among individuals" (1996a: 184). However, like most who write within the sociology of social movements, Melucci dismisses (or overlooks) subaltern modes of resistance as bearers of social movement status. The ambulant, quiet, surreptitious, and persistent activities of people cognizant of their disproportionate lack of power and resources, who act in ways to disguise their activism, are merely "deviants" according to Melucci (1996a: 30). This is a kind of group behavior that without an expressed commitment to system-directed conflict, or an interest in amassing organizational resources (both monetary and bureaucratic) can be dismissed, one presumes, as little more than periodic nuisances that lack staying power. Specifically, "in order for an action of this kind to have any long-term and significant impact, structural changes must take place in society which create new resources and political channels for the institutional implementation of the effects of the action" (1996a: 185). This assumption follows from Melucci's longstanding reliance upon system-directed conflict, what he refers to as "breaching system limits," as the primary litmus test for social movement status (see especially Melucci, 1996a: 22–41).

Like Melucci, Jenson (1995) claims that to succeed social movements must engage ideological and semantic struggles over "naming." Since the struggle over naming both the movement actors and their core issues produces "winners and losers," actors must realize that to maximize political efficacy social movements must "mobilize a collective identity within the movement [and] seek to compel recognition of that identity by public institutions" (1995: 115).

So what kind of collective behavior qualifies as a social movement? For Melucci social movements are: (i) collective actors defined by specific solidarity; (ii) engaged in conflict with an adversary for the appropriation and control of resources valued by both of them; and (iii) whose action entails a breach of the limits of compatibility of the system within which the action itself takes place (1996a: 29–30). I will elaborate on these points below in an effort to construct my own analytical guide to the recognition of social movements.

Recognizing the Subaltern: Redefining Social Movement

As I have commented elsewhere (Schehr, 1997), while it is clear that members of intentional communities (ICs) have cultivated modes of behavior culminating in various kinds of rituals, they have resisted directing their efforts toward the transformation of dominant cultural steering institutions. Furthermore, I believe the dualism of "winners" and "losers" is conceptually flawed. It is clear that globally, resistance movements persist in a perpetual struggle to reclaim civil society, accentuating a vast spectrum of perceived needs and desires that are different from simply "winning" and "losing." Indeed, how does one measure victory? As with most new social movements (NSMs), the impact of ICs' mode of social movement is extremely difficult to calibrate since they attempt transformations in diverse and multiple ways: for example, identity construction, love, sexuality, play, conflict resolution, work habits and distribution of resources, relations to nature and technology, spirituality, and so on. By what measure have ICs "lost" if encounters with their modes of living impact the lives of only a few nonmembers? Below I suggest an alternative designation for such "successful" social movements.

The definition of social movement used throughout this chapter follows two significant contributions to social movement theory. The first derives from the work of Alfred Schutz, the second from mythistory. I will discuss the latter in the conclusion of this chapter.

The Contribution of Alfred Schutz

Somewhat surprisingly, Schutz articulates the essence of subaltern resistance that can be related to the work of social theorists writing on the persistence of resistance within the lifeworld (e.g., Benjamin, 1969; Bloch, 1995 [1955]; Bond and Gilliam, 1994; de Certeau, 1984; Gross, 1992a, 1992b; Gyani, 1993; Nandy, 1987; Rao, 1994; Scott, 1990; Welch, 1985). Unlike the restrictions placed on social movement designations by theorists like Melluci and Jenson, Schutz constructs a constitutive definition of agency that includes an elaboration on his concept *conduct*. For Schutz, the concept conduct, unlike that of behavior, refers to both overt and covert qualities including both intentional outwardly directed action, and subjective reflexes. Thus by conduct he means "all kinds of subjectively meaningful experiences of spontaneity, be they those of the inner life or those gearing into the outer world" (1971: 210). *Action* is conduct that has been preconceived, thought about in advance, and this can be either covert or overt. Schutz also refers to actions which have been preconceived, and thus require bodily movements to place in motion, as *working*: "Working is action in the outer world, based upon a project and characterized by the intention to bring about the projected state of affairs by bodily movements" (1971: 212).

For the social actor to move from covert intrasubjective fantasy to overt expressions of fantasy requires a quality of being that Schutz referred to as the "wide-awake self," that is, being here, now. Much like the philosophical teachings of Zen Buddhism, Schutz contends that the only possibility for self-sameness, that is, self unity, appears in the immediacy of conscious attention to the demands and responsibilities of life within any given temporal moment. Deliberation over past experiences, on the other hand, produces in the reflecting subject the divided self discussed by Mead (1934), Lacan (1977), Butler (1990), I. M. Young (1986), and Cornell (1993). Schutz reveals the significance of the "wide-awake consciousness" as the inauguration in consciousness of the present "reality" confronting actors. For Schutz:

> The state of full awakeness of the working self traces out that segment of the world which is pragmatically relevant, and these relevances determine the form and content of our stream of thought; the form because they regulate the tension of our memory and therewith the scope of our past experiences recollected and of our future experiences anticipated; the content, because all these experiences undergo specific attentional modifications by the preconceived project and its carrying into effect (1971: 213–214).

This quality of mind enables actors to smoothly navigate what Schutz refers to as "sub-universes of reality of finite provinces of meaning." In this way, day-to-day reality is defined by the suspension of doubt, a product of our disinterest in abandoning status quo modes of living. Schutz argues that stasis persists within these sub-universes of reality as long as we can avoid experiences of shock. The "fixation of belief," as C. S. Pierce referred to it, endeavors to drown out the entropy characteristic of natural and human systems.

The suspension of doubt begins to wane, argues Schutz, with seemingly minute perturbations or shocks of the kind experienced in daily intercourse (e.g., moving from awake to dream state; experiences of jouissance emanating from music, film, or theater), producing what I refer to as *fractured consciousness*. This is the prerequisite spatial and temporal episode necessary to produce some movement in a subject's sense of reality; thereby opening them to numerous possible interpretations of future lifeworld configurations. It is at this point that Schutz phenomenological interpretation of interpellation intersects with my interest in the power of nostalgic utopia and dangerous memory.

Nostalgic Utopia and Dangerous Memory

Following Walter Benjamin (1969) and Sharon Welch (1985), nostalgic utopia and dangerous memory are instruments of subaltern resistance constituting the storehouse of cultural artifacts perpetually available for reappropriation by contemporary subjects for use in rearticulating self and group relations to dominant cultural steering institutions. Several social theorists have emphasized the creative appropriation of myth and symbolism to promote resistance (e.g., Hobsbawm and Ranger, 1983; Jamison, 1972; Gross, 1992; Zipes, 1992, 1993; Laclau, 1990; de Certeau, 1984). For example, Bond and Gilliam (1994) promote recognition of mythistoric constructions of the past. Following Nietzsche, they argue that there is no one, true, version of historical events, but rather a multiplicity of interpretations. They argue that the business of liberating the past for subaltern appropriation must begin by "confronting the language of paternalistic domination that resides in the tradition of Western Liberal thought and manifests itself in the common sense terms of spatial, temporal, and geographic subordinations" (1994: 12). Nandy (1987) recognizes in "critical traditionality" efforts by Indian people to convey their hidden transcript through appropriation of Indian folk history. Nandy's work reveals the relevance of deconstructing contemporary power-knowledge regimes to enhance the symbolic re-presentation of cultural selves.

Hidden Transcripts and Schutz's Concept of Dis-belief

Scott's (1990) recognition of the "hidden transcript," employed by oppressed peoples as a surreptitious way to resist power, closely resembles my definition of social movement outlined at the outset. Hidden transcripts consist of three components. They (i) are limited to a particular social site and net of actors; (ii) contain a full range of public expressions from speech to "poaching, pilfering, tax evasion, [and] intentionally shabby work"; and (iii) the "frontier between public and hidden transcripts is a zone of constant struggle between dominant and subordinate" (Scott, 1990: 14).

Important here is Schutz's recognition of the power of dis-belief. Through the retelling of folklore, myth, fairy tales, gossip, jokes, daydreams, and plays of fiction, subjects are capable of suspending the contemporaneousness of their *being in the world*. Schutz suggests that this process, a mode of action in his schema, throws into disarray the more stable and predictable aspects of physical exertion necessary to put thoughts into motion that he calls working. Indeed, "the more the mind turns away from life, the larger the slabs of the everyday world of working which are put into doubt" (1971: 233). What is most important is Schutz's recognition of the constitutive and sensuous experience of "being in the world" that can, at specific historical moments and with reference to mythistory, interrupt the suspension of doubt producing instead a considerably more ambulant and unpredictable experience in nature. I will pursue this aspect of subaltern resistance in the conclusion. For now, I suggest the following working definition of social movements which builds upon Melucci (1996a) but which also takes into consideration Schutz's emphasis on phenomenological aspects of consciousness.

A Working Definition of Social Movements

A social movement exists where:

- there is consensual agreement of purpose among group members,

- group members perceive their efforts as signifying alternatives to prevailing conditions, and

- group members struggle to rearticulate and reappropriate dominant cultural interpretations of political, economic, and cultural phenomena.[2]

In opposition to Melucci's emphasis on system-directed conflict as a prerequisite for social movement status, this definition returns the content of the social movement to the groups themselves. Here I concur with Gusfield (1994) (and indirectly with Schutz), who contends that a social movement exists when the members of a group or organization believe it does. Notice that in my identification of analytical dimensions there is no requisite system-directed conflict necessary to be social movement actors since, with but a few rare historical episodes, this kind of political, economic, and cultural challenge is quite unique. What seems more appropriate to study, but which requires a reconceptualization of the kind offered here, is to identify resistance movements hovering within the lifeworld that typically do not emerge as unified political voices.

The third component of my conceptual dimensions of social movements is similar to Melucci's to the extent that ICs have the capacity to "break the limits of compatibility of the system." However, Melucci's elaboration on this aspect of social movement reveals his tilt toward conventional social movement definitions. Melucci suggests that what he really means when it comes to "breaking the limits of compatibility" is to: "break the rules of the game, it [social movement organization] sets its own non-negotiable objectives, it challenges the legitimacy of power" (1996a: 30). It is apparent that when he speaks of social movement actors he refers to movements of the working class, feminists, students, gays and lesbians, environmentalists, peace activists, and the like. By way of contrast members of ICs would, as I mentioned above, be considered "deviants."

My interpretation of "breaking the limits of compatibility" also includes rearticulation of those aspects of dominant culture that function to interpellate subjects (Althusser, 1969, 1971). Recognizing the emphasis on reappropriation of symbol systems by social movement actors formed the foundation of new social movement (NSM) theory. But NSM theorists have failed to recognize the destabilizing and regenerating capacity of seemingly insignificant group behaviors like those constituting ICs. It is for this reason that nonlinear dynamics, especially chaos theory, offer important insights for social movement theorists.

In their analyses of natural systems (e.g., weather, bees), chaologists pay close attention to instability hovering at the micro level and the macro structural effects it produces. Seemingly minor perturbations (e.g., fluctuations, changes in behavior) at the micro level can produce unanticipated changes at the macro level. The remainder of this chapter will attempt to locate ICs as a social movement within chaos theory. It is to a theory of non-linearity that a truly emancipatory politics may emerge. While I have addressed the relative shortcomings of classical and contemporary articulations of social movements elsewhere (Schehr, 1997), here I wish to establish intentional communities (ICs) as a social movement by applying the insights of chaos theory to generate what I have referred to as a "fourth way" (1997). Building from these initial efforts to metaphorically view ICs as social movement actors, I explore the possible interpretations of subaltern modes of resistance emanating from a chaos model.

Chaos Theory, Postmodernism, and Social Movements

Application of chaos theory to social movements requires social scientists to suspend their belief in linear scientific explanations of behavior. Applications of morphological interpretations of social movements that attempt to tell their story as a linear progression impose artificial temporal-spatial limitations on their subjects. In contrast, chaos theory and its use of fractal dimensions, offers a way to accommodate epistemological shifts in analysis and cognition of social movements. In order to comprehend chaos theory's contribution and difference from conventional linear analysis, it is necessary to briefly define some of its concepts and methods.

Trouser Diagrams and Rhizomes

One useful methodological approach within chaos theory that transcends the limits of linear analysis is the use of "trouser diagrams" (Gregersen and Sailer, 1993). Trouser diagrams provide social theorists with maps of variables far more constitutive and multiplicitous than path analysis. In its configuration a trouser diagram appears as tubes (variables) pointing to the dependent variable in question. Illustrative of the heterogeneity inherent in subject constitution and relations to dominant cultural steering institutions, a Poincaré[3] section of a trouser diagram, can be extracted from any one tube (variable), producing a cross-section that displays the complicated intersection of cognition, identity, power, and desire as these are each related to the composition of a singular methodological construct. Trouser diagrams, therefore, encourage analysis of multiple layers of subject constitution, both as phenomenal actors, and as members of specific groups. Moreover, trouser diagrams typically have no causal arrows directing their flow. This is because systems, both natural and social, are fluid. As a result, assumptions about morphology are avoided in an attempt to see historical events as "always already." This emphasis privileges less the relatively infrequent episodes of political, economic, and cultural upheaval and focuses more on the daily constitution of subjects in group and institutional settings.

In addition to the trouser diagram, I argue that what is needed is a conceptualization of social movements similar to Deleuze and Guattari's (1987) articulation of the rhizome.[4] Rather than limiting conceptual analysis to striated[5] spaces with clearly identified roles and related responsibilities, it is helpful to conceive of social actors within the open field of smooth space. Rhizomes, as the metaphor signifies, are fractal, multiple, unpredictable. As I will attempt to establish in the closing part of this chapter, ICs are rhizomes. They are fractal, unpredictable, surreptitious, ambulant. To apply linear social scientific reasoning, including research methodology, to comprehend subjects' experiences with psychoanalytic semiotic constructions of desire to interpersonal experiences with dominant cultural capital does little to enhance our understanding of contributions made by these actors. That, I contend, can only come from viewing social movements through a fractal lens.

Bifurcation, Fractals, and Torus Attractors

For Prigogene (1980), bifurcation refers to a point in time and space when a path leads to a fork. One can easily visualize a tree from the bottom up. A singular path is travelled upward along the trunk until it reaches the first set of large branches. Continuing along those branches leads to more, but somewhat smaller branches, and so on. Bifurcations occur through the process of iteration (where a system feeds back into itself) that can either maintain stability, or leads to systemic flux and consequent cultivation of a new environment (Briggs and Peat, 1989: 143). With each bifurcation, systems are emersed in flux and appear to be at a crucial stage of decisionmaking. There are, however, parameters designating moments of rupture or stasis. First uncovered by Mitchell Feigenbaum during the 1970s, the Feigenbaum number (4.669) as it came to be known, demonstrated the moment at which complex natural systems, and one could assume social systems, would begin to disintegrate. According to Feigenbaum, when a system reaches three bifurcations at crucial systemic parameters the system becomes unstable.

Understanding bifurcation is paramount to applying fractal geometry to our interest in chaos theory and social movements.

Benoit Mandelbrot, at the time working for IBM, determined that all natural systems were constituted by fractal rather than integral dimensions (Briggs and Peat, 1989).[6] His work on system entropy can be applied to human agency since what is certain in all complex systems is flux. Chaos and order exist in a perpetual dance. This is particularly relevant when it corresponds to ICs or any social movement actors since all subjects are constituted by the complex interplay of subjective expressions of desire (Lacan, 1977), and the expectations of dominant cultural steering institutions; thereby requiring nonlinear hypotheses producing fractal images of reality. Following T. R. Young (1992), fractal geometry provides stimulating evidence of political, economic, and cultural conditions conducive to social movement activity. But how?

Unlike most contemporary social science, chaos theory assumes that non-linearity and flux are as much a part of normal systems as states of equilibrium. Rather than spinning wildly into total disarray, chaotic conditions at the micro level tend toward new systemic configurations, i.e. "order out of chaos" (Prigogene and Stengers, 1984). Bifurcation models, like the one depicted in figure 11.1, illustrate four possible outcomes given a set number of parameters in phase space. The first two, the "fixed-point attractor" and the "limit-cycle attractor," each operate within a narrowly defined phase space with few degrees of freedom.[7] These two bifurcation diagrams are used to illustrate simple ratio-relationships where interactions always return to their initial starting place. When applied to a study of social movements, societies organized in this way would resemble oppressive totalitarian or dictatorial states where opportunities to raise matters of interest are hampered by control over phase space.[8] Little social

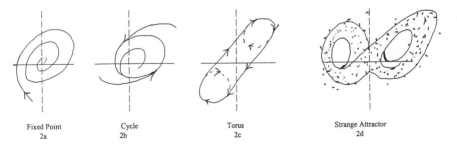

| Fixed Point | Cycle | Torus | Strange Attractor |
| 2a | 2b | 2c | 2d |

Figure 11.1   Bifurcation Model, Constitutive Analysis of Social Movement Actors, Chaos Attractors

movement activity will find *overt* expression under these conditions. It is to the "torus-attractor" and the "strange-attractor" that one must look for opportunities to express oppositional demands.

For most social movement theory, the torus attractor is illustrative. Aside from those rare historical instances where movement actors successfully manufacture a revolutionary transformation in power, most social movements persist within the prevailing mode of political, economic, and cultural contexts in their given societies. Demands for political and spiritual representation, environmental reform, civil rights, military disarmament, enhancements in the welfare state, and the expansion of worker power, each persist within the predescribed negotiated, discourse of dominant culture. The torus attractor is the appropriate example of this most typical mode of social movement since the torus consists of the combination of two limit cycles, thus increasing the size of the phase space. The torus attractor allows us to conceptually map multiple degrees of freedom (Briggs and Peat, 1989) within an identifiable phase space.

Social movements articulating the kind of demands mentioned above do so within a predescribed phase space referred to as civil society (Cohen and Arato, 1992). Recognition and deconstruction of civil society are crucial to any analysis of social movements, but particularly those articulating transformations in interpersonal relations, identity construction, and the like, especially those associated with new social movement theory. This application of civil society to the study of social movements follows the work of Cohen and Arato (1992) who designate it as a cultural space avoiding direct appropriation by political and economic institutions. A thriving civil society is necessary for the cultivation of association and speech, ostensibly providing for multiple manifestations of subaltern interest. Attention to civil society marks a departure from traditional social movement theory in that it deflects attention from those historically rare revolutionary eruptions directed at transformations in political and/or economic relations, privileging instead the kind of sempiternal self-limiting revolution enacted daily by the subaltern.

It is not until interactions within civil society (conceptualized in chaos theory as phase space) move beyond a simple ratio of mostly predictable behavior and state-directed demands, that real systemic transformations are initiated. Here social movement actors articulating demands within relatively stable parameters define the torus-attractor. So, for example, single issue-oriented social movement organizations are not likely to produce systemic instability given the nature of the system's steering mechanisms (as with those in nature) to absorb the weight of their actions.

Complex analyses of the preservation of systemic stability can be found in Bertramsen *et al.* (1991), who argue for a triangular model of system stability that includes the accumulation regime, and the hegemonic block, with the state positioned in the center serving as a "nodal point in bringing about the coherency of a mode of regulation" (1991: 130). The state is viewed as a negotiated set of relationships producing a complex weave of regulatory interests across six large sectors: (1) industry; (2) agriculture; (3) education; (4) finance; (5) the workforce (social security, employment, housing); (6) the relation between central and local government (Bertramsen *et al.*, 1991: 131; Delorme, 1984). Social movements directing their demands to state-based changes in regulatory (administrative), criminal, or civil laws, for example, must contend with the complicated interconnection of these interests.

Consistent with chaos theory and the Feigenbaum number, social theorists can anticipate that social movements demanding changes in between one and three aspects of politics, economics, and culture (producing few outcome basins) will be unlikely to produce systemic instability. But if these same movements place an additional demand on the system (increasing the number of outcome basins beyond the Feigenbaum number), then systemic stability moves toward flux. This can be witnessed in the turbulence created during the mid- to late 1960s when multiple outcome basins were created among social movements, each vying for representation at the level of the state. As long as any one of them proceeded alone, state regulatory mechanisms seemed capable of adjusting to movement demands. For example, during the late 1950s, when the Civil Rights movement and a fledgling student movement seemed to define a resistance culture in America, little in the way systemic instability appeared. As it applies to chaos theory, regulatory changes could be sought in the 1964–65 Civil Rights Bill producing systemic reform within the torus.

In summary, most social movements are illustrative of torus-attractors as they mobilize their resources for the procurement of advancements in politics, economics, and culture below the Feigenbaum number. The constitutive nature of state regulatory mechanisms assures that as social movement actors move within the torus, spaces will open up for the articulation of demands or symbolic expressions of resistance (Bertramsen *et al.* 1991; Jessop, 1990; Freire, 1972; Katz, 1989; Giroux, 1992; Ferrell, 1993; Burawoy, 1979; Armstrong *et al.*, 1989) thus assuring a relative degree of agency. This stage is crucial for theorizing about social movements since it appears that when a torus-attractor bifurcates beyond the third parameter, rather than producing a new dimension within the torus (civil society), phase space acquires a fractal dimension where a state of chaos emerges that may produce considerable systemic instability. The result is a torus-attractor that has begun to break apart (Briggs and Peat, 1989: 51).

Strange Attractors and Postmodernity

Emerging from repeated bifurcation is what chaologists refer to as a "strange attractor." Strange attractors are nonlinear fractal systems whose "geometry is not Euclidean; its turns, twists, skips and reverses chart the nonlinear dynamics of natural and social systems" (Young, 1990: 6). One of the images produced when visualizing strange attractors is that of the butterfly. A single bifurcation or the doubling of options within a phase space produces two outcome basins referred to as a "butterfly attractor."

Most compelling in the emergence of strange attractors is the process that gives them life. In organic systems, the process of perpetual iteration (where its parts feed back into itself) produces progressively greater complexity and uncertainty. Application of this aspect of fractal geometry to the social sciences can be seen in those literatures addressing the complicated constitution of intersubjective and intergroup consciousness, and its relation to dominant cultural steering institutions. For it is the constitution of self, primarily through the vehicle of language but with recognizably numerous non-linguistic signifiers that culturally constructed feedback loops serve to interpellate subjects (Young, 1986; Butler, 1990; Cornell, 1993; Lacan, 1977; Bracher, 1993; Melucci, 1996a, 1996b; Henry and Milovanovic, 1996). The relevance of this point for theorizing subaltern modes of resistance, cultural studies, and their relation to chaos theory can be found in the multiple layers of uncertainty encountered at the level of subject constitution. Arguing for the complex interplay of interpellative aspects of subject constitution argues against any notion of overdetermination.

In a world of hyperreality (Baudrillard, 1981; Kellner, 1989; Luke,

1991) and postmodernity there appears to be a perpetual state of flux, change, repackaging, and instability. Consumer society transforms all functions of mind, body, and interpersonal relationships from parochial experiences of the locale, to hyperreal investments in consumer products with sign values ascribing requisite moods, tastes, attitudes, values, and status (Melucci, 1996a, 1996b; Luke, 1991; Baudrillard, 1981). This has largely been achieved through advances in satellite and computer technology allowing for the widespread dispersion of media imagery, and the globalization of production and distribution. The daily bombardment of advertising media meant to stimulate images of beauty, health, wealth, youth, and power, exists on the same terrain with pedagogical efforts to establish prevailing dominant cultural interpretations of history, science, art, and literature. In each instance it becomes virtually impossible to determine "who one is" at any specific time and place. What we need, want, and desire is, with few exceptions, culturally mediated (Young, 1986; Lacan, 1977; Henry and Milovanovic, 1996; Katz, 1989; Giroux, 1996).

An analysis of subaltern modes of resistance that recognizes this complicated interplay of interpellative forces can be located within the strange attractor bifurcation diagram given the unlimited number of feedback interactions taking place at the intersubjective, intergroup, and system-steering levels of analysis. In this way, predictability of outcome proves far more illusive than in classical and some contemporary interpretations of collective behavior. Moreover, it is this perpetual interplay of constitutive forces that makes the quantum level so unpredictable; thus providing social theorists with ample room to uncover, not only resistance potential, but the kaleidoscopic array of manifested resistance.

Topology Theory, Butterfly Attractors, and Modern Social Movements

Recognition of the persistence of resistance makes social scientific methods of behavioral and attitudinal predictability suspect since they only attempt to account for ways in which linear changes in "x" produce linear changes in "y". Topology theory, a methodological approach that recognizes the constitutive nature of human interaction, benefits from what is referred to as qualitative or "rubber mathematics" (Briggs and Peat, 1989: 84). Topology theory envisions systems as twisting, turning, folding, and curving wholes. A "mobius band" would be a visual representation of a topological mapping of systems that can be contorted in all manner of ways but none-the-less remains whole. Envision holding one end of a long strip of paper in your left hand. With your right hand, twist and turn the strip of paper, without creasing or folding it, returning and joining it to the end held by the left hand. This is a mobius band. Such conceptualization has implications for research methodology. At best, research into social movements must proceed at the qualitative level where layers of subject signification and action can be met with interpretations emanating from the subjects themselves. This micro-level analysis would then be combined with macro-level attention to regulatory steering institutions indicated above.

Signification of unpredictability within the strange attractor locates behavior in one of the two wings of the butterfly indicating two relatively stable options for acting in a specific way. As it relates to social movements, the discourse of the anti-war movement of the 1960s can be viewed as operating in one wing of the attractor, while the master discourse of the Kennedy, Johnson, and Nixon administrations can be seen constituting the other. The most relevant aspects of the butterfly attractor, however, are the regions nearing the edges of each wing, for it is here that instability and flux are more noticeable. This is important for any analysis of social movements but especially ICs since, as I contend, ICs, indicative here of most subaltern modes of resistance, perpetually hover in the space between stability and chaos. The relevance of the spaces characterized by instability is their potential for producing unanticipated outcomes at the macro level. Again recall the decade of the 1960s. With anti-war sentiment growing, by the mid-1960s it was joined by an empowered Civil Rights movement, along with the feminist, environmental, counter-cultural, Black Power, and student movements, each emerging as serious threats to state regulatory mechanisms. This increased the total number of outcome basins beyond the point of systemic stability predicted by Feigenbaum, leading to a state of flux or what chaologists refer to as "far from equilibrium conditions."

With specific reference to ICs, it is clear that the changes they pursue increase the number of outcome basins beyond most social movement actors. Their efforts to reclaim definitions of work, play, leisure, childcare, sexuality, sex or gender relationships, temporal and spatial relations, relations with the environment and technology, spiri-

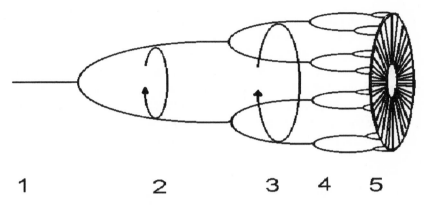

1   2   3   4   5

Figure 11.2 Bifurcation Diagram

tuality, and conflict resolution supersede in their inclusivity most social movements of the twentieth century. Since they exist at the
perimeter of the social system (the edge of the butterfly), they serve
to perpetually generate systemic instability. Previously, I have referred
to ICs as serving a function similar to that of the Southwestern *brujo*.
A brujo, or shaman, exists on the fringe of society as one who is simultaneously of, but not of, that culture. The fringe is the place for
transformation; chaos invites creation. Through the use of fractal
geometry one can visualize the passage from orderly to disorderly
states (See figure 11.2).

Figure 11.2 illustrates a torus attractor in both its state of relative order (2), and when it begins to enter its fractal dimension (3).
It is not until one enters moment (4), where multiple outcome basins
are found, that one truly enters the realm of systemic instability, with
intermittent phases of order. The fifth moment signifies a system in
total chaos. I locate ICs as actors in a subaltern mode of resistance
within moment (4) and (5). It is here that unpredictability reigns due
to the numerous innovations in living, first meant to inhibit, and
then to rearticulate, the dominant cultural interpellative process consistent with their own interpretations of the good. They appear within
the strange attractor bifurcation diagram precisely due to their am-
bulatory nature. As collective actors they seek a progressive reappropriation of lifeworld activities. Moreover, since they avoid direct
confrontation with state regulatory institutions they appear much
more illusive than typical social movement organizations and actors;
thus complicating efforts to construct morphological accounts of their

members (values, beliefs, and motivations), their communities, or their overall impact on society.

It is important to remember that orderly systems do not pass to chaos and remain there, but rather, begin to develop new forms of order (Young, 1992: 16). It is conceivable, as I will attempt to demonstrate in the final part of this essay, that through the application of nostalgic utopia and dangerous memory ICs serve to perpetually introduce notions of transcendence into civil society (torus).

Nostalgic Utopia and Dangerous Memory: Exploring the Hidden Transcript

In this closing section of the essay I would like to return to Schutz's emphasis on the ways in which the creative appropriation of myth, folklore, travel tales, and fairy tales by the wide awake consciousness can stimulate doubt in the minds of the subaltern. It is through these often coded texts that subaltern peoples maintain a sense of solidarity and purpose when faced with oppressive conditions. Indeed, Freire (1972) argued that academics had the responsibility of encouraging subaltern peoples to coalesce, to bring together common interpretations of shared living experiences, a process he referred to as "conscientization."

At stake is the extent to which appropriations of nostalgic utopia (Benjamin, 1969), dangerous memory (Welch, 1985), invented traditions (Hobsbawm and Ranger, 1983), and mythistory (Heehs, 1994) can, when juxtaposed to contemporary conditions, produce images of a more egalitarian past thereby serving as a wellspring of inspiration for resistance. I argue that ICs, hovering as they do within the strange attractor, signify a state of fractured consciousness. Their persistent example of alternative constructions of public and private space, and political, economic, and cultural relations serves as a sort of dangerous-memory. ICs are perceived as constitutive of a complex arborescent historical weave of liberating potential. When juxtaposed to contemporary social conditions, the alternate modes of living exemplified by ICs evoke notable contrast. Determining with any accuracy whether the clash of difference will reverberate with enough perspicacity to initiate transformations in dominant cultural behavior is difficult at best. To further embellish this point I recommend perceiving the kind of resistance promoted by ICs as "afterimages" or "plateaus" (Deleuze and Guattari, 1987). Metaphorically, an after-image is the faint reminiscence perceived by the mind's eye that remains once the original image has disappeared. In reference to plateaus, one can envision both a leveling off following persistent effort, but also the smooth space available for reinscription of additional effort but absent any specific directionality.

What social movement actors generate, regardless of their specific form, are resistance or replacement discourses (Henry and Milovanovic, 1991, 1996; Milovanovic, 1999). A constitutive analysis of social movements would emphasize the virtually incomprehensible combinations of symbolic juxtapositions available to any historical actors as they embrace discursive coalescences compatible with their interpretations of cultural phenomena. That is, simply living in the world and interacting with those around you will generate in memory images of previous events that may or may not correspond with what actually happened. To the extent that actors promote a patterned mode of community association in the manner of ICs, they quite clearly signify, and historically have always signified, alternatives to contemporary modes of living. As such, members of ICs perpetually hover along the edges of the wings of the butterfly attractor. They, like the brujo (Pirsig, 1991), are of but not of. Their legacy is unanticipated. Through their innovations in modes of living, members of ICs generate afterimages for generations of people to come. That is why they are framed within the strange attractor in chaos theory; they perpetually exist in a state of flux characterized both by their heterogeneity of form, and their sempiternal struggle for survival.

Foundation for a theory of subaltern destabilization through the vehicle of nostalgic utopia can be located in the early writings of Sorel (1976) and Bloch (1995). Sorel (1976) contends that constructing utopic visions alone (e.g., novels, songs, folktales, etc.) is not enough to promote destabilization of dominant culture. For that subjects must turn to the liberating potential of mythological reconstructions of cultural capital juxtaposed to contemporary conditions. Thus, myth is valued for its capacity to inspire action, but internal consistency and historical accuracy are irrelevant and purely academic. Myths conjure passion. They offer comprehension of a historical self in association with others perceived to be like them that is more valid (that is not to say more accurate), than their own experiences. For Bloch (1995), the cultivation of utopian consciousness occurs within the "not-yet consciousness," the preconsciousness of what is to come. Articulation of the not-yet consciousness can be seen as a companion concept to Benjamin's (1969) nostalgic utopia, in that consciousness of past and future is a perpetual process of recognition and interpretation. It is constitutive in nature. Like Marx, Bloch conceptualized the manifestation of the future as recognizable in the present and the past. Myths, songs, fairy tales, travel tales, and daydreams, each represent the consolidation of historical images consumed and reconfigured to meet contemporary and future demands. Plaice *et al.* (1995), suggest that the creative appropriation of historical imagery provides for the possibility of "new meaning and fresh synthetic combinations extracted from the thinking of the past, to be discovered and inherited by each succeeding age" (1995: xxvii).

I contend that ICs serve to construct alternative spaces relatively free from penetration by regulatory steering institutions while simultaneously maintaining their own modes of internal control over group and individual conduct. The subaltern, in my case members of ICs, not only create the dialogical space for resistance, but also initiate counter-hegemony by offering alternative modes of living. Within the lifeworld, within the hidden transcript, emerges voices of agency capable of articulating counter-hegemonic interpretations of dominant cultural symbols.

Conclusion

Application of chaos theory to the study of social movements is relevant in that it anticipates the expansion of civil society and the consequent articulation of subaltern concerns anywhere there is systemic flux. Organic systems, and I suggest that possibly even social systems, can typically absorb these demands through bifurcations up to three, as the torus struggles to maintain stability. However, and crucially, continued micrological disturbance within civil society (phase space) will begin to produce macro-level transformations in regulatory steering institutions. If movement actors choose to increase their demands even further, it is likely that systems will reach what chaologists refer to as "far from equilibrium" conditions, a point where predictability of system outcomes is difficult at best. It is at this moment that strange attractors appear. At this point in any system, predictability of outcomes is virtually impossible.

I have located ICs within the strange attractor bifurcation model.

This is predicated on the multiple demands placed on aspects of system steering that may or may not be readily absorbed. Moreover, ICs maintain a political, economic, and cultural existence on the fringe of dominant culture. As such, they hover within those sectors identified in the strange attractor diagram as producing the greatest levels of uncertainty. ICs perpetually exist in a state of flux.

Finally, to more firmly establish their status as social movement actors I referred to those literatures addressing the resistance value inherent in creative appropriations of myth. Like the fractal geometric algorithms used in chaos theory, multiple iterations or system feedback produces considerable instability to the point of chaos. The greater the number of bifurcations, the more a system is constituted by flux. In my estimation, the same can be said for the constitution of subjects within a discursively mediated symbolic-moral universe. Members of ICs, like all social movement actors, engage in *nomination* (Sassoon, 1984), the practice of naming the world around us, of claiming what is real and what is true. ICs exist on the fringe of culture, on the edge of the butterfly's wings, precisely due to their efforts to emancipate human relations with nature, each other, technology, spirituality, and the body. Members of ICs are indicative of a fourth way to conceive of social movement actors because they supersede the torus.

Notes

1. It is useful to characterize the subaltern as the disadvantaged within a specific temporal and spatial period. In twentieth century America, for example, the subaltern would include: (i) women, (ii) black, Indian, Asian, and Latino populations, and (iii) members of the lower middle class, working class, and poor. While there exist variations in each of these classifications (e.g., women who have significant power), in general, when speaking of the subaltern I am referring to any group or subgroup within a specific temporal and spatial period devoid of political, economic, and cultural capital.

2. For example, work, sexual expression, gender, child development, education, conflict resolution, spirituality, environment, race or ethnic relations, war, and so forth may be subject to replacement and redefinition in a manner similar to what Henry and Milovanovic (1996) refer to as "replacement discourse."

3. A Poincaré section, after the French mathematician Henri Poincaré, refers to efforts to identify all of the possible exogenous intervening variables that may impact a dependent variable. It differs from path analysis in its application to the social sciences in that it recognizes even the most subjective of constitutive processes as possible determinants in specific behaviors and thoughts. These constructs are most conducive to qualitative analysis.

4. Rhizomes are literally the roots of trees. I use the concept here to metaphorically denote the way in which roots move away from the tree trunk in unpredictable ways. That is, roots do not move in straight lines, they are ambulant, crooked. I envision members of ICs as acting in similar ways. They do not abide by the typical modes of social movement activism but choose instead to be rhizomatic, moving like roots of trees in unpredictable directions that none-the-less promote growth.

5. Striated evokes the image of lines or pathways dictating specific responsibilities as they relate to roles inherited by actors.

6. Important here is the extent to which Mandelbrot, and by extension my own interests in social movements, privileges the irregular, the fragmented. Understanding fractals and the fractal geometry created by Mandelbrot requires emphasis on the minutia of systemic composition. The point is to emphasize the relevance of micrological compositions of energy, interests, and actions as they too serve to constitute the whole.

7. Limit attractors return again and again to their initial condition. Examples would be violin strings, and a pendulum. These are closed systems. Limit cycles do not return to an initial condition, but rather, move in a cyclic path within a confined space.

8. Perhaps one could consider contemporary Iran, Iraq, China, Cambodia, Honduras, El Salvador, and Guatemala as examples of this kind of limit or fixed point attractor.

References

Althusser, L. (1969). *For Marx*. Harmondsworth, U.K.: Allen Lane.

Althusser, L. (1971). *Lenin and Philosophy and Other Essays*. London: New Left Books.

Armstrong, P. J., Goodman, J. F. B., and J. D. Hyman. (1981). *Ideology and Shop-floor Industrial Relations*. London: Croom Helm.

Baudrillard, J. (1981). *For A Critique of the Political Economy of the Sign*. St. Louis: Telos Press.

Benjamin, W. (1969). *Illuminations*. Edited by H. Arendt, trans. by H. Zohn. New York: Schocken Books.

Bertramsen, R., Thomsen, J., and J. Torfing. (1991). *State, Economy and Society*. London: Unwin Hyman.

Bloch, E. (1995). *The Principle of Hope*. Vols. I and II. Cambridge, MA: MIT Press.

Boggs, C. (1985). *Social Movements and Political Power*. Philadelphia: Temple University Press.

Bond, G. C., and A. Gilliam. (1994). *Social Constructions of the Past*. New York: Routledge.

Bourdieu, P. (1984). *Distinction: A Social Critique of the Judgement of Taste*. Translated by Richard Nice. Cambridge, MA: Harvard University Press.

Bracher, M. (1993). *Lacan, Discourse, and Social Change: A Psychoanalytic Cultural Criticism*. Ithaca, NY: Cornell University Press.

Brand, K. (1990). "Cyclical aspects of new social movements." In R. Dalton and M. Kuechler (Eds.), *Challenging the Political Order: New Social and Political Movements in Western Democracies*. Cambridge, UK: Polity.

Briggs, J., and F. D. Peat. (1989). *Turbulent Mirror*. New York: Harper & Row.

Burawoy, M. (1979). *Manufacturing Consent: Changes in the Labour Process Under Monopoly Capitalism*. Chicago: University of Chicago Press.

Butler, J. (1990). *Gender Trouble*. New York: Routledge.

de Certeau, M. (1984). *The Practice of Everyday Life*. Berkeley: University of California Press.

Cohen, J. (1985). "Strategy or identity: New theoretical paradigms and contemporary social movements." *Social Research*, 52 (4): 664–716.

Cohen, J., and A. Arato. (1992). *Civil Society and Political Theory*. Cambridge, MA: MIT Press.

Cornell, D. (1993). *Transformations: Recollective Imagination and Sexual Difference*. New York: Routledge.

Delorme, R. (1984). "New View on the Economic Theory of the State: A Case Study of France." (Paris: CEPREMAP; memo no. 8401).

Deleuze, G., and F. Guattari. (1987). *A Thousand Plateaus: Capitalism and Schizophrenia*. Minneapolis: University of Minnesota Press.

Eyerman, R., and A. Jamison. (1991). *Social Movements: A Cognitive Approach*. University Park, PA: Pennsylvania State University Press.

Fantasia, R., and E. Hirsch. (1995). "Culture in rebellion: The appropriation and transformation of the veil in the Algerian revolution." In Hank Johnston and Bert Klandermans (Eds.), *Social Movements and Culture*. Minneapolis: University of Minnesota Press, pp. 144–62.

Ferrell, J. (1993). *Crimes of Style: Urban Graffiti and the Politics of Criminality*. New York: Garland.

Foucault, M. (1976). *The Archeology of Knowledge*. New York: Harper and Row.

Freire, P. (1972). *Pedagogy of the Oppressed*. New York: Herder and Her.

Gilmore, D. (1987). *Aggression and Community: Paradoxes of Andalusian Culture*. New Haven, CT: Yale University Press.

Giroux, H. (1992). *Border Crossings*. New York: Routledge.

Giroux, H. (1996). *Fugitive Cultures: Race, Violence, and Youth*. New York: Routledge.

Gregersen, H., and L. Sailer. (1993). "Chaos theory and its implications for social science research." *Human Relations*, 46(7): 777–802.

Gross, D. (1992a). "Rethinking Traditions." *Telos*, 94 (Winter): 5–10.

Gross, D. (1992b). *The Past in Ruins: Tradition and the Critique of Modernity*. Amherst, MA: University of Massachusetts Press.

Gusfield, J. (1994). "The reflexivity of social movements: Collective behavior and mass society theory revisited." In E. Larana, H. Johnston, and J. Gusfield (Eds.), *New Social Movements*. Philadelphia: Temple University Press, pp. 58–78.

Gyani, G. (1993). "Political uses of tradition in postcommunist East Central Europe." *Social Research*, 60 (4): 893–913.

Heehs, P. (1994). "Myth, history, and theory." *History and Theory*, 33 (1): 1–19.

Henry, S., and D. Milovanovic. (1991). "Constitutive criminology: The maturation of critical theory" *Criminology*, 29: 293–316.

Henry, S. and D. Milovanovic. (1996). *Constitutive Criminology: Beyond Postmodernism*. London: Sage.

Hobsbawm, E., and T. Ranger. (1983). *The Invention of Tradition*. Cambridge: Cambridge University Press.

Ingelhart, R. (1990). *Culture Shift in Advanced Industrial Society*. Princeton, NJ: Princeton University Press.

Jamison, F. (1972). *Marxism and Form*. Princeton, NJ: Princeton University Press.

Jenson, J. (1995). "What's in a Name? Nationalist Movements and public discourse." In H. Johnston and B. Klandermans (Eds.), *Social Movements and Culture*. Minneapolis: University of Minnesota Press, pp. 107–26.

Jessop, B. (1990). *State Theory: Putting Capitalist States in Their Place*. University Park, PA: Pennsylvania State University Press.

Johnston, H., and B. Klandermans. (1995). *Social Movements and Culture*. Minneapolis: University of Minnesota Press.

Katz, J. (1989). *Seductions of Crime*. New York: Basic Books.

Kellner, D. (1989). *Jean Baudrillard*. Stanford, CA: Stanford University Press.

Lacan, J. (1977). *Ecrits*. Translated by A. Sheridan. New York: Norton.

Laclau, E. (1990). *New Reflections on the Revolution of Our Time*. London: Verso.

Luke, T. (1991). "Touring hyperreality: Critical theory confronts informational society." In P. Wexler (Ed.), *Critical Theory Now*. New York: Falmer Press: 1–26.

Mead, G. H. (1934). *Mind, Self and Society*. C. W. Morris (Ed.). Chicago: University of Chicago Press.

Melucci, A. (1996a). *Challenging Codes*. London: Cambridge University Press.

Melucci, A. (1996b). *The Playing Self: Person and Meaning in the Planetary Society*. London: Cambridge University Press.

Milovanovic, D. (1999). "Catastrophe theory, discourse and conflict regulation: Generating a 'third way'." In B. Arrigo (Ed.), *Justice at the Margins: The Maturation of Critical Theory in Law, Crime and Deviance*. New York: Wadsworth.

Nandy, A. (1987). "Cultural frames for social transformation: A credo." *Alternatives*, 12: 113–23.

Pirsig, R. (1991). *Lila: An Inquiry Into Morals*. New York: Bantam Books.

Plaice, N., Plaice, S., and P. Knight. (1995). "Translators' introduction." in E. Bloch, *The Principle of Hope*. Translated by N. Plaice, S. Plaice, and P. Knight. Cambridge, MA: MIT Press.

Prigogene, I. (1980). *From Being to Becoming*. San Francisco: W.H. Freeman.

Prigogene, I., and I. Stengers. (1984). *Order Out of Chaos: Man's New Dialogue with Nature*. New York: Bantam Books.

Rao, N. (1994). "Interpreting silences: Symbol and history in the case of Ram Janmabhoomi/Babri Masjid." In G. C. Bond and A. Gilliam (Eds.), *Social Construction of the Past*. New York: Routledge, pp. 154–164.

Sassoon, J. (1984). "Ideology, symbolic action and rituality in social movements: The effects on organizational forms." *Social Science Information*, 23 (4/5): 861–73.

Schehr, R. (1997). *Dynamic Utopia: Establishing Intentional Communities as a New Social Movement*. Westport, CT: Bergan and Garvey.

Schutz, A. (1971). *Collected Papers*. Vol. I. Martinus Nijhoff: The Hague.

Scott, J. (1990). *Domination and the Arts of Resistance*. New Haven, CT: Yale University Press.

Snow, D., and R. Benford. (1992). "Master frames and cycles of protest." In A. Morris and C. McClurg Mueller (Eds.), *Frontiers in Social Movement Theory*. New Haven, Yale University Press, pp. 133–55.

Sorel, G. (1976). *From Georges Sorel: Essays in Socialism and Philosophy*. Edited by J. L. Stanley. Translated by J. and C. Stanley. New York: Oxford University Press.

Touraine, A. (1988). *Return of the Actor*. Minneapolis: University of Minnesota Press.

Young, I. M. (1986). "The ideal of community and the politics of difference." *Social Theory and Practice*, 12 (1): 1–26.

Young, T. R. (1990). *Chaos and the Drama of Social Change: A Metaphysic for Postmodern Science*. Publication of the Red Feather Institute Weidman, MI.

Young, T. R. (1992). *Chaos Theory and Human Agency*. Publication of the Red Feather Institute: 2–22.

Young, T. R. (1999). "A nonlinear theory of justice." In B. Arrigo, *Social Justice, Criminal Justice*. Belmont, CA: Wadsworth.

Welch, S. (1985). *Communities of Resistance and Solidarity: A Feminist Theology of Liberation*. New York: Orbis Books.

Zipes, J. (1992–93). "The utopian function of tradition." *Telos*, 94 (Winter): 25–29.

T. R. Young

12

A CONSTITUTIVE THEORY OF JUSTICE: THE ARCHITECTURE OF AFFIRMATIVE POSTMODERN LEGAL SYSTEMS

Introduction

Given that human beings, collectively, constitute justice systems, the question arises, what kind of justice system should a people create. The architecture of a postmodern theory of justice offered here relies upon the new sciences of chaos and complexity. The substance of a postmodern theory of justice is constituted with a complex algorithm informed by the concept of praxis. The concept of praxis used here respects the need to protect and sustain the natural environment upon which all peoples depend while it honors diversity and human agency. In short, I offer an outline by which an affirmative postmodern theory of justice can be constituted.

When one puts the deeply organized world-view of language, self and Other into a larger socio-cultural framework, the task of a postmodern and affirmative criminology theorist becomes to help reconstitute entrenched ideologies, knowledges, and truths along in order to dissolve and repair personal alienation, repression, and marginalization. Mindful of these dialectics of struggle and linguistic control, several postmodern criminological theorists have called for the development and articulation of replacement discourses; that is, codes of speech more compatible with the stories and points of view of various disenfranchised collectives (e.g., Henry and Milovanovic, 1991,

1996; Arrigo and Young, 1997; Howe, 1994). This is one such replacement discourse.

Postmodern Understandings of Law

Those of us who work out of a postmodern critique of law and justice reject the basic assumptions of both modernist and pre-modern groundings of legal principles and associated theories of justice. There are no natural laws given by god(s) or by divine fiat with which to solve the human problem of order and distribution of resources. There are, as well, no natural imperatives such as asserted by those who offer grand theory as a way to justify class, status or power arrangements. All are, equally, human products. All are, equally, fraught with politics and filled with special interests. All justice systems give a gloss of legitimacy to some of the best and some of the worst arrangements of social life found in the ever-changing history of peoples, countries, nations and states. This chapter is no exception. I fully recognize the human and cultural sources of both the structure and content of this theory of justice. The difference is that, in other systems of justice, human agency is denied in favor of either divine or natural imperative.

The role of human agency does not mean that the concept of justice is to be discarded; still less that, absent a founding god or objective laws of nature, that one thereby can justify anything, that one must embrace nihilism and solipisic self interests. Rather, an affirmative postmodern theory of justice argues that human beings can and should build systems of justice; systems of law; systems of social control. It is just that the architecture of such systems should be explicitly political; that they should be open to collective critique, collective change and accommodating of diverse social forms.

Diversity and collectivity seem impossible from a modernist point of view emphasizing as it does uniformity, predictability, generality and rationality. Collectivity and diversity seems evil from a pre-modernist perspective permitting as they do alternative ways to do marriage, family, economics, politics, religion, education and other distinctly social work. It is the particular genius of complexity theory that diversity and collectivity can occupy the same regions of time and space.

I would like to suggest how this is possible in the sections below. We will start with a look at the architecture of justice from the point of view of chaos theory, the short version of which is that an algorithm which permits pattern in the same moment that it contains surprise; that permits individuality in the same moment that it guarantees stability—of a sort; that honors human agency in the same moment it provides for predictability and dependability, such an algorithm is possible to adopt as a grounding for a postmodern architecture of justice. Let us begin.

A Constitutive Theory of Justice

Stuart Henry and Dragan Milovanovic (1991; 1996) have set out constitutive theory in general. They explain that a postmodern approach to both knowledge and society emphasizes the provisional and situated emergence of truth. In the case of a constitutive theory of justice, one would view each law, arrest, each indictment, each trial and each judgement as well as the actual experience of the accused in the social context in which each emerged.

While the sociology of law and justice is most complex, still the general point can be made that law and the principles of justice upon which law is grounded follow the political and economic arrangements of the social order in which they are found. In stratified societies, law and justice tend to reproduce existing patterns of privilege. In religious societies, i.e., ecclesia, law and justice are given divine sanction—mere mortals cannot argue with either the law itself nor the interpretations of divine law made by a religious cadre arrogating that sanctity to their own interpretations.

A postmodern constitutive theory of justice holds that given peoples can, within rough limits, create just about any system of justice they care to create. The limiting conditions are set by two interacting and quite different sets of concerns. The first set of concerns are to be found in the non-linear dynamics of complex systems. I will lay out these in just a moment. The second limiting set of principles are found in the nature of social relations. In a word, some attention to group needs must be embedded in justice systems else, as Hobbes put it, a war of each against all subverts and degrades the human project.

Chaos Theory and Justice Systems

In a complex society a constitutive theory of justice must take into consideration the essential features of non-linear dynamics. In order to make this essay manageable within the limits set, I will confine myself to a few major features of nonlinear dynamics:

1. *Nonlinearity*: Small changes in key social variables can give rise to very great changes in legal codes and in control practices in a given political economy.

2. *Bifurcations*: Given critical values in key parameters within a socio-economic formation, two or more differing legal systems can arise.

3. *Chaos and Social Control*: In times of deep chaos, traditional methods of social control fail.

4. *Chaos and Creativity*: In deep chaos, uncertainty increases and human agency becomes problematic. However, entirely new systems of norm and order-maintenance emerge. Some have survival values and may become the base of new legal codes and new ways of seeking justice.

I will discuss each point to help give flesh and bone to the major ideas emerging in complexity theory. Again, this is in aid of building a postmodern philosophy of law which recognizes both the social sources of law and the human role in creating and interpreting law. I will end this essay by addressing the most interesting question at hand in a time of uncertainty: upon what foundation does one ground a thoroughly postmodern theory of law. This new science of complexity offers something of a guide as to form if not content.

Nonlinear Justice Systems

Modernist justice systems make much of routine, rationality and uniformity in treatment before the law. Postmodern justice systems, grounded upon chaos or complexity theory make room for creativity and variety in both the making and the enforcement of law. On the surface, non-linear justice systems appear to be an open invitation for bigotry, personal animus and for hostile discrimination in policing and in courtrooms. This would be the case were it not for the overriding principles of praxis and empowerment which continue to inform legal principles in affirmative postmodern theories of justice.

The case for non-linearity, irrationality and irregularity is powerful. In the first instance, it is impossible to embody the regularities and rationalities required for a thoroughly modernist system of justice. No criminal case is precisely, entirely, exactly like another one. No two police officers will respond in precisely the same way to a given action. No two judges will make precisely the same rulings to the same questions. No two juries will make precisely the same judgment to the same act of murder, rape or theft. No two prisons will treat a given prisoner exactly as ordered by the court. Variation is part of the human process; a modernist justice system of the sort required by rationality is impossible.

Nor is rationality particularly desirable. There is much to be said for variation and creativity in policing, judging and sanctioning those who offend legal codes. It is not that special conditions may alter judgments; they do. It is not that sameness and similarity may be impossible; they are impossible. It is rather that mercy, forgiveness, clemency and acceptance are larger, more powerful resources for a transcending justice. Some people will not, can not respond to mercy and forgiveness. All people will, at some time, treat pro-social irrationality as weakness and as an exploitative opportunity. Still most people, most of the time, do fit such nonlinear response into a discourse of forgiveness and redemption. Parents, friends, police, judges, wardens, teachers and others charged with social control make such nonlinear responses with good effect to the human project. A thoroughly postmodern system of justice should accommodate itself to the capacities of complex human beings to transcend causality and to move to entirely new patterns of life and living.

Perhaps the most interesting feature of complex non-linear systems is that very diverse systems can occupy the same time/space continua without conflict. Of considerable interest here is that very different justice systems can co-exist and work their different social magics to enable the human project. In the United States, one can find some seven or eight parallel and very different systems of justice; religious, political, economic, medical and psychological. While it may seem redundant and inefficient to have parallel justice systems and, may in fact, be so, still the possibility of co-existing justice systems best meets the human need for redemption, for reparation, for restoration and for rehabilitation.

Bifurcations

If small changes in key parameters can trigger large changes in crime rates; murder, theft, arson, fraud, pollution and other most serious forms of behavior hostile to person and to community, large changes in social control tactics seem sensible. Yet, it well may be the case that a small change in social policy can forestall the need for large changes in such social control resources. The work of Hübler (1992) at University of Illinois has shown, in principle, that non-linear regimes can be controlled. Control requires a light touch at the right time but, given wisdom and judgment, such intervention in the life of a family, in the routines of a school, in the habits of police officers and in the policies of a business may prevent large changes in juvenile delinquency, in ethnic violence, in vandalism or in consumer fraud.

Then too, there are some bifurcations which affirmative justice systems would defeat. Bifurcations in variables which trigger gender violence, racist crimes and crimes against workers and/or customers by corporations are cases in point. If uncertainty in employment or income are key to racist crime and gender violence, then in order to prevent these from exploding to fill the social space available to them, an affirmative postmodern justice system would, in the first instance, see to policy which stabilizes these at minimal value.

Chaos and Social Control

The United States is, arguably, the most heavily monitored, analyzed, reported and described society in human history. Much of that knowledge is used within the dozen or so control systems which permeate every domain of social life. Modernist criminology, oriented to formal theory and to scientific control theory, supports rank after rank of social control. Modernist states, oriented to political legitimacy, supports a wide variety of control institutions from the criminal justice system itself—now the largest in the world, to the various state regulatory agencies—far more than most societies, to the increasing use of psychology, medicine and psychiatry to find and control those who murder, rape, steal and burn in the most affluent society in human history.

Chaos theory teaches us that efforts to predict and to control fade and fail as ever more chaotic regimes appear. If social processes are indeed non-linear, then the vast effort to control the effects of racism, gender violence, class inequality and corporate hegemony over the production and distribution of essential social goods are doomed to failure.

Affirmative postmodern jurisprudence and criminology requires a research design with which to ascertain the points at which key variables bifurcate. Affirmative postmodern justice systems enjoins a political process by which a society selects, between alternative dynamics regimes, those which most fully answer to the human project.

Below I will offer an outline of a non-linear but affirmative approach to a distinctly postmodern practice of justice but just now, we need to consider one more most interesting feature of non-linear regimes most relevant to social change and renewal.

Deep Chaos and Human Agency

In other work I have tried to think through the effects of differing dynamical regimes on human agency (Young, 1992). I would like to revisit the topic and think about how chaotic regimes affect the human quest for change and renewal and, at the same time, the human need for order, predictivity, and planning. In short, whatever system of justice we humans create through our norms, laws, sanctions and policies, we need to celebrate the diversity and potentiality of human agency in any distinctly affirmative postmodern system of justice.

The implications for a constitutive theory of justice are most interesting. It may well be the case that any system dynamics having fewer than four attractors may be too confining to the human interest in change and renewal. That interest keys off the fact that all human societies dwell in an inconstant world. The global environment is a complex adaptive system which affects the welfare of human society. Food supply, climate, weather patterns including storms, floods and earthquakes, all affect the human project. The global economic system is a complex adaptive process which greatly affects employment, health, pollution and conflict not excluding warfare. Political Blocs such as the European Union, the North American Free Trade Agreement and the Pacific Rim countries are all complex adaptive systems whose ever-changing dynamics affect the welfare of peoples around the earth.

Both modern and pre-modern justice systems attempt to reduce variety and to confine attractor basins to two or four; two genders, four races, two degrees of kinship, four strata of status honor. It well may be the case that the degree of uncertainty embedded in the number of attractor basins available in legal codes defeat the human need for change and renewal in that they forbid options which, in times of uncertainty, answer better to the human project than behaviors sanctioned by legal codes.

At the same time, social policies which drive a society into deep chaos may well increase uncertainty so much that collective responses to common problems are displaced by privatized, short-term responses: theft, robbery, genocide, fraud and other behaviors hostile to human agency. The case of the Ik people in north-east Uganda serves as point (Young, 1971). They were forbidden to hunt game by the government which used their ancient hunting grounds as a game preserve to attract tourists and foreign currency. The Ik society collapsed; children abandoned or prostituted, elderly people cast out, marriage forms collapsed.

I tend to think that people can handle two or three uncertainties in work, health, personal relations, school and religion but four or more are too many. One of the findings of chaos theory is that four or more interacting variables place a system at the edge of deep chaos where a small change can make great differences in one's life (Gould and Gould: 1989). Some make recourse to new, perhaps anti-social behavior to bring a bit of certainty back into their lives.

This may mean that, while eight or sixteen attractor basins may be appropriate for a whole society in a complex environment, fewer attractors may be appropriate for particular individuals or firms. It may be the case that complexity requires differing sets of attractors for differing sectors of a given society; institutions as well as such population groups as age cohorts or occupational specialties. A postmodern theory of constitutive justice may require far more complexity than the simple binary justice systems found in modern and pre-modern societies.

Finally, I want to point out that deep chaos itself is a dynamical region in which, sometimes, the human interest in change and renewal is served. Deep chaos does not mean the end of social life; rather it may well mean the beginning of new and most accommodating forms of justice; forms which augment and enhance human agency and human dignity. The point of an affirmative postmodern theory of justice is, nontheless, an effort to avoid the costs of deep chaos while keeping the benefits of variety, uncertainty, change and renewal.

A Postmodern Praxis Society

The concept of praxis has an ancient and honorable history. Markovic (1974) sets five most interesting and most useful aspects of praxis which I want to use as a grounding for a the postmodern theory of justice offered here. By praxis, I mean a complex activity in which individuals, in collectivities, create culture, society, and create themselves as "species beings," i.e., as human beings. The moments of praxis, as Markovic set them, include self-determination (in contrast to coercion), intentionality (in contrast to blind reaction), sociality (in contrast to privatized nihilism), creativity (in contrast to sameness), and rationality (in contrast to blind chance).

These five "moments" of praxis constitute a very complex algorithm which sets limits at the same time it permits variety. This particular algorithm, having five interacting variables, offers a very, very complex unfolding of human social forms which, at once serves the human interest in pattern and reliability while at the same time permits for variety in language, in love and in work. The unfolding process, complex and changing as it is, moves knowledge making and knowledge using off the dead centers of modern and pre-modern sensibility over to a constantly changing quest for certainty and close control to tolerance and respect for those who, in their wisdom, take differing pathways through the future of history.

Non-Linear Feedback.

Ordinarily, one would expect that, given acceptance for variation in social forms embedded in a postmodern theory of justice, one would find a great deal of conflict, animus and confusion. Chaos theory has one more valuable lesson to offer those who would build distinctly postmodern systems of law and justice. Very different systems can occupy the same regions of time and space if, and only if, the feedback between them is non-linear. I have discussed the idea of non-linearity above but this time want to explicate its meaning for various and very different social life worlds.

Modernist social theory presumes convergence of all cultures toward one universal culture contained within a global political economy. The rich legacies of French, German, Japanese, Innuit and Russian culture are, in the modernist scenario, blended and baked into one common ubiquitous culture. And, given a modernist legal theory and justice system, that effort at sameness is constituted. In the premodern scenario, one religious tradition triumphs and all others are relegated to the dustbin of history as myth and superstition. Not so in an affirmative postmodern architecture of justice. Competing, contradictory and coterminous systems of marriage, politics, religion and economics can retain their structure.

Non-linear feedback means that different rules apply to differ peoples as long as the five moments of praxis are honored. The emphasis on each moment can vary within a given social-life world as might the degree of non-linearity. Still, given non-linearity, we might see Islamic peoples living side-by-side with peoples who embody Christian, Hindu, Buddhist and Jewish religions. Given non-linearity, we can create a system of justice and distribution in which the advantages of capitalism can be extracted while its negativities are moderated by very different economic systems. Again, non-linearity between systems is the key to the integrity of each system.

Modern and pre-modern justice systems insist upon one and only one way of doing marriage or doing gender. Given non-linearity in a justice system, conventional marriage forms can exist side by side with very different forms of intimacy. Again, the over-riding moment of sociality informs and limits such diverse marriage forms; one cannot in the constituted form of justice offered here, sustain brutal, exploitative forms of marriage or religion.

The same variety is possible in sport, in schooling, in art as in music and literature. Affirmative postmodern sensibility rejects uniformity and universality in standards of creating, of sponsoring and of evaluating the art of living. If we use chaos theory to constitute our theory of justice and to inform our making of laws, we can retain most the rich diversity, the rich legacy of ethnic and national cultures. To that end, I commend future generations of lawmakers, law enforcers and those who study them.

References

Arrigo, Bruce, and T. R. Young. (1997). *Postmodern Criminology: Theories of Crime and Crimes of Theorists*. Weidmar, MI: Red Feather Institute.

Gould, James, and Carol Gould. (1989). *Life at the Edge*. New York: Freeman and Company.

Henry S., and D. Milovanovic. (1991). "Constitutive criminology: The maturation of critical theory." *Criminology*, 29: 293–316.

Henry, S., and D. Milovanovic. (1996). *Constitutive Criminology: Beyond Postmodernism*. London: Sage Publications.

Howe, A. (1994). *Punish and Critique: Towards a Feminist Analysis of Penality*. London: Routledge.

Hübler, A. (1992). "Modelling and control of complex systems: Paradigms and applications." In L. Lam (Ed.), *Modeling Complex Phenomena*. New York: Springer.

Markovic, M. (1974). *From Affluence to Praxis*. Boston: Beacon.

Young, T. R. (1971). "International terrorism and public opinion policy processes," *Co-Existence* (July): 22–34.

Young, T. R. (1992). "Chaos theory and human agency." *Humanity and Society*, 16:441–460.

Stuart Henry and Dragan Milovanovic

CONCLUSION: CONSTITUTIVE CRIMINOLOGY ENGAGES ITS CRITICS—AN ASSESSMENT[1]

Since the initial statement "Constitutive Criminology: The Missing Link" (Henry, 1989) and our first substantive statement "Constitutive Criminology: The Maturation of Critical Theory" (Henry and Milovanovic, 1991), constitutive theory has grown into a significant theoretical position within critical criminology, as the contributions to this book testify. As our work developed and began to be discussed we became mindful of the need to address the issues raised by this commentary. Up until the culmination of our joint project *Constitutive Criminology* (Henry and Milovanovic, 1996) we had resisted the temptation to address this growing corpus, believing that doing so prematurely would likely draw us into a distracting debate. However, now that we have laid a firm basis for our ideas, and have welcomed the diverse scholars who have joined with us on the constitutive journey[2] we feel the time is ripe for a first response to our critics' interest and concerns. At the time of completion of this book in the Spring of 1998 there have been numerous reviews in journals, book chapters and substantive articles, and the contribution of the theory has been seriously discussed in ten different texts on crime and deviance (See Gibbons, 1994; 160–64; Beirne and Messerschmidt, 1995: 533–35; Einstadter and Henry, 1995: 277–300; Naffine, 1996: 75–77; DeKeseredy and Schwartz, 1996: 275–76; Akers, 1997: 176–79; Lanier and Henry, 1998: 282–85; Deutschmann, 1998: 378; Barak, 1998: 219–234; Vold, Bernard, and Snipes, 1998). Here, by way of conclusion, we take the time to address some of the issues raised in this discussion. We take the opportunity to address some of these different concerns and diverse directions with a view toward clarifying and enumerating the constitutive project's continued development. Moreover, we look forward to continuous critical dialogue in this endeavor, for it is a crucial component in the emergence of new vistas.

We saw in the introduction that several commentators had recognized that this theory was saying something new and something different. However, most commentators have pointed to constitutive theory's relatively unresearched state (until now). Gibbons (1994) questioned the future impact of the theory and, while acknowledging its critical challenge to mainstream approaches, speculated that it was more likely to be incorporated by mainstream criminology than to result in a revolutionary transformation. Similarly, DeKeseredy and Schwartz (1996: 276) conclude that, despite its important presence, it is not yet developed enough to be called a school of thought. And while Colvin (1997: 1449) saw its "most provocative discussions" as "those concerning the definition and causes of crime," Nelken, in his kaleidoscopic review of new theories, concluded that it will be difficult for constitutive criminology to reach one of its goals of changing the meaning of crime unless the approach is spelled out in more detail (1994: 13). Nelken pointed out that the main burden of any such transformation is on "the theoretically reflective practitioner rather than the theorist" (1994: 29); we agree and this book is aimed to contribute to just such a transformation. Others are less sympathetic, however.

Different Takes

Critical responses to the constitutive project have taken a variety of forms. Unfortunately, one of the underlying themes shared by critics is their focus on parts of the project rather than the project as a whole. Indeed, it is somewhat disconcerting to us that, in spite of our urging that the harm of crime is a dialectical *coproduction* and that ceasing such production requires a holistic response at *multiple* levels, some commentators have sought to reduce the project to its component "parts." Yet Swingewood (1975: 57) has pointed out in his analysis of Marx's dialectical method, "the point is that the totality is always part of something larger and the part is simultaneously a totality." From the perspective of dialectical analysis, "the part cannot be abstracted from the whole and sociologically examined apart from it and then mechanically inserted again after analysis." Rather, the parts, "must be integrated into a whole or they remain abstract and theoretically misleading" (Swingewood, 1975: 44–45). We should also point out that the abstraction "parts," itself is misleading; parts themselves are dialectically and interrelatedly constituted as well as being in a dynamic state of flux. Relatedly, Roger Matthews and Jock Young's left realism (though ultimately divergent from our direction) has similarly argued that only by completing the "square of crime" is it possible to depict the interactive nature (i.e., among agencies of social control, the public, the offender, and the victim) involved in the construction of the social reality of crime (Matthews and Young, 1992: 24–68).

Here we address a variety of "problems" of this kind, pointing out that by separating off aspects for analysis, without relating them to the whole project, critics undermine the integrational objective that we and others set out to achieve (see Barak, 1998).

The Problem of Complex Prose

A recurrent theme among critics of postmodernism, deconstructionism in general, and constitutive criminology in particular, is expressed in the internet joke: "What do you get if you cross a deconstructionist with a mafiosi? An offer you can't understand!" One commentator, for example, questioned "whether the complexity (and apparently obscurity) of the terminology and schemata. . . . is fully warranted, and whether the propositions could be more concisely stated" (Friedrichs, 1996: 125). He goes on to say that "this is a difficult work, dense and even bewildering in places, and especially likely to be challenging to those who come to it with no direct familiarity with the work of the various contemporary critical and postmodern writers cited" (*Ibid.*). The same sentiment was echoed by another who said, "The reader not already familiar with postmodern work and its often obscure language . . . will find it exceedingly difficult to extract the author's ideas" (Colvin, 1997: 1450). And in an otherwise very positive assessment another concluded, "The most vexing problem awaiting readers . . . is the esoteric language used" (Bohm, 1997: 16).

Interestingly, in their own critique of postmodernism's "semantic challenge," Schwartz and Friedrichs (1994: 227–228) usefully summarize some of the arguments in favor of what they describe as "dense and abstruse . . . gratuitously obscure, incoherent, and undisciplined," prose. These include its greater responsiveness to complexity and a playfulness that enables readers to construct their own meaning from the text, thereby empowering them (for additional arguments see Bérubé, 1997). While dismissing these arguments (in favor of addressing the needs of victims suffering the reality of crime), Schwartz and Friedrichs also stumble upon a third argument in favor of complexity, but they ultimately neglect to address it. Thus they ask rhetorically,

> [Is] the obstacle the fact that the rest of us are unable to liberate ourselves from the constraints of interpreting the world in the familiar idiom of rational, contemporary social science? If we reorient ourselves, would we find modes and styles of understanding that are ultimately more valid and more revealing in a changing, endlessly complex world? *(ibid.)*.

This glimpses the central issue. When readers of these materials find them difficult to comprehend the question is, why? The answer is not as self-evident as it seems. The difficulty is not merely unfamiliar prose but an outcome of the modernist scientific tradition which divides the world into ever-more specialized corpses of knowledge, and then comes to believe that immersion in any one of these language fragments is universal. To put it more concretely, someone who speaks in mathematical formulae can chirp merrily and comprehensibly to a fellow mathematician but is incomprehensible to the poet. Similarly, the sense of poetry may resonate among poets but confound the mathematician. In short, when theorizing is vested in single disciplines or subdisciplines it becomes very difficult for those outside to understand. Normally that's alright because academics rarely read outside their own discipline and most intradisciplinary prose is understandable; in contrast, most interdisciplinary prose presents problems of comprehension.

These problems are complicated by the challenge postmodernism makes to the modernist practice of dividing knowledge into disciplines and to the myopic and fragmented knowledges such disciplinary division produces. This fragmentation occurs not only between disciplines but, in the case of those like criminology, within them (Ericson and Carriere, 1994; Barak, 1998). In seeking to integrate insights and build transcending concepts, it has become necessary both to incorporate some prose from the diversity of disciplines *and* to invent some overarching concepts designed to capture social life's complexity (Bérubé, 1997). The result is that the prose becomes largely unfamiliar to the narrowly invested reader. This is particularly so when one sometimes comes across neologisms, mathemes, ideographs, phase maps, outcome basins, bifurcations, algorithms, isomorphisms, homologies, and butterfly attractors! So why were several high school students able to grapple with and understand this work? (See p. 3 of this book). The answer is that they had yet to be "trained." As a result our text was no more difficult to them than the single disciplinary work, all being somewhat incomprehensible. Yet to the "trained" (disciplined) academic this work was difficult.

Indeed, that we have a wide range of disciplinary coverage has been recognized by some of our critics. For example, Friedrichs (1996: 124–25) admits that in "advancing a novel integrative approach," *Constitutive Criminology* incorporates a "vastly ambitious engagement with a wide range of especially challenging and difficult theories in social thought." These include not only the familiar mainstream theories and those of several generations of critical scholars, postmodernists, and educationalists but,

> going wholly outside of the boundaries of social theory and the literature of the humanities, they consider the relevance of innovative theoretical approaches and propositions emanating out of the physical sciences and mathematics such as chaos theory, quantum mechanics, Godel's theory, catastrophe theory, and topology for the concerns of criminologists! Altogether, the range of exceptionally demanding ideas, concepts and positions in this book is simply awesome.

Further focusing on where the problem of prose may lay is Ruller's paradoxical judgement that *Constitutive Criminology* "is hard to understand for a 'modern' (pre-postmodern) reader who believes the world can be characterized in terms of order, perfection, essentialism, causality and individual autonomy" (1997: 496). Yet Ruller also says "[Henry and Milovanovic] describe the traditional or 'modern' criminology with considerable conciseness and clarity" and reiterates that while, "[t]he authors write with great clarity" "what they present in this field (about chaos theory, corel sets, etc.) will not be understandable to the great majority of criminologists" (1997: 496–97). Thus, the issue is not that presentation of constitutive ideas lack lucidity but that they reflect the complexity, ambiguity and uncertainty of the social world and the artificial limits of disciplinarity, itself the hallmark of modernity. So it seems that difficulty is at least partly in the eye of the reader, and yes, reading outside one's discipline would considerably lessen the problem of prose.

In addition, the question of innovative language use has earned the dubious honor of "esoteric" (Ruller, 1997: 497; Bohm, 1997: 16). However, innovative language use has been recognized by those in critical pedagogy as necessary if we are to transcend our present power-knowledge relations. Giroux, for example, has said "every new paradigm has to create its own language because the old paradigms, through their use of particular language forms, produce knowledge and social relations that often serve to legitimate specific relations of power" (1992: 21). He goes on to say that a clarity versus complexity binarism is an artificial construct in that it overlooks "how language and power come together in complex ways to exclude diverse narratives that rupture dominant codes and open up new spaces and possibilities for reading, writing, and acting within rather than outside of a democratic politics of difference" (1992: 25). The call for "clarity," therefore, assumes a consensus whose continuous invocation fuels the politics of containment not liberation.

The Problem of Marriage

It seems that not only are different disciplines incompatible, but so to are different positions within any one discipline. Now we take the view that integration of knowledge involves complimentarity. It is not that contradictory positions must be resolved, synthesized or pitted against one another to the glory of the vanquished. Rather, it is that contradictory positions are contributory explanatory frameworks, often explaining different aspects or dimensions of an issue. Such positions, and not limited to two, are co-contributors to the totality and must be examined both in themselves, in relation to counter positions, and in relation to the whole that they are each a part of. We can illustrate this by considering critiques of the constitutive project's notion of the "marriage" of structure and agency. For one commentator (Naffine, 1996: 75), we "seem to be suggesting, in Marxist fashion, that economic structures formed by the logic of capital . . . determine the fate of the individual" which leads to the conclusion that "their criminology appears to be pure instrumental Marxism." Naffine continues, "But then they endeavor to complicate their account of power by suggesting that the economic and social structures which oppress, are the products of our imagination, which we can therefore reimagine," a position that leads them, unlike Foucault, to deny the reality of power (Naffine, 1996: 76). And further:

> As Marxist materialists, however, Henry and Milovanovic evidently are not persuaded that the life of the mind can have real effects. It is the economy that is real, while our understanding of the world—our "imaginings"—can never be truly constitutive of reality. So while they flirt with Foucault, at heart Henry and Milovanovic seem unconvinced by the Foucauldian account of power as knowledge preferring an oddly-adapted Marxist formulation of power and its relation to crime (*ibid*).

Union, it seems, is difficult to sustain when some readers are intent on separation. The idea that both these notions are co-constitutive as we clearly and categorically assert, is not enough. There needs to be certainty, commitment; no "flirting" *a la* Matza (1964: 28) is allowed.

Similarly with Matthews and Young's critique of (skeptical) postmodernism where they say "strangely enough, however, the postmodernist critique has indicated some points of overlap between left realist and feminist criminology" (1992: 13). Why is this strange? And again we find an essentialist and reductionist position in Howe (1997) who indicates that any cross-over to modernist thinking from poststructuralist thought is equivalent to sleeping with the enemy. In short, this "wedding," Howe (1997: 89) tells us, cannot be a happy one.

Such essentializing is troubling. However, others reading the constitutive project seem to find a different truth, one reflective of a non-essentializing position. For example, compare Bohm's (1997) comments with Naffine's reading of us as "Marxist materialists." Bohm (1997: 15) argues that "by focusing on the linguistic production of reality, the authors tend to down play (but do not ignore) the material conditions of production (e.g., the ownership of private property and wealth)." Indeed, in a succinct statement of our basic position he demonstrates that *Constitutive Criminology*:

> assumes that human beings socially construct their world primarily through language and symbolic representation but, at the

same time, are also shaped by the world they create. Two contradictions of this process are that people come to "reify" the world they create . . . and that the institutions and structures people create frequently become the source of social constraint and domination as do attempts to oppose them. The optimism of Henry and Milovanovic's theory lies in the belief that, as creators, human beings are capable of changing the institutions and structures that dominate and constrain them. For Henry and Milovanovic, people are the "co-producers" of reality and their actions can be both constraining and liberating (Bohm, 1997: 15).

In spite of this empathetic reading of our position, the notion that such seemingly contradictory ideas, and even the integration of insights from diverse disciplines, can be mutually constructive, let alone constitutive, is rejected by many of those committed to particular disciplines. Indeed, the unwillingness to accept that disciplines can provide contributory insight to our understanding of the totality is not confined to the structure versus agency debate. From a feminist postmodernist perspective Howe (1997) rejects any notion of a marriage between modernism with postmodernism and sees our constitutive project as fundamentally flawed: "criminology offers no insights into crime. Postmodern theories cannot be happily wedded with the modernist, positivistic paradigms of criminology . . . that is what I tell my students" (Howe, 1997: 89). Howe asks the question, "Can criminology and postmodern feminism meet and have a nice day?" and she replies, "I don't think so" (Howe, 1997: 92). Yet it is precisely such a wedding that others want to arrange. As Barak (1998: xi) says in the "Preface" to his *Integrating Criminologies*: "one of my purposes for writing this book includes trying to help criminology overcome its historical tendency to succumb to one or the other of the competing social and behavioral sciences . . . [a] state of affairs that has contributed to separate bodies of knowledge. Therefore, this book is an attempt to reach out to those estranged bodies of knowledge. It is also an attempt to help unify them." Indeed, Barak goes on to argue that the most promising insights about crime and justice are emerging in the overlapping spaces between disciplinary perspectives . . . [where] there is a convergence of material and spiritual forces; the conscious and the unconscious; the body, the mind, and the environment; and between society as we know it, as it has been, and as it could be."

We find much work sympathetic to this thrust in recent theorizing in critical pedagogy, "border pedagogy," and "postmodern pedagogy." Giroux (1992), for example, advocates that intellectuals become "border crossers." "Borderlands," he observes, "should be seen as sites for both critical analysis and as a potential source of experimentation, creativity, and possibility" (1992: 34). Similarly, recent research by critical race theorists and feminists suggests that we should not merely investigate singular forms of oppression such as gender, race, class but also the intersecting nature of such subordination (Schwartz and Milovanovic, 1996; Simpson, 1991).

The Problem of Logic and Causality

The tendency among those invested in particular disciplines or theoretical positions to divorce agency and structure, and to separate modernism and postmodernism is also reflected in readings of the constitutive take on causality. Several commentators highlight the point that *Constitutive Criminology* is not content to settle for traditional conceptions of linear causality. For example, Croall (1996) says that the constitutive project "rejects uni-causal theories, recognizes that there are no determined structures, rejects the social construction of crime and sees those attracted to crime as being affected by multiple influences in a socio-economic and cultural context" and she goes on to claim that much of this has long been recognized in more "modernist" critiques. Now if that is the case it must be news to leading mainstream modernist theorists like Akers (1997: 178) who complains that "constitutive criminology has not yet offered a testable explanation of either crime or criminal justice" and who treats our rejection of mainstream criminology's traditional search for the causes of crime, while simultaneously accepting the notion that crime is "codetermined," as reflecting "some internal logical inconsistencies" (Akers, 1997: 177). He rhetorically asks:

> If the search for causes must be abandoned, as clearly stated by Henry and Milovanovic, or if crime does not exist as an objective reality in the discursive process as they may imply, then how can crime be enabled and constrained . . . and at the same time have reciprocal "shaping" effects on social structure . . . It would seem that constitutive criminology has not really abandoned the search for causes, because crime, victims, and control are "shaped" by both micro-level events . . . and macro-level structural arrangements (*ibid.*).

Now why is considering the relevant contributions of mutually interrelated events, activities, arrangements, structures etc., considered contradictory? As we have repeatedly stated, the concept of causality that seems best able to capture this notion of duality is that of dialectical interrelationships or coproduction. Indeed, rather than reject social construction as Croall claims, we consider the social construction process critical. Thus we argue that "Crime is not so much caused as discursively constructed through human processes of which it is one" (Henry and Milovanovic, 1996: 170). As Colvin's (1997: 1449) reading of *Constitutive Criminology* explains:

> these processes comprise relationships that are not deterministic but dialectical, a dialectic that assumes nonlinear development and a movement, through human agency, toward instability of social forms . . . Whether a particular situation or interrelationship will result in criminality cannot be determined with any precision since the dynamics of human relations are indeterminate, can be altered by seemingly small events, and are part of an historically situated, on going process that is also indeterminate (*ibid.*).

So whether it is the indeterminacy of social life or constitutive criminology's reflection of that indeterminacy which some critics find uncomfortable, is unclear. What should be clear is that *Constitutive Criminology*, "assumes that the very notion of 'cause' is problematic and . . . [i]mportantly, while not totally abandoning the notion of causation . . . dialectically assemble[s] causality from the perspective of 'mutual influences,' 'structural couplings,' 'strategic essentialisms,' 'relational sets,' 'psychoanalytic semiotics,' 'gendered analyses,' and 'chaotic transformations' " (Barak, 1996: 157), to which we would add, "contingent universality" and "non-linear iteration."

Unlike much of modernism's dualisms such as free will versus determinism, conflict versus consensus and order versus chaos, constitutive theory sees each as operative. Indeed, according to the insights generated by chaos theory, we can have order and disorder in the same system. This does not mean despair, resignation, nihilism; rather it poses new challenges in ways we conceptualize complexity. Thus, the challenge will be to further integrate ideas such as non-linearity, feedback, fractal geometry, attractors, phase space, self-similarity, indeterminacy, and iterations into our scholarly horizons.

The lack of receptiveness of new critical initiatives in academia is reflected in Matthews and Young's (1992: 11) comment about the "slowness with which postmodernism has permeated criminology." They argue that it "may largely be due to the current low level of theoretical debate in the subject" (1992: 11). Is it no wonder that some such as Smart have advocated abandoning criminology to sociology (1990: 77); as if sociology is any less myopic? This said, it is unfortunate that there exists great resistance to change, once debate has been engendered. Take again Matthews and Young's (1992: 13) position that "rather than modernity having failed, the truth is that it has never been fully implemented." They see the modernist thrust as an "unfinished project" and any abandonment of its linear progression would be "regressive" (1992: 13). Unfortunately this dualistic thrust omits the potential gains of the emergent and ossifies and reifies what has developed in the past. It is not that the affirmative postmodern approach of constitutive criminology rejects the gains of the past. Rather, it builds on what has been in creating new conceptual tools for future analysis and offers new visions of change, such as those painted by postmodernist feminists such as Cornell (1991) and Butler (1990, 1996).

Our own development of causality is built on various perspectives drawn from both the modernist and postmodernist initiatives. In *Constitutive Criminology*, for example, we developed the idea of constitutive interrelational sets which has its source in the work of constitutive theory (Giddens, 1984), complexity theory (Mandelbrot, 1983; Gregerson and Sailer, 1993; Pickover, 1988), structural coupling (Luhmann, 1992; Teubner, 1993), strategic essentialism (Spivak, 1988; Jessop, 1990), relational sets (Hunt, 1993), critical race theory and intersections (Matsuda et al, 1993), autopoietic systems (Teubner, 1988, 1993; Cornell, 1992), dialectical materialism (Marx, 1975; Sayer, 1979), topology theory (Lacan, 1961) and social constructionism (Schutz, 1967; Berger and Luckmann, 1966). It is not, therefore, that complexity cannot be understood, but that it cannot be captured solely within the prevailing categories of much of modernist thought. Nor can the idealization of prediction be our goal. Constitutive criminology is an ongoing search for understanding complexity over time. It is not to say that we cannot develop useful conceptualizations which can provide the basis of social action. To this end, modernist and postmodernist insights need to be both critiqued *and* integrated. At best we can offer only "contingent universalities." Anything more is tantamount to creating potentially reified structures; anything less is to regress back to the nihilistic forms of postmodern analysis.

The Problem of Crime as a Constructed Reality

Related to the problematic nature of causality is the nature of the reality of what is constituted through the dialectical process. Some commentators seem to assume that because *Constitutive Criminology* sees crime as socially constructed, this necessarily denies it having real effects. For example, Akers argues that constitutive criminology seems to "take the extreme position that denies crime as such really exists. Crime exists only because it is a 'discursive production,' that is, a product not only of the interaction of offenders, control agents, criminologists, or other people, but also simply by their talking about it . . . This implies that there is no such thing as crime as an objective behavioral reality to be explained . . . Does this mean that criminal behavior would not exist if we did not talk about it?" (1997: 176–77). But consider the critique of (skeptical) postmodernist thought by some prominent left realists. On the one hand, they offer the "square of crime" indicating that " 'crime' arises at the intersection of a number of lines of force" (Matthews and Young, 1992: 17), (a position coming quite close to the notion of crime as a social construct) but yet also argue for an "objectivism" (*ibid.*: 14–15).

At issue here is what is meant by "talk" or more precisely "discursive practices" in the social construction of reality. The critics assume there is a neat separation between reality and our talk about it. Our argument is that practices are part of the process that produces what then seems to be a separate reality. However, the critical issue for criminology is not whether the discursively produced representations have some underlying and independent existence, but that people act toward them *as if* they possess this quality. As such, categories based on socially constructed difference become invested with energy from those who treat them as real. Investors then act toward these categories to either defend their interest in that reality or oppose others' notion of reality. It is people's (and agency's) actions that produce harm. Take the simple example of religious belief. History is replete with examples of people persecuting and abusing those who have different beliefs. That religion might readily be seen as a social construction does not deny the harm of those acting toward it as a reality. To be clear, it is not that the harm of crime is unreal, but that the constructions that lead to its effects are the outcome of discursive practices.

Consider the thrust of the left realist's point that: "an adequate explanation of crime and control needs to incorporate the particular and the general, and to locate specific and discrete phenomena within a framework which locates and explains the relation between the parts" (Matthews and Young, 1992: 12). From our view such concepts as the "particular," "general," "specific," "discrete," and "parts" are problematic and should not be taken as self evident. Rather, these are discursive constructions, presented as particular contextualized concepts. We accept that different "levels" are operative. However, we criticize the thrust of arguments that invest energy in nominalist categories without further investigation. From the constitutive view these very "self-evident" nominalist categories in their continuous use reify bodies of knowledge and reduce our investment in the creation of alternative vistas.

Consider race, ethnicity, sexuality, gender, and class, all socially constructed, reified categories produced by the creation of distinctions based on perceived difference. Actions of people based on these differences (e.g., impositions, reductions, repressions, etc.), whether men against women, straights against gays, etc. (all themselves constructed categories) produces avoidable harms. It is for this reason that we define crime as "nothing less than moments in the expression of power, such that those who are subject to them are denied . . . their worth, and simultaneously reduced and repressed in several ways" (Henry and Milovanovic, 1996: 116). Crime, therefore, is the expression of the power to create harm based on socially constructed differences. The pain of that expression is real; its constitution is socially constructed. Thus, we are not arguing that crime (as harm) will disappear if we stop talking about it, but that harm will cease to be the outcome of a world that does not invest in the realities of difference. This leads directly to the problem of policy.

The Problem of Policy

The fundamental policy problem confronting the constitutive project is how, as a society, it is possible to stop investing in structures of oppression whose manifestation channels and sustains the very use of the power to harm, without at the same time exercising power. The subtext of this issue underlies the anti-death penalty position which becomes reduced to the argument that the state's use of capital punishment is as bad or worse as that of the murderer. A related problem is how, given the nature of power and social structure, is it possible to change the reified products of discourse that we take to be structure, culture, nature and so on?

In responding to these policy questions some believe the constitutive project meets its Waterloo: "Most disappointing is the discussion of how to overcome the problem that local action cannot transform wider structural, state and institutional systems. While [Henry and Milovanovic] argue that superliberalism and chaos theory can create an 'empowered' democracy they provide few practical strategies to indicate how this can be achieved . . . and many of the strategies seem little more than old wine in new bottles" (Croall, 1997). But in considering policy, the connection between resistance and reconstruction here is vital. Unlike some relevant critiques levied against the nihilistic forms of postmodern analysis—"its skepticism about 'progress,' its deconstruction of the concept of crime, its antipathy towards grand theory, mean that it can too easily lead towards nihilism, cynicism and conservatism" (Matthews and Young, 1992: 13)—our affirmative version sees deconstruction *and* reconstruction as necessary foci; separate one from the other and the roads to nihilism or romanticism are seductively inviting.

Given that the basis of crime (as harm) is the socially constructed and discursively constituted exercise of power through difference, it follows that human subjects whose investment in power relations harms others have the potential to reconstitute their use of human agency to be less harmful or have the potential to be reconstituted through interactive relations with the wider culture or structure. Such a perspective, as Colvin (1997: 1450) says: "opens the possibility for transformation of human subjects and the social structures we construct."

One of the means to achieve this reconstruction is through replacement discourse that fuels positive social constructions. Replacement discourse is designed to displace harmful moments in the exercise of power with discourses that tell different stories about the world. This is not simply saying that if we stop talking about crime it will go away. Rather it is to say that if human discursive practices cease to construct differences as a basis of power (see Cornell, 1992) the site for investment will be deconstructed, and investment and defense of it as a reality will be less possible. This is because the perception of people as less than fellow human subjects, as "others," will be dissipated. Harming others will be tantamount to harming oneself. This is why we advocated a policy of "social judo" in which the use of power is turned away from harm production, and toward reinvesting in positive connections with a relationally oriented community of fellow human subjects. As Bohm (1997: 16) says, "The judo metaphor is apt here because, on the one hand . . . using power to reduce the power of others only replaces one excessive investor with another. On the other hand, when using judo as a means of self-defence, the power of the aggressor is turned back against the aggressor."

The problem of policy, then, is not one of merely applying strategies but of teaming deconstruction and reconstruction so that appreciation of difference rather than domination based on difference, pervades the spirit of social life. Difference without domination is to be celebrated (see Cornell's point about an "ethical feminism," 1991). Nor should the classical economic equivalency principle be quickly embraced, because subsuming difference within notions of formal equality is to deny the variability and polyvocality of the human condition and to ride roughshod over substantive inequality (Young, 1981). The problem is not to remove existing institutional and social structures that reproduce these differences whose investment with power results in oppression and inequality. Instead, the problem is how to cease our unreflexive rebuilding of these social forms and structures while reinvesting energy in alternative, connective interrelational social forms. That we are doing just the opposite is symbolized in the current prison building program, as if by building prisons we are not deeply harming ourselves as well as those incarcerated (Milovanovic and Henry, 1991). That this is taking place in late-twentieth-century America is indicative of how far we are from dealing with the fundamental issue and why societal and structural transformation require continuous and relentless struggle.

So is this tantamount to "old wine in new bottles"? We think not. What we are suggesting is that "dissipative structures," that is, structures that are extremely sensitive to their environment and its perturbations and consequently undergo continuous change while still providing horizons for social action, have much in common with the notion of "contingent universalities" (Butler, 1990). Here provisional truths may become the basis of political action and social policy, but these are always contingent; subject to change, refinement, substitution and deletion when faced with historical conditions and further reflective investigation. In short, in our view the problem of policy should remain a problem; there are no answers, only working solutions; no wine, new or old, only wine in the making.

Notes

1. Originally presented at the conference: Social Dynamics and Regulatory Order in Modern Societies—New Theoretical Perspectives on the Causes of Crime and Social Control, Onati, Spain, Oct 23–24, 1997.

2. Many of those who have applied these ideas are represented in this book but others, such as Russell Smandych, Trent Kane, Patricia Ewick, Susan Silbey, George Pavlich and Chris Stanley have taken account of it in their own work.

References

Akers, Ronald. (1997). *Criminological Theories: Introduction and Evaluation*. Los Angeles: Roxbury.

Arrigo, Bruce. (1997). "Review of Stuart Henry and Dragan Milovanovic's Constitutive Criminology." *Theoretical Criminology*, 3: 392–96.

Barak, Gregg. (1998). *Integrating Criminologies*. Boston: Allyn and Bacon.

Barak, Gregg. (1996). "Review of Stuart Henry and Dragan Milovanovic's Constitutive Criminology." *Social Pathology*, 2: 154–59.

Beirne, Piers, and James Messerschmidt. (1995). *Criminology*, 2nd ed. Fort Worth, TX: Harcourt Brace.

Berger, Peter, and Thomas Luckmann. (1966). *The Social Construction of Reality*. New York: Doubleday.

Bérubé, Michael. (1997). "In praise of obscurity." *The Chronicle of Higher Education* (February 21): B4.

Bohm, Robert M. (1997). "Review of Stuart Henry and Dragan Milovanovic's Constitutive Criminology." *The Criminologist*, 22: 15–16.

Butler, Judith. (1990). *Gender Trouble*. New York: Routledge.

Colvin, Mark. (1997). "Review of Stuart Henry and Dragan Milovanovic's Constitutive Criminology." *American Journal of Sociology*, 102: 1448–50.

Cornell, Drucilla. (1991). *Beyond Accommodation: Ethical Feminism, Deconstruction and the Law*. New York: Routledge.

Croall, Hazel. (1996). "Crime: Understanding more and condemning less?" *Reviewing Sociology*, 10(3).

DeKeseredy, Walter, and Martin D. Schwartz. (1996.) *Contemporary Criminology*. Belmont: Wadsworth.

Deutschmann, Linda B. (1998). *Deviance and Social Control* 2nd ed. Toronto: ITP Nelson.

Einstadter, Werner, and Stuart Henry. (1995). *Criminological Theory: An Analysis of Its Underlying Assumptions*. Fort Worth, TX: Harcourt Brace.

Ericson, Richard, and Kevin Carriere. (1994). "The fragmentation of criminology." In David Nelken (Ed.), *The Futures of Criminology*. London: Sage.

Fitzpatrick, Peter. (1984). "Law and societies," *Osgoode Hall Law Journal*, 22: 115–38.

Fitzpatrick, Peter. (1992). *The Mythology of Modern Law*. London: Routledge.

Friedrichs, David O. (1996). "Critical criminology and progressive pluralism: Strength in diversity for these times" *Critical Criminology*, 7:121–28.

Gibbons, Don C. (1994). *Talking About Crime and Criminals*. Englewood Cliffs, NJ: Prentice Hall.

Giroux, Henry. (1992). *Border Crossings: Cultural Workers and the Politics of Education*. New York: Routledge.

Gregerson, H., and L. Sailer. (1993). "Chaos theory and its implications for social science research," *Human Relations*, 46: 777–802.

Harrington, Christine. (1988). "Moving from integrative to constitutive theories of law: comments on Itzkowitz," *Law and Society Review*, 22: 963–67.

Henry, Stuart. (1989). "Constitutive criminology: the missing paradigm," *The Critical Criminologist*, 1(3): 9, 12.

Henry, Stuart, and Dragan Milovanovic. (1991). "Constitutive criminology," *Criminology*, 29: 293–316.

Henry, Stuart, and Dragan Milovanovic. (1993). "Back to basics: A postmodern redefinition of crime," *The Critical Criminologist*, 5(2/3): 1–2, 6, 12.

Henry, Stuart, and Dragan Milovanovic. (1994). "The constitution of constitutive criminology: A postmodern approach to criminological theory," in D. Nelken (Ed.), *The Futures of Criminology*. London: Sage.

Henry, Stuart, and Dragan Milovanovic. (1996). *Constitutive Criminology: Beyond Postmodernism*. London: Sage.

Howe, Adrian. (1997). "Criminology meets postmodern feminism (and has a nice day)." In Brian D. MacLean and Dragan Milovanovic (Eds.), *Thinking Critically About Crime*. Vancouver: Collective Press.

Hunt, Alan. (1993). *Explorations in Law and Society: Toward a Constitutive Theory of Law*. New York: Routledge.

Jessop, Bob. (1990). *State Theory: Putting the Capitalist State in its Place*. Cambridge, UK: Polity Press.

Lacan, Jacques. (1961). *The Seminar of Jacques Lacan: Book IX: Identification 1961–1962*. Translated by Cormac Gallageur (unpublished).

Lanier, Mark M., and Stuart Henry. (1998). *Essential Criminology*. Boulder, CO: Westview Press.

Luhmann, Niklas. A. (1992). "Operational closure and structural coupling: The differentiation of the legal system," *Cardozo Law Review*, 13: 1419–41.

Mandelbrot, B. (1983). *The Fractal Geometry of Nature*. New York: W.H. Freeman.

Marx, Karl. (1975). *Early Writings*. Translated by Rodney Livingstone and Gregor Benton. New York: Random House/Vintage.

Matsuda, M. J., Larence, C. R., Delgado, R., and K. W. Crenshaw (Eds.). (1993). *Words That Wound*. San Francisco: Westview Press.

Matthews, Roger, and Jock Young. (1992). "Reflections on realism." In Jock Young and Roger Matthews (Eds.), *ReThinking Criminology: The Realist Debate*. London: Sage.

Matza, David. (1964). *Delinquency and Drift*. New York: Wiley.

Milovanovic, Dragan, and Stuart Henry. (1991). "Constitutive penology," *Social Justice*, 18: 204–24.

Milovanovic, Dragan. (1992). *Postmodern Law and Disorder: Psychoanalytic Semiotics, Chaos and Juridic Exegeses*. Liverpool, UK: Deborah Charles.

Naffine, Ngaire. (1996). *Feminism and Criminology*. Philadelphia: Temple University Press.

Nelken, David. (ed.) (1994). *The Futures of Criminology*. London: Sage.

Pickover, C. (1988). "Pattern formation and chaos in networks," *Communication of the ACM*, 31: 136–51.

Ruller, Sibo van. (1997). "Review of Stuart Henry and Dragan Milovanovic's Constitutive Criminology." *Contemporary Criminology*, 26:496–97.

Sayer, Derek. (1979). *Marx's Method*. New York: Humanities Press.

Schutz, Alfred. (1967). *The Phenomenology of the Social World*. Evanston, IL: Northwestern University Press.

Schwartz, Martin, and Dragan Milovanovic (Eds.). (1996). *Race, Gender, and Class in Criminology: The Intersections*. New York: Garland Publishing.

Schwartz, Martin, D., and David O. Friedrichs. (1994). "Postmodern thought and criminological discontent: New metaphors for understanding violence." *Criminology*, 32: 221–46.

Silbey, Susan. S. (1992). "Making a place for the cultural analysis of law." *Law and Social Inquiry*, 17:39–48.

Simpson, Sally S. (1991). "Caste, class and violent crime: Explaining the difference in female offending" *Criminology*, 29:115–35.

Smart, Carol. (1990). "Feminist approaches to criminology, or postmodern woman meets atavistic man," in L. Gelsthorpe and A. Morris (Eds), *Feminist Perspectives in Criminology*. Milton Keynes: Open University Press.

Spivak, G. (1988). "Can the subaltern speak?" In C. Nelson and L. Grossberg (Eds.), *Marxisms and the Interpretation of Culture*. London: MacMillan.

Stitt, B. Grant, and David J. Giacopassi. (1992). "Trends in the connectivity of theory and research in criminology." *The Criminologist*, 17: 1, 3–6.

Swingewood, Alan. (1975). *Marx and Modern Social Theory*. London: Macmillan Press.

Teubner, Guenther. (1992). "The two faces of Janus: Rethinking legal pluralism," *Cardozo Law Review*, 13: 1443–62.

Teubner, Guenther. (1988). *Autopoietic Law: A New Approach to Law and Society*. New York: Walter de Gruyter.

Teubner, Guenther. (1993). *Law as an Autopoietic System*. Oxford: Blackwell.

Young, Jock. (1981). "Thinking seriously about crime: Some models of criminology," in M. Fitzgerald, G. McLennan, and J. Pawson (Eds.), *Crime and Society: Readings in History and Society*. London: Routledge and Kegan Paul.

Vold, George B., Bernard, Thomas J. and Jeffrey B. Snipes. (1998). *Theoretical Criminology* 3rd ed. New York: Oxford University Press.

LIVERPOOL JOHN MOORES UNIVERSITY
Aldham Roberts L.R.C.
TEL. 051 231 3701/3634

ABOUT THE CONTRIBUTORS

Bruce A. Arrigo is Professor of Criminology and Forensic Psychology and is the Director of the Institute of Psychology, Law, and Public Policy at the California School of Professional Psychology-Fresno.

Andrew Bak graduated with a master's in Criminology and Criminal Justice from the Department of Sociology, Anthropology and Criminology at Eastern Michigan University.

Gregg Barak is Professor of Criminology in the Department of Sociology, Anthropology and Criminology at Eastern Michigan University.

Mary Bosworth is Assistant Professor in the Department of Sociology at Fordham University.

John Brigham is Professor of Political Science at the University of Massachusetts-Amherst

Dion Dennis is a lecturer in the Division of Social and Policy Sciences, Department of Sociology, University of Texas-San Antonio.

Stuart Henry is Professor and Chair of the Department Sociology at Valparaiso University.

Victor E. Kappeler is Professor of Police Studies and the Director of Graduate Programs in Criminal Justice at Eastern Kentucky University.

Peter B. Kraska is Associate Professor of Police Studies at Eastern Kentucky University.

Dragan Milovanovic is Professor of Criminology in the Department of Criminal Justice, Sociology and Social Work at Northeastern Illinois University.

Lisa Sanchez is Assistant Professor in the Department of Sociology at the State University of New York-Buffalo.

Robert C. Schehr is Assistant Professor in the Criminal Justice Program at the University of Illinois at Springfield.

Jim Thomas is Professor in the Department of Sociology at Northern Illinois University.

James W. Williams is a graduate student in the Department of Sociology, York University, Ontario.

T. R. Young is Founder and Director of the Red Feather Institute, Weidman, Michigan.

INDEX